CW01391651

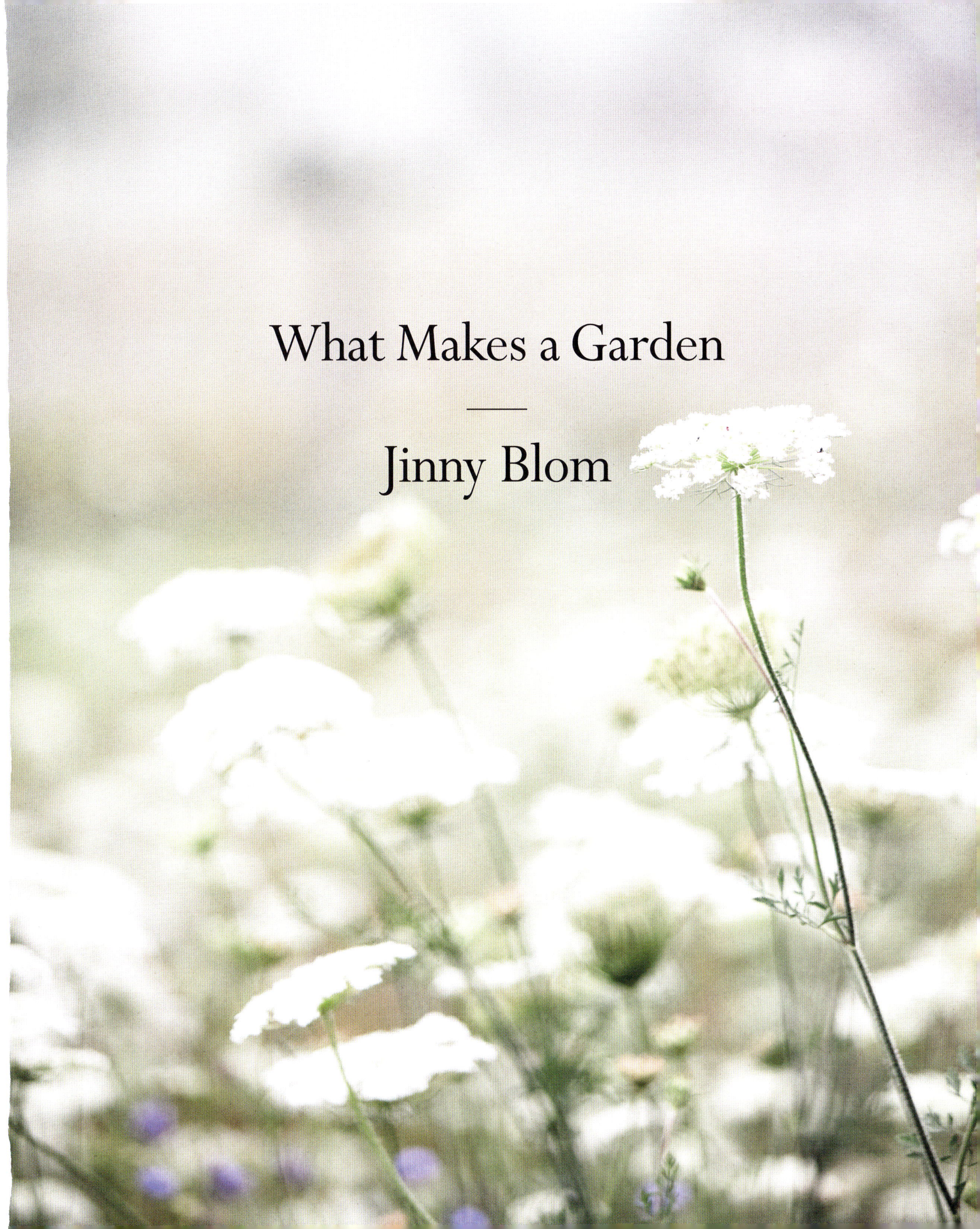

What Makes a Garden

Jinny Blom

What Makes a Garden

Jinny Blom

FRANCES LINCOLN

THIS BOOK IS DEDICATED WITH LOVE TO MY NIECES
HAZEL AND ZOE BLOM

—

And my Godchildren
Octavia Nancy Dean
Felix and Celeste Haughton

Quarto

First published in 2023 by Frances Lincoln, an imprint of The Quarto Group.
1 Triptych Place
London, SE1 9SH
United Kingdom
T (0)20 7700 6700
www.Quarto.com

A catalogue record for this book is available from the British Library.

ISBN 978-0-7112-8295-7
Ebook ISBN 978-0-7112-8296-4

10 9 8 7 6 5 4 3 2 1

Design by Here Ltd
Commissioned by Philip Cooper
Edited by Anna Southgate/Laura Bulbeck
Photography by Britt Willoughby; supplemental photography by Jinny Blom/Jinny Blom Studio, except where stated otherwise on page 247.
Picture Research by Jinny Blom/Frances Costelloe

Printed in China

Endpapers: I designed a huge limestone table to stand in a rather unique listed courtyard garden. I'd seen a pair of gilded Italian gryphon legs on an antique console table and thought they would be a good starting point. So, with the help of my friend Paul Jakeman, a master stonemason and fellow Brother of the Art Workers' Guild, I set to work. These are carved in Portland limestone and sit on wonderfully fossily plinths.

Title page: This is the first summer for this young garden, photographed a matter of months after planting. It never ceases to amaze me how quickly plants shoot up if the environment offered to them is carefully considered and well prepared. The garden will continue to grow and flourish and simply to improve with time and age.

Introduction: *Cercis canadensis* 'Forest Pansy', or redbud as it is known on its native continent, is a beautiful small tree. The flowers emerge on the twiggy stems in early spring before the rich mahogany-coloured leaves. It needs space to give off its elegant best.

FOREWORD

To be a designer, whether it be of landscape or buildings, is an immense privilege. We strive instinctively to leave something that we hope will outlive us, offering a legacy of worth, and providing some pleasure and – dare I say it – even amusement, to subsequent generations. After all, this is very much what we have inherited, where so much of what we see is derived from layer upon layer of generations of often unselfconscious but careful husbandry of both land and buildings. While we appreciate the serendipity of things, the parts of any contribution that are most likely to survive are those that harness the natural materials that surround us and bring them into useful or uplifting harmony. Derelict buildings, like overgrown landscapes, can be beautiful to look at and are also 'very good for nature'; but you cannot very comfortably live in or with them. In any case, although nature always and eventually wins, we should not feel ashamed to introduce elements of use and order, adding something of value to pass on.

To do this successfully requires greater understanding than just responding to a brief or a budget. The evidence of that binary approach is all too manifest in the acres of thoughtless sprawl – visible through the window of this train as I write, and which we all try to ignore for much of the time. But even here, looking carefully, patches of moss under a leaking gutter here, wild sapling tree growth there, offers reassurance that the end for some of these shoddy and unworthy places has already begun. With humility and modesty, we might create things that people will think worth maintaining.

Refreshingly, this book is not really about the gardens that Jinny Blom has created, beautiful and numerous as they are. They will outlive her, and will doubtless offer good doctorate-material for generations of landscape students to come. It is instead more about the philosophical journey that she has taken to arrive at a plateau where all the various threads, references, ideas, watching, reading and experiences have somehow come together to form a coherent vision of what is best to do. This is an informed thesis of what life's journey offers to those who wrestle with the numerous challenges that are presented in the world of gardens. The gardens are easy to photograph, but the ideas are much harder to express, and how wonderful that she has managed to get them onto the printed page. The wisdom, wit and insight that she passes on are a true legacy.

–PTOLEMY DEAN OBE

WHAT IS A GARDEN?

Creating a garden is, initially, an introverted process. It takes a while to imagine a garden and to develop it into its final form. For much of that period your thoughts are just part of an evolving dream of a future reality. It takes longer to build a garden and a whole lifetime, or more, for that garden to mature. To embark on making a garden is an act of faith. The creative journey is made unique by the relationships we have with those we enlist to help us. Without other people there would be no garden. Together, we generate a great alchemical soup of ideas, we consider constraints and we discuss details that ultimately coalesce into the new garden. Landscape gardens can express themselves in myriad ways. I have always enjoyed the freedom landscaping offers to explore what the land, the people and the circumstances ultimately reveal.

Recently, and seemingly in response to increasing warnings about our effect on the planet, gardens appear to be having an identity crisis. Evocations of an imagined lost wilderness peppered with wildlife are at the fore in contemporary garden culture, while gardens with perspective and order seem, for now at least, consigned to history. Any form of art or innovation seems shamefully wasteful of natural resources, as though we have forgotten, briefly, about our impending fate. What on earth are we doing? This 'hair shirt' hubris about how we gardeners alone can offer a *mea maxima culpa* to the earth seems odd. With our eyes raised imploringly towards heaven are we wriggling ourselves off the guilt hook?

English gardener and author Christopher Lloyd once said the countryside in May cannot be beaten, so why try? Appreciating and supporting the wider ecological structure of the countryside, and finding harmony with it, has been around for centuries as a design concept. I do think, however, that the natural world and the gardened world are very different things. From a practical stance, the constant encroachment of the natural world onto our hard-won cleared ground is inexorable; ceaseless work is needed to keep it and its denizens at bay. For any landowner, however much or little they have, maintaining it is a challenging experience. I have a friend whose land, one summer, became too tinder-dry to cut hay. The merest spark from a tractor blade could trigger a wildfire, so all machine work in the region was stopped by legal decree. The moment cultivation slowed however, the parched land filled with tiny trees. To our modern, non-agricultural eyes, this is a marvellous act of 'rewilding', yet to a subsistence farmer it represents a life's work slipping through their fingers.

For as long as we have cultivated land, we have sought a point of division between us and the wild. The invention of boundaries was our first step towards establishing some sort of control over nature, ultimately creating gardens. But what is a garden? A garden is paradise on earth, made by humankind for the deeper exploration of who we are, what life means and how to prepare for the inevitability of death. A garden invites a tender exploration of beauty, of geometry, of divine inspiration and a searching for inner peace through meditatively caring for something beyond us. It allows us to express our reverence for trees, flora and fauna for their own sake in a place of good order – emphatically not the wilderness. Every garden encapsulates, in microcosm, the cycle of life through the seasons. It is inescapable. Gardens have always existed behind their high walls and fences, in imperfect worlds of war, destruction, plague and famine. Every generation before us, without exception, has faced existential threats. We are, perhaps, only different because we finally understand, albeit too late, that we have brought many of the problems we face on ourselves: global warming, nuclear war, habitat destruction, over population, asset stripping, mass extinction. We do not much like the prospect of having to undo things and go without. We have too much, expect too much, want too much, give too little. Are we, with this latest trend, actually craving limitation so that we can find peace?

There was a case, in 2008, of a property developer in Suffolk furiously cutting down a mass of saplings he deemed inappropriate. They belonged to an elderly neighbour who in turn claimed the developer had vandalized their garden. The case made it to the High Court. Lord Justice Moses offered in his summing up: 'The *Oxford English Dictionary* states that a garden is an enclosed piece of ground devoted to the cultivation of flowers, fruit or vegetables. That definition is clearly now too narrow, as the current fashion for wild gardens and meadow areas amply demonstrates. The reality is that no description will categorically establish whether a piece of land is a garden or not. It is incumbent on the fact finder to determine its use. It is important to look at the relationship between the owner and the land, and the history and character of the land and space.'

So, there we have it. We have evolved. If you think it is a garden, it is a garden.

Unfettered by definition, please join me in a romp through the vast and complex constellations of what makes a garden. What follows reveals much about my approach to garden-making, beginning with all things human – how we develop our cultural understanding of the world around us and our unique responses to it and how we define our personal style. I explore our sensory realms that bring us so much pleasure and satisfaction, then move on to the fundamentals of the alchemy of garden-making using inanimate and animate materials to bring ideas to life. Finally, and most important of all, I consider how the passage of time brings beauty to the finished article. What I hope to share through this process, is that the freedom of expression, the generosity of spirit, the pillaging of art, architecture, history and culture that lie within the subject are bountiful and free. Every one of us can make a garden, whatever that might suggest; classless, priceless, peerless.

Humanity

Part 1

1. CIVILISING THE EARTH

Look deep into nature, and then you will understand everything better.

–ALBERT EINSTEIN (1879–1955)

← There is a close companionship between the *Cercis canadensis* 'Forest Pansy' and the irresistible *Rosa × odorata* 'Mutabilis'. Not only do their colours support each other beautifully, but they share a spare open habit that oxygenates a border. Strong colours like these do better without too much competition.

THERE IS A TERM WE USE IN LANDSCAPING when what we are building is in a filthy, mud-splattered and semi-constructed state. If we need to tidy it up quicky, we call it 'civilising'. This generally means knocking out potholes and throwing down some cheap gravel to make the terrain navigable and clean. However, the word has stuck in my mind in terms of the wider discussion about what makes a garden. Isn't garden-making a considerate relationship between us and nature? In making a garden, we are offering to 'civilise' a small part of the wilderness, to refine it according to our tastes. Our intention is to borrow it, fashion it, care for it in a stylised manner, and enjoy it.

'To civilise' means to bring something from a wild state to one of enlightened development. To transform the original, natural condition into a more cultured, polished and refined form – as judged by human standards, of course. The wild manages perfectly well without us imposing ourselves on it. Conceptually, it is interesting to read the definition of 'civilisation' today as it feels at odds with much of contemporary culture. The messaging these days is strongly in favour of us 'liberating' nature. I still feel the reverberations of excessive human pride in us 'allowing' nature full freedom. The fact is, we don't, we are forever exploiting it and tinkering with it. We claim we are not imposing ourselves and yet we still do. But here we are, discussing the interstices between wildness and civilisation.

Humankind has been creating stylised landscapes and gardens for millennia. At its best, I see the relationship as a courteous one. It can work beautifully if decisions are scrupulously considered and carefully made, and if the end result is then cherished. The most successful landscape designs are those in which people meet nature more than halfway with sensitivity, desire, nurturing and respect – like a good love affair.

Culture

Through the love affair we have with making gardens, we discover much more about ourselves and each other. As the poet John Donne put it so beautifully: 'No man is an island entire of itself; every man is a piece of the continent, a part of the main.' We need each other in order to flourish. Ideas thrive when we share them. Wars have been won and lost in the pursuit of freedom of speech – that's how important this need is. It is hard-wired into humans. We need the liberty to contribute to, and evolve our common experiences, to create and uphold our mutual culture.

What is culture? Culture is unique to us, as far as we know. It is born of our human capacity for rational and abstract thought, combined with a highly developed shared language. Language doesn't not necessarily mean words. Behavioural traits unique to human beings develop as we work together in groups. This includes spoken language, shared beliefs and customs. Often, humour is based on whip-fast recognition of niche cultural references. Humour unites us. However, our culture isn't simply defined by where we live. We develop ideas, codes and institutions with great enthusiasm. We use material objects, tools and techniques to create works of art and develop rituals and ceremonies. This instinctive ordering of our shared world benefits from our ability to collaborate swiftly in order to create structures. As a simple example, the Mediterranean Garden Society, of which I am a member, regularly produces a beautiful little pocket journal. It connects members who garden in or appreciate Mediterranean climates around the world. The society originated from a simple desire to share and disseminate information, and to develop a cultural hub for common interests and enjoy the pleasures of hearing of new discoveries. It also serves as an early-warning system for dangers, such as plant diseases. This unique cultural thread is like a live nerve. We are interdependent creatures and become stronger when the collective nervous system is working well.

Culture makes all men gentle.

–MENANDER (c. 342/41–c. 290 BC)

Shared Threads of Interest

Global cultures vary considerably in their depth and appearance. Cultural details and norms can be hard to understand for people born outside them. They are communicated from birth, formed over a lifetime and handed on. However, increasingly with the use of the internet, travel and the connectivity of our 'global' culture, things are changing. We are ever more unified by shared threads of interest. My own studio is made up of people from seven distinct cultural backgrounds. Within each are subdivisions based on where in our countries we come from, our social experiences, our political leanings, our education and the routes we have chosen for ourselves. We are united by our love of a common subject, and this is broadened and made richer by what each of us brings to it. Our collective knowledge and experience become our mutual cultural expression.

I'm fascinated by the controversy that surrounds cultural appropriation. In gardening, the cross-pollination of plants is considered vibrant and exciting. It offers a route to new discoveries, to variety, to minimising attacks from predators, to gaining strength and beauty. It can go wrong of course; we have made lots of mistakes. Yet why shouldn't cross-pollination be received with equal enthusiasm when it comes to understanding, learning and borrowing from other cultures. It doesn't diminish anyone, as far as I can see. I had reservations about trying to ape Japanese gardens after reading a very detailed academic tome on the subject. The esoteric nuances of true Japanese gardens are astonishing and require lifelong study. I felt that making copies of these gardens without a profound understanding was best avoided. A chance conversation with my friend Atila changed all that. Atila is Turkish and Muslim. He's a highly regarded jazz singer. Unbeknown to me, he is also obsessed with creating bonsai. Given what I perceived to be the cultural gulf between Turkey and Japan, I asked him why bonsai meant so much to him. 'Bonsai allows me to disassociate from life and connect with nature on a spiritual level,' he said. 'I get totally lost in creating an art piece while feeling a personal connection with each tree I work with. In some ways it's just another way of being meticulously artistic without singing a single note, which I find to be one of the most tranquil and peaceful practices I have ever embraced.'

Whatever form they take, gardens and garden-making are integral to most, if not all, world cultures. Deep down in the human basal ganglia, our reptilian brain, lies a primitive drive to create gardens. The next rung on the ladder, the paleomammalian brain, develops our feelings of warmth, our emotional connection to the modified landscape – our desire to tend and care for it. And finally, the newest part of us, the neomammalian brain, enables us to reason, plan and communicate through language and abstraction. This is when we become artists. Fluent in our cultural understanding, we can now start to create. But what shall we create?

↗ Dolly Parton understands the need for her style to support her music and her philanthropy. She has said of herself that she'd have been a drag queen if born a man. Her look is instantly recognisable. Beneath her outward appearance, this tiny woman is a powerhouse of intellectual curiosity. Style and substance go hand in hand.

Valley Curtain, Rifle, Colorado, 1970–72, Christo (1935–2020) and Jeanne-Claude (1935–2009)

Style

God is really only another artist. He invented the giraffe, the elephant, and the cat. He has no real style; He just goes on trying other things.

–PABLO PICASSO (1881–1973)

Style, at its most simplistic, means an approach to doing something in a way that is typical of a person, a place or a historic period of time. We can easily identify someone's style of dress, of decor and of gardening. It becomes a signature. In some cases, a style is so intoxicating that it triggers a movement that defines a period. History will, I'm sure, remember Piet Oudolf for his original imprint on the contemporary gardening psyche. He paints with plants; his fluent style is much copied. His generous spirit doesn't mind at all – he encourages sharing. I asked him about his feelings on the subject and he said: 'There should not be secrets about how one gardens or creates them. In many ways, it is so related to how you are yourself and sharing is not the pleasure of giving away but getting back much more than you give.'

I'm intrigued by the two quotes here. Picasso says God has no particular style; I like this, there is freedom and self-confidence in it. Matisse conjures up the prison of style, of ego, of success; this is a sorry state of affairs. Imagine inadvertently creating something so popular, so identifiable, that it defines you and by extension limits your desire or ability to strike out into new creative pastures. I sometimes wonder how Dolly Parton feels about her wigs.

When I first started thinking about making gardens, I wanted to do things very differently. It was possibly about twenty years before I actually started making them, and I was more fascinated in installations than gardens. One of my early imagined schemes involved planting a kilometre of dry riverbed with the rusty, evergreen grass *Anemanthele lessoniana*. I had dreams of filming it with the wind running through it (like Pier Paolo Pasolini) to a soundtrack by Ennio Morricone. My scheme was almost certainly triggered by a combined love of the artwork of Christo and Jeanne-Claude, a recurring image of Zabriskie Point in Death Valley from Michelangelo Antonioni's eponymous film, and a passion for Italian film directors of the 1960s. However, I had a mortgage to pay and the practicalities of achieving the elusive moment were, well, elusive.

It did make me start to think, though. I definitely wanted to be creating landscapes. These disparate ideas had not come from the *tabula rasa* of my mind, but from a knobbly kit bag of references: my own, unique, cultural encyclopaedia of things I'd seen and heard, stories, conversations, films; kilometre after kilometre of European landscapes viewed from train windows; shared enthusiasms with friends; and trends that had passed through the air before evaporating. I understood, too, that neither Picasso nor Matisse had emerged fully fledged as artists but became themselves gradually. Picasso had been trained by his father, an academic painter, from the age of seven. He, of course, had immense natural talent, but it was supported by the inescapable skeleton of technical skill. So, Picasso's style emanated from substance. His gift was to evolve his way of painting constantly from the well-grown roots of his early training, secure in his ability to extemporise.

I realised that, before I could make the artistic installations of my early dreams, I needed to master the skills of the discipline and see where that journey took me. Gardens are pragmatic, and the tailoring of them more earthly, more practical, slower. We garden-makers are literally tied to the ground and all its vagaries. For me, it has become an all-consuming interest and the style of my work is as varied as the circumstances I encounter.

An artist must never be a prisoner. Prisoner? An artist should never be a prisoner of himself, prisoner of style, prisoner of reputation, prisoner of success, etc.

–HENRI MATISSE (1869–1954)

Style is a simple way of saying complicated things.

–JEAN COCTEAU (1889–1963)

Finding Your Voice

Whenever I am in the south of France, in Villefranche, along that Riviera coast, I think of Jean Cocteau and his quick, eloquent pen-and-ink sketches of the sailors he so loved. The faded pinks and blues of the stuccoed buildings in the strong Mediterranean light is somehow fused into these simple expressive works. Walking through the narrow streets, I'll notice the turn of an agave leaf that seems to capture the exact same gesture as his sailor's arm flung behind his head. The place and the people are so inexorably bonded together in Cocteau's effortless sketches. It is fascinating how his seemingly nonchalant hand has created such an indelible mark on style. His suggestion that style is a simple way of saying complicated things is interesting. It takes a lot of understanding and love of a subject to confidently distil it down to a uncomplicated design, or sentence, and he could do this literally with a flick of his wrist. Cocteau created visual mnemonics that we all know, love and understand. Madonna owed one of her better remembered looks to the fashion designer Jean Paul Gaultier who in turn owes a huge amount of his design sensibility to Cocteau. No one denies the train of events. Cocteau has also affected me, inspiring me to conjure something simple, believable and seductive. Some of my hotter gardens play simply with the space between things, proportion and louche naturalness.

Human nature is inquisitive and acquisitive. No matter what we are doing ourselves, we like to go and peer over a neighbour's wall and make sure they're not doing something better or more interesting. And if they are, we will most likely plagiarise it. Or we will feel anxious about not conforming and before you know it every street in every suburb will have an identical tree planted in the front garden. When I was a child in England, you could identify these gardens of Acacia Avenue very easily. You could assess who liked buying the houses, what they wore, the cars they drove, what they ate, where they went on holiday. The garden style spoke volumes about the need for postwar stability and social conformity. Plant a neat row of hydrangeas, mow the lawn and relax.

Cottage gardens, on the other hand, evolved from shared seeds. They were simple expressions of beauty in humble surroundings long before they became a fashion. They were just what people did to embellish their homes alongside the hard work of staying alive.

It's pointless to embark on a descriptor of garden styles here – this is a study in itself, and we are all familiar with Italianate gardens, French garden style, the English plagiarism of the two and our own home-grown heroes such as Humphry Repton, 'Capability' Brown, and later Harold Peto, Edwin Lutyens and Gertrude Jekyll. The subject is well trodden. It highlights the fact that the garden was often hijacked as a necessary expression of status for the insecure nouveaux riches. The landscape – and the choice of landscape gardener – told the world that you had understood and were getting it right. Some of our greatest gardens are soused in materialism and were coded fashion victims of their day. That said, the legacy of impressive building and attention to detail is undeniable. Had I been there, I doubt I'd have turned down a commission like Blenheim Palace if it had come my way. Importing and exporting 'style' around the world has long been something humans have done. It is interesting to note that the world's richest man, Bernard Arnault, earned his wealth by selling style.

So, in the end, the style you like is yours to discover. As John Ruskin said, quality is never an accident; it is always the result of intelligent effort.

Boy and Lyre, 1958, Jean Cocteau (1889–1963)

2. PLEASURE – PARADISE REGAINED

Having always believed that gardens were synonymous with pleasure, I was surprised to discover that the word 'pleasure' only came into use in the fourteenth century. It is the state of being pleased, gratified, delighted and content. This book takes a somewhat circuitous journey to arrive at that state, the destination being . . . a garden.

The old Persian *pairi-daeza*, meaning 'surrounded by a wall', gave rise to the word we use today: paradise. Ancient gardens of paradise were self-contained refuges for exquisite flora and fauna, with humans as their nurturing attendants. Within their walls, carefully conceived, poetic topography was enhanced by, among other things, the flow of water. The presence of running water, both a luxury and a necessity in the arid countries in which the form originated in the sixth century BC, allowed the gardens to become places where humans could get lost in mystical idealism. Typically, the waters were split symbolically into the four rivers of life, becoming calming metaphors to sweeten the inevitable pain of life and fear of death. These gardens with their water systems – *chahār bāgh* in Persian – were secluded, precious places.

In many cultures, gardens represent a heaven on earth – a place in which our mundane cares and physical ills wash away, uniting us joyfully, if temporarily, with a higher plane of consciousness. That ecstatic heightened state creates a longing that supports us through the tribulations of life. Islamic gardens, for a clear example, have never lost sight of their core principles. The garden is intended to provide quiet, shade, perfume, cool water, beauty and pleasure; all purely sensual experiences.

Any garden ought to set out to achieve these physical goals if it is to succeed at all as a pleasure ground. I add to this a gentle cartographical disorientation – a good garden takes away your desire to know where you are – liberating you to meander through changing experiences safe in the knowledge that another hand has mapped the journey with your pleasure in mind.

Being in a garden is a sublime experience. A good garden will stimulate all five senses, delighting, stimulating and teasing each one in turn, yet how that voluptuous feeling of abandon in a garden is reached is uniquely personal.

← It's worth looking at a real Persian garden rather than a subtle historic painting. Here, at Qavam House, Shiraz, in Iran, the use of strong colour is at once surprising and charming.

Freedom

Eliciting a brief for a new garden can be fascinating. Often, at the start, there is a relatively predictable list of objects, most of which are easily bought. As the designer, I need to place these things – that is a matter of common sense and doesn't always make an especially stimulating basis for discussion. Where the deliberations become more interesting, is when true personal desires start to emerge. People are understandably shy to express what really matters to them. Gardens are not, however, a typical material commodity, but require exposure of the commissioner's true self. It can take a little while for people to feel confident in expressing the less tangible aspects of why they are asking for a garden. This is the beginning of a long relationship that progresses slowly and with care.

As we start to dig deeper, different evocations of sensual pleasure start to emerge. 'My husband and I want to be able to make love in the garden without worrying about people seeing us.' Or 'I would like a Japanese outdoor bath made of wood and I want to be able to get from the house to the bath, naked, without disturbing anyone else.' Absolutely. Nakedness is a decisive physical luxury in a garden for many people, especially German people like my husband. I'm planning our garden now. One key preoccupation is how to create a suitable maze of hedges that enables his unpredictable and unseasonal naked sunbathing without traumatising the postman. Such thoughts were never far from the minds of garden-makers in the past, especially in pre-Victorian Britain before we all became neurotic about sex. Carnal pleasures are very welcome in my gardens. Original sin is well documented so there seems little point excluding it now the damage is done.

Almost everyone wants a hot tub or plunge pool. I could never really understand why until I was trapped in a small mountain-side hotel in Mallorca in a freak summer storm. Sea fog rolled in. At breakfast, an English couple at the next table muttered darkly, 'We should have gone to Scotland.' The fog rapidly developed into a violent storm, the worst the island had experienced for many years. We were told to stay indoors as the steep and narrow mountain roads were too dangerous to navigate in the whipping winds. The hotel staff, all Mallorcan, looked cheerful – the storm had broken a fifteen-day heat wave through which they had worked like Trojans. My room was too gloomy to read in, the windows being small so that the room stayed dark and cool. What should I do, I asked them? Go and sit in the hot tub, they chorused. So, I did. The tub was set into the now abandoned cliff side and had picturesque views out over the roiling stormy seas. The rain was torrential, steam rose gently from the surface of the warm tub mixing ethereally with mist from the sea. The staff charmingly brought me a glass of wine to celebrate the eccentricity of it all and we all laughed heartily. I felt like Neptune's daughter presiding over the waves. This delightful experience banished forever my sense that hot tubs are ghastly.

Years ago, I made a garden for a stucco-fronted villa in the leafy area of Maida Vale, London, a smart part of town in which the detached cottages dating from the 1820s all have attractive high-walled gardens. The listed building needed some rigorous research to support the changes we wanted to make. A local council officer told us that the small pavilion we wanted to include was unacceptable as, originally, the gardens opened out onto farmland and that bucolic view (now long lost in central London) was important. I set to work rummaging through the City of Westminster archives as something told me this was unlikely. What I discovered made me laugh out loud. A far cry from the politeness of the district today, these lovely villas were built by City businessmen flush with new cash from their colonial enterprises. They were not, of course, their principal residences. Instead, these handsome houses and gardens housed mistresses – often several at a time – to whom the city gents could rush for some lunchtime pleasure. The lushly planted gardens had uniformly high walls of 2.5 to 3 metres (8 to 10 feet) and, more often than not, small Regency latticework pavilions for post-prandial hanky-panky. These frolicsome gentlemen had absolutely no interest in gazing at the grazing animals on the surrounding lands owned by St John's College, Oxford.

Perhaps these gardens of earthly delights were the first domestic dilutions of the great English landscape gardens of one hundred years earlier. Surely, the private pleasure gardens created by William Kent at Chiswick House for Lord Burlington, just 10 kilometres (6 miles) from Maida Vale, had settled into the public consciousness. Everyone in London and the provinces must have heard lasciviously embellished tales of what went on in the grounds with their temples, cascades, grottoes and, most thrillingly, Lord Burlington's bagnio. A wealthy merchant could certainly build for himself, in a reductionist form, his own little patch of idealised nature, replete with fountains and follies and fun; a pleasure ground of his own.

My mother-in-law loved sunbathing and gardening in equal measure. As she grew older, the joy she got from sitting in her battered garden chair, in a sunny spot and surrounded by her flowers, was exquisite. Her year-round brown skin craved the vitamin D of a long sunny day as much as her nostrils quivered at the scent of magnolia blossom. She would sit for hours in complete peace, face raised to the sun, her fingers stroking the flower petals near her chair. It looked and felt as though she was mainlining pure solar health! She, like many of her generation, had lived through the war. Her experience of the firebombing of Hamburg and its gruelling aftermath was particularly extreme. The overwhelmingly traumatic experience never fully left her, yet her love of plants, gardens and gardening was certainly a balm throughout her life. She experienced pure peace outside in her garden, the skies no longer a source of fear and pain. The deep value of that innocent peace can only be understood by others who have experienced its opposite condition. Gardens are synonymous with domestic harmony and order; even after that terrible bombing, Germans were found to be fulfilling their gardening habits, raking ash and embers where their gardens had been, continuing the automatic response to care for their ruined landscape as though it were still there.

General View of Hampstead, London, 1822, Thomas Mann Baynes (1794–1876)

↗ I love looking for historic images of places I'm working in to see how they appeared before we smothered them in buildings. This is a view over Hampstead Heath from c. 1822. The gentle rolling hills and copses have since been replaced with lumbering buses and numerous speed cameras.

I saw the angel in the marble and carved until I set him free.

–MICHELANGELO (1475–1564)

Unfettered Imagination

Imagination plays a fundamental role at the outset of garden-making. My two young nieces, Hazel and Zoe, spent a day with us at the studio in London. We agreed that they would design the garden at their own home, a typical terraced Victorian townhouse with a rectangular outdoor space to the rear. Before the girls arrived we sent them instructions on how to survey their garden. They made a surprisingly accurate measured evaluation that we translated into a scaled CAD plan, which we printed onto large sheets of paper, one for each niece. We structured the day as though they were clients. 'Firstly, we must have your brief, what is it you really want from the garden?' They proceeded cautiously at first, 'nise brics [sic], no paving slabs (unless approved by Hazel and Zoe Blom) . . . and then whoosh, we were off, twelve trampolines, a trampoline built into a tree, goldfish, a crystal cavern, NO LITTER, a tunnel leading to secret meeting place (kids only), a library and coat rack, and strorbrees [sic].' On and on they went, bossy and brilliant by turn. After that, they drew their plans with a rare intensity that lasted the whole day. As they packed up to go home, Zoe asked in amazement, 'Jinny, is this *really* your job?' For weeks afterwards, back in the studio, we were fired up with the imagination they had brought. Unfettered by practicality, they had allowed themselves freedom to roam around in the subject pulling all manner of contradictory elements into the chronicle of their gardens. As adults, it is far harder to access this unbounded realm between fantasy and reality and yet we must try not to lose it. Subsequently, Zoe has taught herself to use the computer programs we use in the studio and is quite focused on taking over the business should I ever retire.

So, here emerges the fact that a garden needs to be suitably planned to allow the senses true freedom. The ability to get lost in a space, to feel so comfortable that your senses and emotions can drift effortlessly beyond corporeal bounds requires the absolute safety of a well-structured space. Physical experiences outside are wonderful and they stimulate the imagination, whether they're in a suburban back garden or a fantasy wonderland.

Fountain
strawberries
THE BRIEF
Ivy hanging over a table and chairs!
Little trampoline on a tree (built in)!!
Four tyre swings
LED lights!!!
BIG Pond
Vines!!
Cave with fake grass/grass ivy hanging over the eternce (View Prince Charles idea (with glowing eyes at the back)).
Small hot Pool!!
Secret tunel leading to a Secret meeting area (KIDS ONLY!)
flowers!!
Lilly pads!!
Lits for the dark
Play house (Not Plastic, real building)!!
ducks
Strorbrees!!
Nice bricks
Barbicue
tabell and Chairs!!
bunny caje!
Vegetalle patch
BIG tramplean!!!!!!!!!!!!
nise Brics!!
Frogs
Big tree! (to climb)!
Lots of trees!!!!
NO LITTER!!!
No Slabs!!
(only ones approved by Hazel and Zoe blom.)!!

← This marvellous old postcard shows the Fife Arms Hotel in its heyday – a Victorian granite colossus deposited beside the rushing Clunie Water in Braemar, Aberdeenshire. As solid as the granite hills from which it was drawn, even back then it could have been called an 'organic' hotel. Under the floorboards we found spent furnace clinker reused as insulation. Everything in the building was made from natural materials and in my garden there, I wanted to tie the high Victorian love of plant hunting and exotica with the natural riches of the Cairngorm Mountains.

↙ View of Taggia, an Italian town in the Liguria region of Italy, 1895. Rising up behind the town are the Ligurian Alps, once home to spartan villages in which life was extremely hard. After the Second World War the remote villages here – and across Europe – gradually emptied as people realised they needed to make their lives in the rapidly growing and industrialising towns. In France, in the 1970s, we were acutely aware of the way of life in the deeper recesses of the countryside dwindling. I remember hill towns with almost medieval populations gradually falling still. Today they have become tourist attractions filled with second homes, the old way of life romanticised, reinvented and viewed through distinctly rose-tinted spectacles.

↱ pp. 20–21: Sometimes little is needed to make a garden sing. This is an espaliered *Malus* 'Evereste', one of the best trees for the purpose as it is pliable and giving. Blush-tipped white blossom in spring is followed by abundant little crab apples in autumn. Spiders add their decoration that is made uniquely seasonal by the heavy morning dew.

Positive Influences

I've made more than a few large vegetable gardens, from simple vegetable beds cut into lawns to rather more elaborate confections with glasshouses, vine tunnels and espaliered fruits and livestock. This approach seems to be gathering momentum as the hard bite of how our food is mass-produced touches us almost daily. Few of us relish the air miles, the abject misery of edible sentient creatures, the plastic wrappings, the destruction of soils through intense farming and inordinate mountains of waste. How could we? Food is a pleasure that becomes almost sinister when handled badly. Growing delicious edibles at home is the new rock 'n' roll. Gardens are redolent of this desire for freshness, health and proper nutritional values. Old pop stars are making cheese and beer. Chichi farm shops are sprouting like mushrooms up and down the country. Motivation, means and method are creating some amazing results.

I think particularly of friends Manuela and Iwan Wirth, owners of the international contemporary art gallery Hauser & Wirth, who have combined modern art, contemporary gardens and organic farming to create their new concept: Artfarm. Their commitment to a holistic experience of hospitality is driven by their own personal generosity. They commissioned Piet Oudolf to create a now very famous garden at their Somerset gallery. Some months after the opening, Iwan said – with genuine astonishment in his voice – 'I had no idea how popular gardens are!', as hordes of visitors streamed down the drive for the pleasure of seeing Piet's planting in typical grey British drizzle. Subsequently, we worked together in Royal Deeside, where I created a small garden of mixed wild and cultivated plants on drumlins for their Scottish Baronial art hotel, the Fife Arms.

The Covid-19 pandemic and excellent Wi-Fi combined to create huge shifts in people's beliefs about what constitutes a good life. The collective unconscious spoke. We discovered that we don't like being in cities anything like as much as we thought. We crave sweet fresh air in our lungs. We want to wander through gardens foraging for herbs and salads, to be surprised by the unexpected burst of sharp sweetness from a fresh-picked plum. We want to see for ourselves the field in which the cow grazed before being served as roast beef, feeling cautiously optimistic that if we looked the bullock in the eye our shame would be lessened. Gardens, in the current climate, have become far more than a lawn and some flower beds or a place for bottom-pinching lasciviousness. They are gradually extending to meet a bucolic desire for paradisical completeness and self-sufficiency. They are becoming Roman again (about which, more later.)

Many of us have little or no experience of living in harmony with nature and growing food for ourselves. Older friends and relatives who might have known the ropes are no longer with us. I think of two men in their seventies. The first, my friend Živile's father, still shins up apple trees to collect the highest fruit and to prune every branch. The second is our own Hortulanus Rex, King Charles III, whose hands are the only testament needed to his love of the work. Generally, though, we are alone in the wilderness of domestic inadequacy, reliant on foragers blogs, shiny internet teachers and 'allotmenteering' enthusiasts. Perhaps, if we could learn to work the land together and share our knowledge and skills again, we might find ourselves on the brink of returning to Eden. Though, the harsh reality is, of course, that paradise is a psychological construct. Life is easy there. The truth is, 'living in harmony with nature' is a lot harder, colder, wetter and more worrying than any of us know. Subsistence-level farm-steading is something that humankind has fought hard to escape. In the process we have lost our sensitivity to the land with devastating consequences for the planet.

Reading *Thin Paths* by the English author Julia Blackburn on the lives of the *mezzadri* or 'half people' in Liguria, Italy, plunges you back into the pre-Second World War hardships of a life before plastic, piped running water and abundant fossil fuels changed everything. It is barely eighty years ago. Expectations of life were modest, work was gruelling, the pursuit of enough to eat was everything. A notable discovery in this extraordinary book is that throughout the hardships described and the endurance of the characters shines a generosity that is almost as extinct as the way of life itself. Despite the scarcity of food, there was an underlying principle of sharing with those less fortunate. A local 'hermit', a young man horribly disfigured during a farming accident, fled the village to live in a cave to spare those around him of having to see his terrible deformity. He gathered food for himself, foraging chestnuts, these being the basis of all diets in the mountains. At a discreet distance, villagers left him food, a blanket and on one occasion a beehive so that his connection to them remained as a slender thread.

It is challenging to think of living in such a small, reductionist way given all we have become used to. Yet the hermit, damaged and alone, still received love from the village, still carved beautiful images into his cave and still created for himself a small pleasure garden. 'Heaven on earth for all eternity' he had written beside the cave mouth.

Wood engraving showing the manufacture of Chartreuse by the Carthusian monks of the monastery, La Grande Chartreuse, near Grenoble, France, c. 1888, artist unknown.

↙ Carthusian monks, working hard below ground to make Chartreuse in elegant copper stills. My understanding is they, like the champagne-making Benedictines, favoured the caves for their even temperature. The earth has all the answers.

The Physical Body

Hard work is an inescapable fact of making gardens. There is an unrelenting stream of things that need doing, often testing physical thresholds of strength and agility. We find ourselves teetering at full stretch at the top of a ladder to tie in a stubborn rose or heaving on a fork to try and lift tenacious, matted roots. Much of this work is done in questionable weather. Yet this very physical labour is one of the great pleasures of gardening. The ever-twitching brain switches off for a while, allowing the senses and sinews full freedom.

It is interesting to reflect on the role of the garden in institutions of worship such as monasteries. Think of all the marvellous gifts that nuns and monks have bestowed on us over time and how they have created and refined products from soap to linen cloth to pottery and comestibles, all made in confinement and using their own produce. Favourites of mine include dear Dom Perignon and his marvellous champagne and the Carthusian monks who created Chartreuse. The recipe for the liqueur dates to 1605 when a French diplomat, François Annibal d'Estrées, is said to have presented the Carthusian order of monks with a manuscript containing the recipe for an unusual elixir that reputedly conferred a long life on its consumer. Eventually the recipe containing 130 botanical elements ended up being grown and cultivated at the Grande Chartreuse monastery gardens not far from Grenoble. This '*Elixir végétal de la Grande Chartreuse*' is distilled with grape *eau de vie* and despite its lurid colour and questionable flavour remains immensely popular. Its life-extending qualities remain undocumented. I would love to have seen the garden in which the components grew in their order beds.

The balanced diurnal rhythm of prayer and work – in Latin, *ora et labora* – forms the backbone of life in a monastery. Little change is required, little extra from the outside world needed. The monks, much like the Romans, chose the most beautiful areas in which to build their long-term homes. The environment they created was a highly adapted smallholding that ran like clockwork in harmony with its surroundings. The land required quite specific characteristics to support the monks' way of life, sustaining the household and its dependants with sufficient left in store to support a wider community or to provide for them when times were lean. The monks paid careful attention to the topography, choosing sheltered spots beside fast-flowing rivers beneath protective wooded escarpments and with water meadows. They would then canalise the river and channel water to wherever they needed it, through beds of watercress – the cress cleans toxins naturally from the water – into high-sided fishponds for live trout that need running water to stay healthy, then on, via an overflow, into water meadows where the grass and herbs grew sweetly for the small herds of dairy cattle and sheep to feast on, and for hay. The monks dug wells in their large walled gardens to irrigate the vegetables. A pig or two would be housed with the chickens, for they are the best companions. Chickens remove parasites from pigs and pigs remove parasites from the soil. Chickens also enjoy nesting on a shelf above pigs in a sty, the pigs keeping them warm as they snooze below. The pigs would run in the orchards at the first windfall, snuffling up the bitter fallen apples, releasing nitrogen into the tree roots to hasten the ripening of the main harvest. The nearby wild woodland would also supply firewood for bread ovens and hazel coppice for the vegetable garden supports and basket weaving. It also yielded wild mushrooms and herbs for medicine and flavouring. Each monk had his tasks, up early for prayer followed by long hard hours of work. Meals were homemade and simple, using produce from the potager within the grounds. It is hard to imagine there being any waste products from a system like this. Everything was used and reused.

This harmonic way of life has much to commend it. It closely resembles, in both its design and function, descriptions of the actual Garden of Eden: a literal shared 'garden' of highly productive land in a natural depression in the landscape bordered by four great rivers, the Tigris, the Euphrates, the Gihon and Pishon. Again, the production of food was not segregated from the cultivation of plants for pleasure and the social uses of a garden.

The Troubled Mind

...The cure for this ill is not to sit still,
Or frowst with a book by the fire;
But to take a large hoe and a shovel also,
And dig til you gently perspire;
And then you will find that the sun and the wind,
And the Djinn of the Garden too,
Have lifted the hump—
The horrible hump—
The hump that is black and blue.

–RUDYARD KIPLING (1865–1936)

In some parts of the world, living in a small, closed loop of domestic production and consumption – like that of monks – is still happening. Physical work is second nature and human bodies are rarely still. There is always something to be done and inertia is not an option if you want to stay alive with a thriving family. I am unaware of the broad mental health statistics for people living in this way. The Western way of life is almost entirely passive, not to say immobile. Work is largely static and cerebral. Our bodies must coerce us to find things to occupy them, such as gardening, having an allotment, going to the gym, running, hiking, and so forth. Developed and fast-developing countries worldwide are seeing an unprecedented rise in levels of depression. Is it because being deracinated from the earth to live much more solitary lives in urban conurbations makes us lonely and unwell? Could there be a link?

The headline types of psychological conditions are as follows:

- anxiety disorders
- personality disorders
- psychotic disorders, such as schizophrenia
- eating disorders

My personal experience working in mental health, as I did for many years before becoming a landscape gardener, focused on psychosis and anxiety. I worked in residential care. Severe psychological disorders are almost without exception lifelong conditions requiring regular medication. Our ethos, because it does help to have an ethos, was to ensure that every day was structured. It may sound dull, but eating, sleeping and working with some regularity brings great benefits to our body chemistry. Our daily work involved sustaining this rhythm. It is much harder than it sounds when opposing forces of psychosis, fear and depression are exerting strong gravitational pulls in other directions. Anyone who has even the remotest experience of what I'm talking about will understand that. Severe mental health issues are gruelling for those who have them.

We had strong links to various occupational therapy units for our people to visit during the day and to work there. One very good one was a horticultural therapy unit – a series of glasshouses and a tiny garden where seeds could be planted, nurtured, potted on and ultimately planted out in the garden. Seeing the effects of this unit, I decided we could rebuild our own gardens at the residences – we had three – and plant them up. It would be wrong to describe what happened next as a miracle because it wasn't really, though it was very exciting to be part of! There was an increase in energy and focus among our residents. We had ten people living in each house – we felt that ten was a good-sized group for feeling 'familial'. Everyone had something to contribute, from laying slabs to making tea, to planting. The group activity alone was mood altering. Changing our physical environment was stimulating. We were having fun. We all laughed a lot. It was quite rigorous exercise, in turn releasing endorphins – hormones that are literally a self-made morphine that makes you feel good. One of the most seriously clinically depressed people, a man who would spend weeks lying on his bed if allowed (which he wasn't), voluntarily went and bought everyone cakes. Small as it sounds this was a big thing.

During my time in this career, I also trained as a psychologist. It gradually dawned on me that the benefits of the 'structured day' we insisted on for our residents was also immensely helpful for me. I suffered badly with post-traumatic stress disorder, a condition that triggers acute anxiety attacks that are unpredictable and hard to manage. I hid my condition more or less effectively and just moved on if anything became too much, which I had done every six months on average over a ten-year period by this point in my life. But I didn't want to move on from this work, so things had to change.

Cycling 15 km (10 miles) to work and back every day, the rhythm of the working day and gardening at home in the early mornings did a lot to mitigate my highly nervous state. Learning simple coping techniques in this way was literally life-changing. Gardening was a key part of it and for several years I wouldn't leave home in the morning unless I'd done at least an hour outside.

Nebuchadnezzar as a Wild Animal, c. 1400–10, artist unknown

↗ Babylonian king Nebuchadnezzar is shown here as the madman he is reputed to have become after God struck him down with madness to counter his increasingly hubristic behaviour. Apparently, God instructed that he must walk on all fours and graze grass like an ox until he regained his right mind. A modern-day interpretation might suggest he was bipolar. I find this image very moving; psychological disorders can strike hard and at their most florid are difficult to live with.

Problems of Isolation

Isolation is usually the most serious form of punishment in prison, yet in the civilised world more and more people are living alone. No amount of material goods or fat income or medication can compensate for human companionship or shared experiences. Isolation leads to inhibition and makes the barrier to forming relationships much harder. There is a brutality to isolated living in an urban environment, especially in an apartment without access to the earth. In one UK city, residents fought with the local council when they tried to turn a fairly nondescript patch of lawn around their tower block into allotments. The council's resistance was immense, yet eventually the residents won. This was such a healthy outcome. An allotment is a universal type of garden. People from most cultures will be familiar with a domestic vegetable plot and see it as a natural activity with collective responsibility. The chats, the weather, the size of Percy's pumpkin, the sharing of seeds and vegetables, discussions about cultural preferences, the almost daily care needed for plants – all of which bring people together around a shared interest.

Perhaps pertinent to mental health is having a sense of who owns what in a city. The contested lawn was 'owned' by the council who, for whatever reason – health and safety, drains and power lines – had felt the status quo was being threatened. In much the same way, our local doctors' practice wouldn't let us make gardens of their lawns, the unspoken fear being that no one visiting the practice wanted to have to run the gauntlet of a number of peculiar old men growing tomatoes. The Inclosure Act of 1773 changed forever access to land in the British Isles. There were differing types of land described in the act, the lowest of which was 'waste' ground: waste land that the landless could use freely. Invariably it wasn't much use, or it was dangerously inaccessible, such as on cliff edges, but it was better than nothing. But, today, there is no longer any waste ground. I would be fascinated to sit with MPs to discuss changing the law to allow urban waste ground, such as these pointless snippets of civic grass, to have a communal loan status. That, in one fell swoop, would give purpose and community to people, diminish isolation, create a sense of personal autonomy, increase biodiversity and improve the air in built-up areas. There would be no need for big social intervention or government funding. Just rip up the lawn and commandeer the land.

3. FIVE SENSES

Scrambled Senses: Synesthesia & Neurodiversity

I experienced synesthesia as a child. It is quite hard to explain the effect it had on my senses of sound, smell, taste and proportion. Things I saw three-dimensionally either felt right or wrong. When they felt wrong, they affected me so strongly, physically, that I'd be sick. It might be the acute angle of a row of terraced houses or the textural weave in a coat that created a chaos of colour, or music that could suddenly bring peculiar tastes into my mouth. I could also see structures that weren't there, but I felt needed to be. For example, I might sense a barn missing in a farmyard and could virtually see its outline; I still get this impulse with buildings today. I had no means of making sense of my experiences and it was clear that neither my family members nor my friends were experiencing the same. I found the condition acutely embarrassing and kept quiet about it. Eventually I trained, or willed, myself out of it and into the conformity of more 'normal' responses. However, I would say that synesthesia definitely informs how I design today. I still feel very strongly the rightness or wrongness of a place and what it takes to make the wrongness right! I see finished gardens and landscapes instantly on arrival at a site. Often, I can't articulate what I see and waves of that isolating weirdness of my youth rush back unbidden.

These days, in the studio, we take the synesthesic's instinctive 'rightness' of ideas through a process of 'due diligence' to make the matter real, accurate and communicable across all the disciplines we need to work with. The key to unlocking the stigma of neurodiversity is to allow people to speak freely. It is important to develop common languages.

The reason for mentioning this relates to my desire for my colleagues to have free creative expression at work. It takes effort to be yourself and to feel accepted. Being a 'freak' child meant I was bullied and ostracised at school. While painful, it was possibly the best thing that could have happened to me. I made friends outside the norm and had a better insight into the ways in which humans absorb and process information. It also made me self-sufficient. Ultimately, it led me into psychology and mental health work and once you have spent years working alongside people with psychosis, only awe of what the human mind and perceptions can generate remains. There are many realities, many ways of processing the world around us, many ways of expressing it. Neurodiversity is becoming more widely discussed and better understood. Other traits that fall under the umbrella are dyslexia, colour-blindness, autism spectrum and left-handedness. In my landscaping life, I have encountered a huge number of people who 'didn't do well at school'. Being one of them, I am always interested to chat about how we all managed to cope with our incomprehension of our respective conditions. Being termed 'thick' or 'not academic' is challenging, yet neurodiverse people are not wired the same and have very different thought processes – often hugely creative and left-field ones. Many have gone on to achieve great things and have had to plough their own furrow to get there. We could thank them for their inventive contributions – they are not insignificant.

↖ These are the skilled hands of my studio members. Each makes images in their own way to express themselves. I prefer this to a list of achievements — though, of course, each of these individuals can claim many. During human evolution, the development of dexterity in the hands is thought to have occurred simultaneously with an increase in brain size.

Smell

Our noses govern much of our relationship with hedonics – the area of psychology that deals with both pleasant and unpleasant states of consciousness and their relationship to organic life. Pleasure and emotion are also heavily influenced by our nostrils. Smell is a potent emotional barometer. A certain scent trigger can last longer and be more fulsome than a memory. Memories tend to fade and distort over time and are often kept alive by retelling them, making them unreliable, as the game Chinese Whispers or Telephone has long proven.

Scent turns us on or off other people. They might not smell bad, yet they don't smell 'right' to us. It is an unambiguous emotional and psychological shut down if the nose says 'no'. According to detailed scientific research into the subject, we learn a great deal about food, other people and our physical environment through scent. Even though human noses are unsophisticated compared to those of dogs, they are, nevertheless, our mainline to all matters organic: danger, sex, enemies, food, pleasure, nature. In a word, the nose tells us whether organic things are happening or rotten. As many people learned from the coronavirus, to lose our sense of taste and smell is to be robbed of all pleasure. Those who experienced it learned to appreciate the link between scent and taste. Without smell, food is experienced as a purely textural substance rather than a flavourful one. Our brains aren't used to it, and it becomes unpalatable.

Remember Marcel Proust and his madeleine dunked in his tilleul tisane? It is the most universally recognised literary account of the link between scent and memory. My own is an unknown brand of French disinfectant – one whiff and I'm 'back there'. And fear, we can smell fear. Our noses shoot complex scents straight into our limbic system, which rapidly triggers an emotional response. It is not difficult to understand, then, the impact of smells in people with post-traumatic stress disorder. Shock can link scents very quickly to our responses, as odours increase the recovery of autobiographical memories. To balance the equation, scent also triggers happiness and good responses.

Nowhere is the sense of smell more alive than when we are out in nature – scent is one of the principal pleasures in a garden. It tells us so much. The subtle changes in the seasons are borne on the air, snuffled up by our alert nostrils. A crumbly handful of compost, inhaled deeply, tells us it is sweet and ready to use. The health of water, sweet or stinky, usually lets us know if it's safe to use, and for what, while stagnant, anaerobic soil shoots alarm right up our proboscises. Count how many times in a gardening day you hold something to your nose. It is surprising. Without due reference to all matters olfactory, a good garden cannot be a success.

I spent most summers as a child on the garrigue in the Languedoc, southern France, a rough limestone scrubland near the Mediterranean coast. Dense thickets of kermes oak, *Quercus coccifera*, punctuate the landscape. Juniper and stunted holly oaks, *Quercus ilex*, and holm oaks, *Quercus rotundifolia*, fill the landscape with their intense aroma. Pungently aromatic shrubs such as lavender, sage, rosemary, wild thyme and *Artemisia* are also common garrigue plants. The air is thick with spicy volatile oils, and with a sonic and visual accompaniment of bees, hummingbird moths, butterflies and hornets. The human nose is a remarkable organ, and a landscape of this kind is a dream come true for mine, forever etched in great detail in my olfactory memory.

↗ This is the garrigue landscape of the Hérault department of France, where my aunt and uncle owned vineyards close to the coast and where I spent a very great deal of time as a kid. Looking at this, I can smell the saline air mixing with aromatic oils; I can feel the place. The plants were all very twiggy, and so tough that they could pierce my feet, even through the soles of my sandals. However painful though, the smells and sounds were so intoxicating that I'd be gone for the whole day, day after day, scrambling about in my personal version of rock pooling.

Scent and Seasonality

Gardens benefit from aromatic diversity. It's worth considering scent as a separate subsect when designing planting. The seasons bring wave after wave of unique scents. Winter has some of the best smells, with sweet box, *Sarcococca hookeriana, Mahonia* ssp., *Chimonanthus praecox*, or wintersweet as it is known, and shrubby honeysuckle, *Lonicera* x *purpusii*. I don't know why the winter flowers are so narcotically fragrant, yet they are a mainstay in my garden plans. Generally, winter-scented plants are shrubs. They bring a structural depth to a space and provide shelter for small birds and mammals, especially as many plants are evergreen, or almost.

Spring brings greater subtlety and a little more crawling around on all fours as these floral whiffs tend to be very low down – the pretty floral scent of primroses, *Primula vulgaris*, buried deep among the mosses, and the rather more startling scent of apricot that emanates from their taller cousin, the cowslip, *Primula veris*. Perhaps my favourite spring scent is from the widow iris, *Hermodactylus tuberosus.* I first came across it in a small bouquet on my birthday in February. Not only is the widow iris an extraordinary colour combination of glass green and black, it is also exquisitely scented. Mine must have been grown in a hothouse as they usually flower in late spring. I plant them whenever I can in appropriately warm, stony land, where they won't get swamped by other things and can naturalise steadily.

Spring scents are quite refined, much like those of winter, yet they veer into the floral with an undertow of green crispiness. Think of hyacinth – it's possible to smell the thick, slippery sap in the stem just as much as the sweet, almost overpowering fragrance of the flower. The same applies to scented narcissi, the juicy stems contributing a great deal to the overall impact.

Heading into summer, the floral aromas warm and intensify. Among my favourite scented plants to bridge the seasons are perennial wallflowers, which I keep in great pots on the front doorstep. As the last of the tulips fades, the remarkable scent of the wallflowers through which I grow my tulips persists. Another unassuming summer vine that contributes far more than expected is *Lonicera periclymenum* 'Graham Thomas' – a sport of a wild honeysuckle that was found in a Warwickshire hedgerow by its namesake. No scent is sweeter or more transporting for me. I was given a tiny bottle of *chèvrefeuille* (French for honeysuckle) eau de cologne when I was small and the smell is forever fixed with happiness in my mind. I plant it everywhere, in every hedgerow, garden wall, trellis.

Autumn deepens into musky earthy aromas, fungal and forest-like. Woodsmoke and long-smouldering dampness join with the delicious greasy smell of fresh apple skin. I love the resiny aroma of pungent chrysanthemums whose sticky leaf smell is almost impossible to wash off. And then there are the daphne flowers, stretching their rich couture perfume far across the garden from their unassuming little parent bushes.

The great olfactory arc of the year leaves you with deep reserves of stored memory and stirring desires to smell it all again.

↲ pp. 30–31: All gardens need an orchard. This one is a beautiful relic. The trees, though old, still bear abundant fruit. In spring, the scents of fresh nettles and grass mingle with tender wafts of sweet apple blossom accompanied by birdsong. Exquisite.

↗ I have steadily increasing colonies of cowslips in my garden. As the primroses start to go over, the stems of the cowslips start to lengthen, indicating that the tumbling race into spring is really underway.

PERFUMERS SCENT WHEEL

- FRUITY
  - CITRUS: GRAPEFRUIT, LEMON
  - BERRY: BLACKBERRY, RASPBERRY, STRAWBERRY, BLACK CURRANT (CASSIS)
  - (TREE) FRUIT: CHERRY, APRICOT, PEACH, APPLE
  - (TROPICAL) FRUIT: PINEAPPLE, MELON, BANANA
  - (DRIED) FRUIT: STRAWBERRY JAM, RAISIN, PRUNE, FIG
  - OTHER: ARTIFICIAL FRUIT, MEHTYL ANTHRANILATE
- VEGETATIVE
  - FRESH: STEMMY, GRASS CUT GREEN, BELL PEPPER, EUCALYPTUS, MINT
  - CANNED/ COOKED: GREEN BEANS, ASPARAGUS, GREEN OLIVE, BLACK OLIVE, ARTICHOKE
  - DRIED: HAYSTRAW, TEA, TOBACCO
- NUTTY
  - NUTTY: WALNUT, HAZELNUT, ALMOND
- CARAMELIZED
  - CARAMELIZED: HONEY, BUTTERSCOTCH, DIACETYL (BUTTER), SOY SAUCE, CHOCOLATE, MOLASSES
- WOODY
  - PHENOLIC: PHENOLIC, VANILLA
  - RESINOUS: CEDAR, OAK
  - BURNED: SMOKY, BURNT (OAST/CHARRED), COFFEE
- EARTHY
  - EARTHY: DUSTY, MUSHROOM
  - MOLDY: MUSTY (MILDEW), MOLDY CORK
- CHEMICAL
  - PETROLEUM: TAR, PLASTIC, KEROSENE, DIESEL
  - SULFUR: RUBBERY, HYDROGEN SULFIDE, MERCAPTAN, GARLIC, SKUNK, COOKED CABBAGE, BURNT MATCH, SULFUR DIOXIDE, WET DOG, WET WOOL
  - PAPERY: FILTER PAD, WET CARDBOARD
  - PUNGENT: ETHYL ACETATE, ACETIC ACID, ETHANOL, SULFUR DIOXIDE
  - OTHER: FISHY, SOAPY, SORBATE, FUSEL ALCOHOL
- PUNGENT
  - HOT: ALCOHOL
  - COOL: MENTHOL
- OXIDIZED
  - OXIDIZED: ACETALDEHYDE
- MICROBIOLOGICAL
  - YEASTY: FLOR-YEAST, LEESY
  - LACTIC: SAUERKRAUT, BUTYRIC ACID, SWEATY, LACTIC ACID
  - OTHER: HORSEY, MOUSEY
- FLORAL
  - FLORAL: LINALOOL, ORANGE BLOSSOM, ROSE, VIOLET, GERANIUM
- SPICY
  - SPICY: CLOVES, BLACK PEPPER, LICORICE ANISE

Perfumed Gardens

A perfumer's scent wheel breaks scents down into easy-to-understand groupings. Almost without fail, these are scents found in nature and, more specifically, in gardens. I've not applied the same scent theory directly to gardens, myself, though it is probably a natural by-product of any planting design that it will encapsulate the same notes at some points during the year. Having looked more closely at the scent wheel, I feel it could be interesting to apply its olfactory sequencing to a planting design and see how it works.

'Perfumers' gardens' – historically in the region of Grasse in southern France – were once the source of many raw plant materials for the perfume industry. The region is still considered the world's perfume capital and makes for an interesting visit. Typically, the old stone terraces that line the steep hills of the area would be planted with aromatic trees such as fig, avocado and bitter orange for their leaves, flowers and fruit, and lilacs. Winding behind these, and probably trained on wires, would be great trusses of honeysuckle and jasmine. The Moors introduced jasmine to the flower farmers of the area in the sixteenth century. Queen of all the flowers were the carnations, *Dianthus caryophyllus*, tall cultivars grown in the open fields and also under glass to keep the blooms perfect. Then came the shrubby aromatics such as thyme, sage, rosemary, savory, myrtle and lavender. The flowers grown were treated purely as crops. Even today in Grasse, roughly 27 tonnes of jasmine flower are harvested every year. Great blocks of roses are also still grown, usually *Rosa* x *damascena*, for both Chanel and Dior have their own dedicated production sites. Violets, tuberoses, poppies, paeonies and *muguet*, the sweet lily of the valley so beloved of the French, are also still in production.

In 1921, Coco Chanel made a trip to Grasse, in search of a scent she could call her own. Local perfumer Ernest Beaux made a series of scents for her to try and she chose, of course, No5 – perfection when it comes to balancing the 'notes' of a scent. Top notes are aldehydes: ylang-ylang, neroli, bergamot and lemon (Beaux was something of a revolutionary using these chemical compounds to fix the scents); middle notes are iris, jasmine, rose, orris root and lily of the valley; base notes are civet, amber, musk, sandalwood, moss, vetiver, vanilla and patchouli. Civet comes from captive African civets that typically produce 3–4 grams of the substance per week. Amber is usually derived from the resin of *Styrax benzoin*. Musk was originally harvested from the musk deer and is now produced synthetically. Orris root was grown in Italy, where *Iris germanica* and *I. pallida* roots are both dried for use. They can take anything from three to five years to dry properly and the scent of the dried powder is a heavy pungent floral with myriad uses in perfumery and other scent-based trades. It was, and still is, used in potpourri, that marvellous semi-composted mix of wildflowers, roots and herbs that was made, often by monks, to stifle the stench of unwashed humans. The best of these is still made in the traditional way in Florence, at Santa Maria Novella, an apothecary founded in 1221 by Dominican friars. Their perfumes and potpourri are still made using raw, natural ingredients, many of which grow wild on the Tuscan *maquis*. The majority of herbs and flowers used in the potpourri are still extracted from the pharmacy's garden, much as they were more than eight hundred years ago. So, a huge array of plant aromatics that could, broadly speaking, if planted out, make a rather beautiful garden.

The Palace of Versailles has recently opened a new perfumers' garden, laid out much in the manner of a large potager or cutting garden, with capacious rectangular beds and hothouses. As an aside, I hadn't realised that the seventeenth-century court of Louis XIV is considered by some to be the official birthplace of 'perfumery'. My French granny, an excellent historian who loved all the wrong bits of history, delighted in telling me that Versailles reeked of urine. There was a single water closet for the Sun King and everyone else ducked behind the tapestries that lined the great chambers. None of these marvellous textiles survived – they all rotted away, but not before the stinking *tapisserie* give their name to the term *pissoire*. So, perhaps it was a matter of needs must that perfumery and its associated gardens shot to prominence. I might contest the Sun King's court as the origins of perfumery, however, as it is easy to find accounts of plant aromatics being used for perfume throughout history, while the word's derivation from the Latin *per fumum* meaning 'from smoke' is also something of a giveaway. But it is a fun story and fits with the big old ego Louis had! Cicero apparently said the 'best scent for a woman is none at all', as he choked on some worthy matron's dense *fumum*.

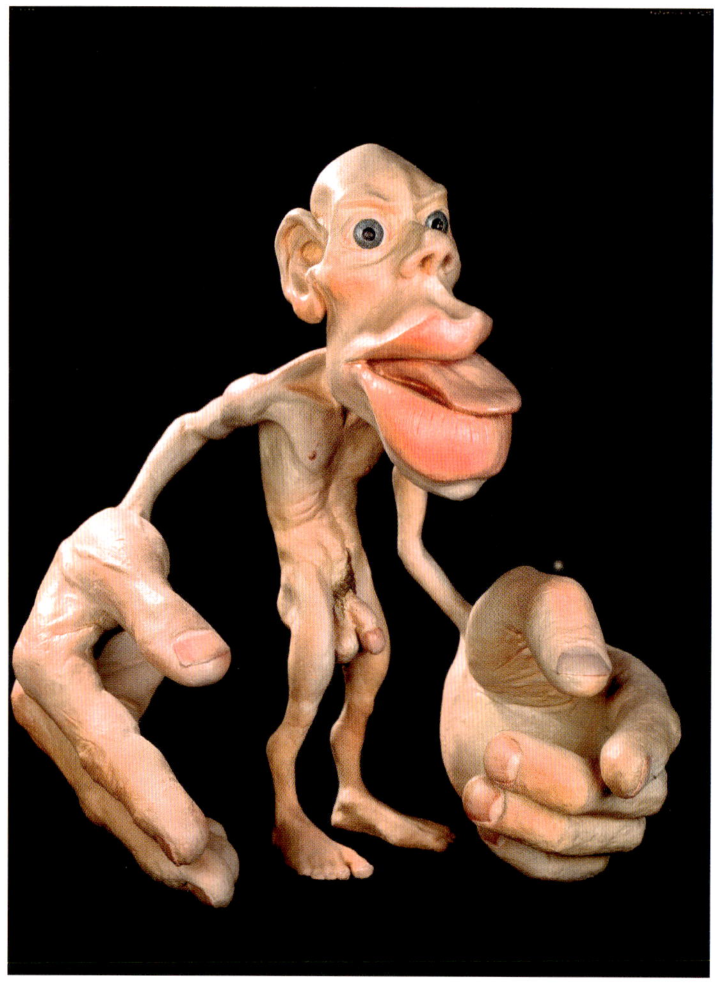

Sensory Homunculus, twentieth century, English School

↖ Meet Mr Sensory Homunculus. This model represents a technical map of the most sensitive receptors in the human body. Take a good look, as things are not quite as you might imagine. He shows the relationship between the brain and the amount of information it receives from different body parts – the larger the body part, the greater the number of sensitive receptors. Certainly, I'd not given much thought to my bottom lip before.

Touch

The sense of touch is the physical root of human development. Newborn babies, human or animal, deprived of touch if their vulnerable little bodies aren't warmed, stroked and held closely, can fail to thrive. This vital sense communicates safety, love and care immediately and non-verbally. It is the starting point of sincere relationships with others as well as a confidence in the bigger world around us.

The largest organ of the body, our skin is the sensory organ for touch. Nerve endings in the skin occur in combinations that respond to specific types of pressure and temperature. The sensations that are typically generated and communicated through our skin are heat, cold, pain and pressure. Skin is also the vital communicator in proprioception, the ability to sense the correct position and movement of our body parts, and also our awareness of problems via pain. It is a term any gardener, builder or landscaper is likely to become familiar with after endless trips to the osteopath. Proprioception is accomplished by neurons in the skin, joints, bones, ears and tendons sending messages about the compression and contraction of muscles throughout the body. Without this feedback from our bones and muscles, we would be unable to walk, work, go to the pub or even stand upright.

Garden-making and the creation of architecture, art and food are heavily dependent on our sense of touch. Touch is an immediate link to a qualitative assessment of materials. I am a firm believer in the idea that, by touching something, we have an immediate sense of its quality, its truth. For example, I was at a very famous, large modern art gallery in America once. It is awe inspiring, it is designed to command attention and convey greatness. Visually, it is entirely convincing and many 'oh wow's' were uttered, until I put my hand on the handrail to steady myself on yet another colossal stone staircase. It was a scaffold pole! Hastily installed on completion of the job, either because the architect hadn't wanted or had forgotten a handrail, it had been painted to mask its true identity. And yet, I've been up enough scaffolding in my life to recognise the sensation of cheap extruded metal in the palm of my hand. My reaction was immediate and in that brief moment I lost my faith.

A creation of any description must, in my view, take authenticity seriously. Whatever your choice of expression, make sure you see it right through to the most irrelevant details or it will fail you. I completely agree with the modernists on this. Arne Jacobsen's masterpiece St Catherine's College, Oxford, is close to my home. Jacobsen designed everything down to cutlery, doorknobs and, of course, the gardens. With sensitivity and precision, he planted the gardens with great care, mindful of how they would develop. They are now registered along with the Grade I listed building. The interesting thing is how much he cared about the sensory experience of this building for students. He must have understood the fragility of being away from home, the pressures of learning, the weight of expectation, the desire to have fun, the need for calm. He balanced the design of the building with these tender young people in mind and didn't let his ego forget the purpose of the task. The result, whether one appreciates his architecture or not, is easy to enjoy. Everything the hand touches has a material and considered truth. I carry this principle of physical authenticity right through my garden building. Touching is believing.

Touch in Gardens

How is the sense of touch relevant in the making of a garden? So much of making and enjoying a garden is sensory that how the garden feels is necessarily inherent in the structure. Take, for example, the use of stone. Stone is a marvellously malleable substance, its range of surface textures alone allowing it to be used in very many ways. I spent roughly five years working on the restoration and redesign of a ruined *castello* in Italy. The walls for the olive terraces on the land were made from local stone – worn volcanic boulders, naturally rounded over the millennia. Fragments of everything from smooth granite to light raspy pumice and fractured, angular limestone could be seen – and felt – in these stones, a symphony of physical sensation that was absolutely unique to the location.

It was important that the new gardens were absolutely in accord with the locale, maintaining a subtle sense of ancientness. To me, this would be conveyed through the physical sensations generated by the new design. After some travelling around and reading I fell upon an old black-and-white photo of a similar hilltop village in the same area. The paving was simply vast slabs of stone with weeds and tufts of grass emerging from the cracks between them. It stands to reason that the stone was quarried not too far away; no farmer of old would ever have hauled unbelievably heavy materials over a great distance as both their and their animals' bodies were needed for the more essential work of earning a living. We too found a local quarry and laid huge slabs, interplanting them with herbs. The sensation of the stone underfoot was unique – smooth yet uneven, it awakened the need to trust your instincts, alert to the unpredictable surface. Even with eyes shut, the feel of the stone immediately informed the brain of the nature of your surroundings.

I also found ancient stone troughs for holding water and incorporated them into the garden. Here, the stone had been worked, and you could feel with your fingertips the chisel marks made long ago as the mason swept in busy little diagonal lines across the stone's surface. Today, the troughs have the added texture of lichen and the odd worn down chip where a cow's bell might have clanked against the rim as it drank. The combined history of these objects helps build the textural essence of this new-old place.

Typically in this province the principal walls – by which I mean the walls highest in the hierarchy of importance to the castle – would have been topped with travertine. This detail is seen again and again in the local hilltop towns, the stone quarried and then worked to a smooth, sophisticated finish worthy of its importance in conveying wealth and beauty. We did the same. The travertine was quarried, cut to size using modern water-jet cutters and worked using high-pressure water jets to give a beautifully soft and undulating, almost polished finish, exposing fossilised leaves, shells and other natural detritus in its calcified sediments. Travertine is formed of calcium deposits, often accumulating around the hot springs that occur naturally in this volcanic region. It is irresistibly tactile. Drawn to the cool, comfortingly beautiful touch of it, I also made a huge table that we ate and worked at under the shade of ancient pleached holm oaks. On baking sunny days, the constantly cool stone was almost magnetic to our hot human skin.

The planting was also tactile, designed to be brushed against to release its scents. We planted enormous old mulberries with huge, gnarled trunks within stroking distance. Visually they announced age and the desire to touch them was irresistible. We used large volumes of aromatic plants, most of them edible, making them appealing to all *cinque sensi*, five senses.

For another garden in a different country, I worked on a design for a large naturalising rocky hillside, all made from scratch. The combination of managing the extreme rainfall, creating little rocky stream beds, navigating steep slopes with new rock formations and creating narrow paths through this recently imagined wilderness was exciting. More so, because the small children who lived there loved to clamber over the uneven surfaces, scrambling this way and that. Returning, for a moment, to proprioception, a garden is made so much more exciting when it is a challenge to navigate. Our towns and cities give us plentiful access to smooth surfaces to walk on. In gardens, I like to intervene with cobbles, random slabs and gravels – surfaces that give our muscles and brains that extra jolt of information to keep us alert. There is pleasure to be had in needing to hop from stone to stone or to watch your step on uneven cobbles. And, interestingly, the little children on my rocky hillside choose this less prescriptive play environment, full of jeopardy, mud, leaves, water, stretching, reaching, sliding and scraping, over their fancy play houses, climbing frames and slides! Isn't it odd that designing an urban playground carries such heavy legislation for health and safety, yet playing in the woods carries no health warning? Maybe urban play parks could be much more naturalistic and get round the red tape that way.

→ This old trough has so much character. The diagonal surface texture derives from the chisel strokes used to finish the work by hand. Made in a place and time before mechanisation, this is the work of a skilled, but probably quite lowly stonemason – possibly an apprentice. For a long time, all drinking troughs were carved from stone in this way.

↗ These are fossilised leaves in the travertine that I used to make the coping stones for the walls. The level of detail trapped by the calcium that forms the travertine is exceptional. This plant looks very much like *Carpinus betulus* to me, a native to the area.

← As part of the restoration of this ruined place, I paid much attention to textures of the past. I looked at houses of a similar age nearby and established that the walls were often coped in very thickly cut travertine marble. We used high-pressure water jets to achieve the soft, worn finish that tempts you to run your hands over the stone. The result is tactile and timeless.

Skin

Our skin needs shade to protect it from the harmful effects of too much ultraviolet light, fragile creatures that we are. We appreciate the sun's gifts most from a cool shady spot. There is nothing more inviting than a refreshing pool of shade beneath a canopy of green aromatic leaves on a warm summer's day. Intense aromas of vine or fig leaf in a hot country have left those of us lucky enough to travel with nostalgic traces of holidays in our olfactory memories. Strong sunlight, filtered and dappled by green is a pleasure intensified.

I have a very large weeping willow, *Salix babylonica* 'Pendula', in my garden. Often mistaken for a tree that loves water, it comes from dry areas of northern China and was traded for millennia along the silk route before finding its way to England via Syria. This tree is at once evocative of willow pattern plates and the Victorian parks and gardens in which they grew quickly beside ornamental lakes. Distinguished by having a canopy light enough to allow grass to grow beneath it, the weeping willow provides the best dreamy shade. We profited from forty-odd years of growth before buying the house and the tree is now a perfect size and shape. Beneath the tree we have set up an old, planked trestle table that was going cheap in a junk shop. In summer I sometimes work outside under the benevolent, high-domed canopy. Very often it is the scene of suppers and drinks and convivial social activities. The protective character of the tree relaxes everyone. It has become one of the rooms of the garden and near its trunk lie naturalised carpets of cyclamen. In a new garden, of course, the creation of shade must sometimes take a different form. Obliging trees cannot be magicked out of nowhere.

One important aspect of creating shade is the climate, and how that affects what you are proposing. In places of intense sun, it is impossible to survive comfortably without shade. In equatorial Africa, where I have worked, the weather is predominantly dry. So, given that the near-constant dry periods are close to drought, a green canopy can't be relied upon. It might also become an environment for creatures you'd rather didn't drop into your lap while you're reading. The heat in turn impacts the size of the shade canopy you might need, as well as the materials. A hot, dry country dictates that lots of outdoor activities necessitate shade – whether cooking, eating, relaxing, working, you will need protection. Locally found natural materials are perfect: dry straw, natural fibres and narrow, split-timber batons woven together into a palisade are ideal with a rough pole structure base. I like the aesthetic that is instantly appropriate when local materials are used. All the textures belong together effortlessly, and the colours are right.

The *ne plus ultra* of outdoor shade is unquestionably found in the Mediterranean region, with its long, hot summers, beautiful aromatic climbers and seductive evenings outside as the air moistens and cools. Here, a pergola is often the simplest construction of rusty steel rod bent to a gentle arc by a local blacksmith. The purpose is solely to support a vine or jasmine as a tightly knit canopy. Nothing is easier to make or more delightful to reside under than this.

In the temperate British Isles, a tree canopy works a charm, usually because of its scale and capacity to dry its own leaves relatively quickly in a breeze. However, unless you are brilliant at pruning and fastidiously tidy, British pergolas aren't very nice to sit under. The local garden tradition is one of pergolas and arcades as walks – think of the laburnum tunnel made famous by Rosemary Verey at Barnsley House and copied relentlessly – though laburnum faded from fashion as the seeds are poisonous to children and everyone decided chrome yellow was vulgar. The great pergolas of Harold Peto or Edwin Lutyens are mainly perambulatory. The British do shade rather differently because the unpredictable weather requires a fair bit of dashing in and out of the house. A permanent shade structure becomes easily neglected, gloomy and full of dead leaves. When the sun does come out, it can be surprisingly fierce. Days of consistent warmth are rare – temperate islands are volatile – it's why we talk about the weather so much; you never know what you are getting. Therefore, the time of day the sun appears is inconsistent and the location for sitting in it or hiding from it is necessarily spontaneous.

I once visited Tel Aviv to look at the White City, an incredible collection of Bauhaus architecture. Created by Sir Patrick Geddes between the 1930s and 1950s, the White City feels like a garden city brimming with lush greenery, yet in 1909 it was just a sand dune and a dream. Colonising a hostile environment to create a large urban conurbation (his word) took a good deal of creative thinking. Geddes professed he wasn't designing a 'garden city' as such, but an urban entity. He wanted to create a city around an environmental approach that drew together human needs: physical, social, economic. The architects had mainly trained in Germany before their exodus to Israel. The houses are almost uniquely constructed from concrete and painted white. The architects were aware of the intense desert heat and designed the houses on pilotis, or legs, to create shade at street level. Eschewing a ground floor in favour of shade also created space to cultivate kibbutz-style vegetable gardens. Apparently, the concrete construction made the apartments boiling hot and the complex was for a time considered a dismal failure, although it did make the street-level shade even more popular.

Today, such innovative thinking around climate is driven, to some extent, by climate change. In the French city of Lyon, the annual summer temperature is now close to that of the North African city of Algiers some 2,000 kilometres (1,250 miles) further south. The surface temperature of street benches in Lyon rendered them painfully unusable. In turn, the city sits below the Alps and on the banks of the river Rhone, making seasonal flooding from meltwater a great risk as well. The City of Lyon authorities and landscape architects L'Atelier des Paysages came up with a radical plan to cool the city. They decommissioned a multi-lane underpass, 2.6 kilometres (1.6 miles) in length to create a huge reservoir, channelling rain and meltwater into it. This water, cooling in itself, is used to wash streets and irrigate thousands of new trees planted along the pavements of the city. This innovation has resulted in significant cooling in the city in summer, better air quality and a pleasant environment for the locals. This kind of investment of intelligence, finance and action is sorely needed now. It can also be adapted to gardens. Increasingly, we are investigating ways to introduce plants to influence the overall use of a space. We build fewer shade structures and plant more shade trees and save every drop of water.

↵ p. 40: I spend a lot of my life at work, making gardens for other people. All I really want at home is some shade, birdsong and friends. As a family, we spend virtually the whole summer outside under our willow. I've been thinking about remaking our garden for quite a long time now, and somehow I just keep returning to this spot to mull it over. Mulling is also gardening.

↘ Doesn't this look dated? Not because its black and white but because of the current antipathy to lawns. John Betjeman's wonderful film *Metro-Land* (1973) reminds me of the ubiquity of lawn cutting and car washing on Sundays that until relatively recently united the inhabitants of British suburbia. Calm domestic repetition. Joy in ordinariness.

Grass

Grass has become quite politicised over the last twenty to thirty years. The sweet smell of cut grass in summer is reminiscent of school sports days, garden parties, hay fever and croquet. Those heady nostalgic images are now threatened by the darkening skies of climate change. Grass has taken on a troubling cast.

Big movements in the United States in the 1990s strove to stop, or at least slow, the resources that go into maintaining vast swathes of suburbia as a vivid green sward. Mowing, watering, chemical feeding and bug-spraying were creating green deserts in which nothing else lived, often in places where short grass really didn't belong. Huge volumes of precious water were pumped into keeping otherwise arid lands green. However, lawn is the preferred look for many. It announces that this is a clean, tidy, well-ordered place to live, not a wilderness full of snakes, bugs and things that could sneak up on you, making your life a misery at least and very sick at worst.

With my now broader experience of the American landscape, I have more sympathy with the 'clean and tidy' notion, for the wilderness is not at all like the benign one I grew up with in Britain. I ran off into a wild meadow once in Maine because it was full of the most incredible plants. I could see tall red lilies and I wanted to get a closer look. I sprinted back out minutes later with ticks, leeches, gigantic mosquito bites and deer fly bites like volcanoes – the creatures had feasted on the back of my neck in seconds. I was stunned at the ferocity of the attack. That just doesn't happen in my neck of the woods. If that's what people had to contend with in the past, no wonder they evolved suburbia.

I have a notable American to mention here, apropos grass. His name is Neil Diboll. I first heard him talk at Kew in about 1997. He has been championing the return of the Midwestern tall grass prairie since his university days in the 1970s. Neil runs the very successful Prairie Nursery in Wisconsin. He gave the most compelling speech about ripping up lawns and replacing them with the tall grass prairie species. Certain things he said stuck in my mind like glue – the depth that these plants root to for a start, some more than 2 metres (6 feet). That immense depth describes the enormity of the grass mat. Imagine the depth of typical turf and then picture it at a 2-metre (6-foot) depth and add that to the scale of an enormous landscape. It all makes perfect sense.

The Midwest has become a dust bowl after centuries of being planted with European agricultural crops. Shallow-rooting, annual crops have taken all traction away from the soil surface in these vast sweeping landscapes. The result is horrific erosion and desperate desertification. Neil painted a clear picture of the vast prairie grasslands as they once were: tall, very deep-rooted flower and grass mixtures spread as far as the eye could see, no trees breaking the view. Huge herds of buffalo roamed across the landscape, their weight treading down the soils. Seasonal fires sprang up and swept through in the autumn, reducing the thatch and aiding seed germination for the following year – many of these plants have a symbiotic relationship with fire. The landscape had its own simple, steady rhythm. It was the result of slow evolution and it worked. Thanks to Neil, and others like him, a huge prairie mania took hold. Many native prairie plants are now frequently used in our gardens. I feel they work best with a continental climate where summer and winter temperatures are more extreme.

Depending on what you read, and where you read it, between 20 and 40 per cent of the world's landmass is covered in grassland, and there are roughly 12,000 species of grass. Quite a lot of them are the grasses we humans survive on as food, so I am not referring to lawn alone. Grass is, of course, a mainstay in most gardens, conveniently covering large areas, rendering them manageable and weed free. Grassing over 'dirty' ground, or ground infested with ground elder or bindweed, is a simple, if slow, way of decontaminating it. Mowing over pernicious weeds is an easy chemical-free fix provided you have the patience.

In a landscaping context there's no better plant than grass as a fixative. It is simply a matter of right plant, right place. With the amount of soil disturbance we generate in our landscaping, there needs to be a rapid and reliable way of protecting the soil surface; bare earth erodes at an alarming rate and has to be covered quickly. Invariably, we use a grass or mixed meadow of some kind. This is particularly the case in the United Kingdom, which since the 1970s has lost around half of its biodiversity. Wherever possible, we put back what structure we can to assist its repair.

← The undisputed king of gardens is the weather. Changing light, leaf-rustling breezes, mackerel clouds, mists — this is where the atmosphere lies. Garden photographers like Britt Willoughby get up before dawn to catch the fleeting effects the weather has on the landscape. Mystery and magic lie in these thermal wraiths of vaporous haze.

→ My friend, the photographer Tom Mannion, is, like me, a cloud fancier. Tom is better known for images of stunning interiors, yet his favourite pursuit is cloud spotting and this is one of his. Each cloud has a poetry of its own. They are one of the reasons why flying is so uniquely special. To be up in this ever-shifting landscape of water vapour is one of the best reasons to be alive.

Weather

The British climate is subject to much ridicule worldwide. All too often, there is the perfect English summer's day – soporific weather for sunbathing, lying in garden chairs, chatting and listening to the birds and bees. A soft rustling breeze stirs the air pleasantly at intervals, casting wafts of delicious flowery scents across the garden. Made reckless by the charm of it, the temptation is to organise lunch in the garden with neighbours for the following day. Given the extreme volatility of our island climate these things can never be planned too far in advance. Sure enough the next day dawns beautifully, but by midday a brisk easterly wind kicks up and ominous clouds start building. By one o'clock, the appointed hour, it is grey, cold and a biting wind with spitting rain has arrived. Everyone troops back inside.

Can we predict weather? Anecdotally we can. There are known physical symptoms, such as aching joints when it's about to rain or headaches as storms build and air pressure changes. An ability to predict weather is a gift and, historically it seems, a gift of royalty. In ancient Egypt, for example, the pharaoh was the only person bestowed with the power to speak directly to the sun god Ra.

The Babylonians were using cloud formations as weather predictors as early at 650 BC. The ancient Greeks invented the term 'meteorology', meaning the study of atmospheric disturbances or meteors. A meteor in this instance means something that falls from the sky; it could be a space rock but more likely for the Greeks it was a 'hydrometeor' such as rain, hail or snow.

Around 300 BC, the Chinese created a calendar of weather festivals, dividing the year into twenty-four distinct periods or 'solar terms', each celebrating a specific weather type. Still remarkable to this day it forms a unique gardening calendar. It pre-dates by a significant timeframe the later Western scientists who began charting weather on daily maps to create forecasts.

In the West we have four seasons that seem to do the job when we add in the now fading markers such as solstices and equinoxes. By contrast the Chinese solar terms divide the year at fifteen degree intervals housed within the four seasonal quadrants of the year that we know in the West, so achieving six 'terms' per season. The observations listed for each term were, and still are, relied on by farmers when planning their year. The terms are both poetic and informative. Could they reliably map climate change too? If the seasons fail to correspond to this ancient arrangement might that be cause for alarm?

Degree	Solar term	Zodiac animal	Star sign	Date
315°	立春 LÌ CHŪN, SPRING STARTS Beginning of spring in the South of China.	虎 TIGER	AQUARIUS	DATE IN 2021: 4 FEB
330°	雨水 YŬ SHUĪ, RAIN WATER Rainfall increases from then on.		PISCES	DATE IN 2021: 18 FEB
345°	驚蟄 JĪNG ZZÉ, AWAKENING INSECTS Hibernating insects start to awaken with spring thunder.	兔 RABBIT		DATE IN 2021: 5 MAR
0°	春分 CHŪN FFN, SPRING EQUINOX Mid-spring; day and night are equally long.		ARIES	DATE IN 2021: 20 MAR
15°	清明 QĪNG MÍNG, PURE BRIGHTNESS It is warm and bright (when not raining); vegetation turns green.	龍 DRAGON		DATE IN 2021: 4 APR
30°	穀雨 GŬ YŬ, GRAIN RAIN Rainfall increases greatly and is helpful to grain.		TAURUS	DATE IN 2021: 20 APRIL
45°	立夏 LÌ XIÀ, SUMMER STARTS Beginning of summer in the South of China.	蛇 SNAKE		DATE IN 2021: 5 MAY
60°	小滿 XIĂO MĂN, GRAIN FULL The grain gets plump but is not yet ripe.		GEMINI	DATE IN 2021: 21 MAY
75°	芒種 MÁNG ZHŎNG, GRAIN IN EAR Grain grows ripe and summer farming begins.	馬 HORSE		DATE IN 2021: 5 JUN
90°	夏至 XIÀ ZHÌ, SUMMER SOLSTICE Daytime is the longest and nighttime is the shortest of the year.		CANCER	DATE IN 2021: 21 JUN
105°	小暑 XIĂO SHŬ, SLIGHT HEAT It is hot.	羊 GOAT		DATE IN 2021: 7 JUL
120°	大暑 DÀ SHŬ, GREAT HEAT The start of the hottest time of the year and when rainfall is the greatest.		LEO	DATE IN 2021: 22 JUL

Degree	Solar term	Animal	Zodiac	Date in 2021
135°	立秋 LÌ QIŪ, AUTUMN STARTS Beginning of autumn.	猴 MONKEY	LEO	DATE IN 2021: 7 AUG
150°	處暑 CHÙ SHǓ, LIMIT OF HEAT Marks the end of hot summer days.		VIRGO	DATE IN 2021: 23 AUG
165°	白露 HÁI LÙ, WHITE DEW Temperatures begin to drop and it turns quite cool.	雞 ROOSTER		DATE IN 2021: 7 SEP
180°	秋分 QIŪ FĒN, AUTUMN EQUINOX Mid-autum; day and night are equally long.		LIBRA	DATE IN 2021: 23 SEP
195°	寒露 HÁN LÙ, COLD DEW Turns a bit cold.	狗 DOG		DATE IN 2021: 8 OCT
210°	霜降 SHUĀNG JIÀNG, FROST'S DESCENT Turns colder and frost appears.		SCORPIO	DATE IN 2021: 23 OCT
225°	立冬 LÌ DŌNG, WINTER STARTS Beginning of winter.	豬 PIG		DATE IN 2021: 7 NOV
240°	小雪 XIǍO XUĚ, LIGHT SNOW Starts to snow.		SAGITTARIUS	DATE IN 2021: 22 NOV
255°	大雪 DÀ XUĚ, HEAVY SNOW Snows heavily for the first time of the year.	鼠 RAT		DATE IN 2021: 7 DEC
270°	冬至 DŌNG ZHÌ, WINTER SOLSTICE The shortest day of the year.		CAPRICORN	DATE IN 2021: 21 DEC
285°	小寒 XIǍO HÁN, SLIGHT COLD Gets colder.	牛 OX		DATE IN 2021: 5 JAN
300°	大寒 DÀ HÁN, GREAT COLD The coldest time of the year.		AQUARIUS	DATE IN 2021: 20 JAN

Being a collection of islands surrounded by sea, the British Isles have a unique temperate climate. Traditionally it was never too much of anything and rarely much of anything at all. The constantly eddying airflow was moist, cool, mild and comfortable. Summers were not typically long or dessicatingly hot and winters were not subject to profound hard freezes. While it was not easy to predict the minutiae of the weather, it was safe to assume it would never be extreme. This gentle climate allowed great freedom for gardens and went some way to explaining the British tendency to talk obsessively about the weather. In recent years, the weather has started to become more dramatic, bringing floods and droughts. As a result the British are altering their planting schemes somewhat in response to it, although it is too soon to be conclusive about changes in the weather.

I have a healthy respect for continental weather, borne out of gardening in, among other countries, France, where I have small patch of garden in the southwest. It is incredibly tricky. Summers are baking and the winters so desperately cold that really the only available garden seasons are spring and autumn. It is also damp in winter as our village is on the confluence of two large rivers, so the water table rises hugely. Heavy flooding is not uncommon, killing a great many plants that might otherwise like the heat, such as salvias. The flower market in the village brims with garish annuals in early summer – zinnias rule! So, we enjoy a ravishing spring of irises, wisteria, paeonies and wild orchids that rapidly give way to parched nothingness until September, when a plethora of fruit ripens in the countryside. It's beautiful and enjoyable, but it's not gardening as we know it. Gardens here tend to be more successful if they are either highly structured, like the Gardens of Eyrignac, or given over to fruit and veg.

For a successful garden, gaining an intimate understanding of the specific microclimate of the site is essential. And they really are microclimates. For example, my garden in England faces east and looks out over fields. It is in an elevated position on a hilltop at the edge of a village – ours is the last house before open countryside. My friend Julie lives not more that 120 metres (400 feet) away; her garden has high walls and is within the warm heart of the village. Our two gardens have completely different climates and support very different plants. Not 3 kilometres (2 miles) away in the city at the bottom of the hill, the gardens are below sea level. It is cold and damp and the riverine nature of the location attracts a very different weather from that at the top of the hill. The gardens there get all the rain as it follows the river valley.

Given that my studio makes a lot of gardens, it stands to reason that each one is climatically unique and has to be evaluated as such at the outset. The individual microclimate can be affected by design, of course, and needs to be if the garden is to be comfortable. Every project starts with a full assessment of the weather the location is subject to. Experience tells me the most reliable way of analysing this, apart from the obvious visual and topographic surveys, is by word of mouth. Projects require an enormous amount of talking. It pays dividends to get a group of the indigenous population together and have a good old chat about the weather. Pubs are made for this. Projects are social activities and the shared knowledge is invaluable. Things to assess in the microclimate review are: topography, exposure, aspect, hot pockets, frost pockets, shade and drainage. Once you have a good grasp of these, you can start planning how to get the local weather conditions to work to your advantage. This is why making a new landscape is such an absorbing four-dimensional puzzle – an analysis of pre-existing conditions makes the end result infinitely more comfortable.

→ *Hamamelis*, or witch hazel, flowers in late winter when it can still be very cold. It is not unusual to see its flowering branches covered in snow. Its sweet and spicy scent drifts through crisp, damp air. It is a stalwart of any winter garden and perfumes a room from a single cut stem.

↖ When planting a hot, dry garden, I use prodigious quantities of *Cistus* across lots of varieties, this one being *Cistus* × *argenteus* 'Silver Pink'. These plants love to be hot. Baked by unrelenting sun in unforgiving soil, they offer up their sweet, delicate crinkly flowers and often aromatic foliage without demur.

← An absolute favourite of mine is *Rosa pimpinellifolia*, the burnet rose of Scotland. Again, belying its toughness with its feathery foliage and pretty, single white flowers, this rose can withstand deluges of summer rain, arctic wintery blasts and months of heavy snow cover. It is a ruthless pioneer with the beguiling charms of a doe-eyed maiden.

Taste

Fully exploring the senses is invaluable to the making of gardens. Senses need to be considered in the round and allowed for, filtering opportunities for exposure to each one. Our sense of taste is very much part of garden-making for the myriad of flavours a garden can offer. I have always associated wandering through gardens with a degree of oral exploration. As a child, I would pluck snapdragon and honeysuckle flowers to suck the nectar out of them and chew the sweet, pale green shafts of long grass. Tiny alpine strawberries lurking under their pretty crinkled leaves, weirdly musky and hot nasturtiums, and barely ripe, lip-puckering gooseberries were other favourites.

↓ This is part of a small orchard that links to the vegetable garden on the previous page. The trees are pears, which I bought big and old for two reasons. The first relates to the saying that you 'plant pears for your grandchildren' as they take an age to mature. The second is that I wanted to achieve instant age in this part garden for aesthetic reasons. The trees are underplanted with lavender and rosemary for their scent.

↵ pp. 50–51: I like to include a vegetable garden in every project – it doesn't have to be huge. This one has nine raised beds, some cold frames, a large fruit cage and a small orchard. This garden was entirely newly built and this photo shows the first season of planting up the beds. We have a collection of edible things such as strawberries, chard, squashes, peas, beans, courgettes and tomatoes mixed in with sweet peas, dahlias and herbs. The produce will change year on year and amply feed the family.

Oral Pleasures

The human mouth is an extraordinary organ, closely linked to staying alive through human evolution. The taste sensations humans encounter, categorised as bitter, sweet, sour, salty and umami, have helped navigate food safely since time began. Taste is also very closely aligned to emotions, and strong emotions at that. Literature and experience have enriched our vocabulary to express intense feelings via powerful tastes: the sour grapes of jealousy, the bitterest pill to swallow and uttering sweet nothings to a lover. An hour or two in the company of Shakespeare would certainly develop the analogous list. A deeper understanding of taste sensations can help when designing a fully functional garden of edibles and medicinal herbs.

Sweetness is generated by sugars and alcohols and certain amino acids. Humans have evolved to enjoy sweet things, their sugars signalling an energy-rich food; sweet foods are usually high in carbohydrate, providing us with easily ingested energy. The human brain is a hungry organ, so is constantly alert to the possibility of gorging on such morsels. This has been the case throughout history and it was only natural that a co-dependence with bees developed very early on. Bees fuelled human evolution by offering access to reliable quantities of honey throughout the year. The symbiosis we have with bees was literally life changing. Over time, while our urge for sweetness remains, our sweet foods have changed with dire consequences for our health.

Common salt is found in halite, the mineral salts that gather around saline springs and that are found in evaporated sea water. It is also a trace mineral in some vegetables. Salt is essential for electrolyte and fluid balance in humans and animals and without it we become very ill. The taste sensation developed to remind us that we need it. In places where food is scarce, salt deprivation has devastating consequences on health. On a project we made in Africa, we put agricultural salt licks out in the wilderness beyond the ha ha to attract passing animals. They were very well used, and I'd consider using them for smaller wild creatures too.

Bitterness is usually found in plant-based compounds. Humans learned to recognise it as a warning that something wasn't safe to ingest in quantity – useful in a world where one red berry is delicious, and another could make you extremely unwell. Most human diets benefit from some bitterness and 'bitter salads' were not unusual in the not-so-distant past. Leaves such as dandelion, chicory and sorrel, full of vitamins and minerals, aided digestion. Their slightly over-stimulating properties are recognisable in their colloquial names, dandelion being *pissenlit* in French (I'll leave you to translate).

Sourness, we mainly associate with underripe fruit or things that are going off. It is another warning sensation to hold us back from overdoing it. Sourness is created by hydrogen ions. In many countries the taste is appreciated. In Turkey, for example, shiny, vivid green greengages, or *eriks*, are consumed underripe and sour. I've eaten my way through mountains of them – crispy, tart, and juicy, dipped in salt. Maybe it's the climate that makes them so unexpectedly delicious.

I have left umami until last. It's a Japanese term that broadly translates as 'savoury'. Umami is the detection of carboxylate anion of glutamate on the human tongue. Rather like salt, too much umami would be unpalatable, yet it is essential in flavouring long-cooked broths, seafoods and seaweed.

Tastes have changed. Looking back through the history of food it is easy to see that. For a start, until relatively recently, there were no chemical flavourings in our foods and most of our medicines came from the plant world. Culturally our foods and their flavours defined us as nations. Reading *Toast* by Nigel Slater, his autobiography of English childhood eating, I laughed out loud several times. Presented with the sorts of dried packet foods common in those days, no one would touch them now. My French mother fed us garlic in a country in which it was treated with deep suspicion. 'You stink' was not an uncommon insult at school and I'd hide my lunchbox for fear of derision. Fear of flavour diversity was synonymous with racism. My best friend was Rajasthani, so we could both relax together in our respective worlds of oral ostracisation.

It is hard to believe that there is so much variety in the foods available now. These days many know what agretti, *Salsola soda*, is and eats it without demur. Bitter flavours in fresh foods are back and curious combinations of foods that don't belong together appear in fast food joints, such as pomegranate seeds on potato salad with a hard-boiled egg. But hey, let's experiment, never mind the inappropriateness or the air miles – it's all about umami, mouth feel and marketing!

A Gardener in a Potting Shed with Pineapples and Various Vegetables, nineteenth century, Alfred William Hunt (1830—96)

← A pleasantly instructive image of Aztecs creating a *chinampa* – a woven floating mattress of a garden – with more developed versions, fully planted floating serenely in the background. I find these gardens absolutely captivating, especially with their little pavilions and the *Salix bonplandiana* around the edges.

↗ Endless teams of gardeners plant the annual display of fruiting trees in the eponymous planters at Versailles.

↙ In this charming scene from a Georgian English garden, the gardener is hard at work with his exotic fruit and vegetables. Unusual produce, such as pineapples, were all the rage and had to be shown off to visitors during what I can only hope were excessive and bawdy lunches.

'Versailles: Garden', line engraving from *The Perfect Gardener. Instructions for Fruit and Vegetable Gardens*, Jean-Baptiste de la Quintinie, Paris, 1690

Tasty Gardens

Gardens as paeons to oral pleasures are not unknown. Our very own King Charles III has made his organic vegetable garden into a place of great beauty and productivity. He is not the only monarch to have done so. Louis XIV of France commissioned Jean-Baptiste La Quintinie to build the Potager du Roi in a marsh known as the 'stinking pond'. Never let practicality get in the way of a hungry monarch. The kitchen garden at Villandry, the most famous of the chateaux of the Loire, took vegetable gardening to fresh heights of artistry and husbandry. No longer could the humble vegetable be sneered at simply as a kitchen ingredient to be hidden away out of sight. In Victorian England, the maintenance of walled vegetable gardens was considered a high art. Unique and previously unexplored flavours such as cauliflower were served at smart banquets to pique the jaded palates of the great and the good. At the time cauliflowers weren't unknown in England but required skill and constant warmth to grow them well, and so they became the province of the wealthy with their retinues of sophisticated gardeners.

Some of the most extraordinary and innovative gardens were the *chinampas* of the Aztecs. The hugely unpopular Aztecs were itinerant marauders who fought and pillaged their way across Mesoamerica until, one day, they saw an eagle perched on a cactus with a snake in its claw and took it as a sign (who wouldn't!) to found their first city … on a lake. They overcame the obstacle of water by building vast mattresses of reed and brash with woven panels, probably of willow *Salix bonplandiana*, a naturally fastigiate tree that wouldn't have overshaded the gardens, and swamp cypress, *Taxodium mucronatum*, topped off with soil and rock.

The *chinampas* were vegetable and flower gardens. The Aztecs constructed a woven perimeter using reed and willow hurdles that they then back-filled with soil from the bottom of the lake, and other organic matter, until the finished level was above the waterline. The soil from the bottom of the lake was rich in nutrients and bacteria, making it a good fertiliser. A rather formal layout included willow trees set at intervals around the perimeter of the *chinampa* – their water-tolerant roots matting and reinforcing the edges and offering a ready supply of basket-making material. These gardens were wildly productive with up to seven harvests a year, their rich soil constantly moist in the heat. Typical crops included the 'three sisters' of Mesoamerican cuisine – beans, corn and squash – alongside tomatoes and many other local edibles. Some of the *chinampas* were used only for growing flowers and had small buildings on them, rather like pavilions. I can see a future for this kind of gardening on water. There is a clear logic to it and the level of productivity justifies the initial effort. The Aztecs lived very well and comfortably until 1519 or so when the Spanish came and drained the lakes to get at them – and the rest is history.

Plants That Changed the World

Among the many plant flavours of the world are several that have changed the course of history. Here are some of the most influential:

The potato, *Solanum tuberosum*: Originally from modern-day Peru, this starchy vegetable was first cultivated about 10,000 years ago. The Spanish took it back to Spain from South America in the 1500s and it is now the world's fourth-largest food crop after maize, wheat and rice. Such was the impact of a potato famine in Ireland in the mid-1800s that it led to widescale migration.

Wheat, *Triticum aestivum*, and other varieties: This grass is widely grown for its carbohydrate-rich seed and is the second-biggest global crop after maize. Wheat covers roughly 220 million hectares (550 million acres) of land in the world.

Tobacco, mainly *Nicotiana tabacum*, another member of the Solanacae family: Everyone is familiar with tobacco for smoking, yet in its native South America the plant was a sacred medicine with myriad uses. Introduced to Europe by the Spanish following their conquest of South America, the plant's cultural relevance has since been lost.

Coffee, *Coffea canephora* and *C. arabica*: With origins in sub-Saharan Africa, this bitter drink is high in caffeine and antioxidants. A stimulant, it was originally drunk in the Yemen by Sufis to help them stay awake during their ceremonies. A vital cash crop in African countries, coffee is also the legal tonic drug of choice across the world.

Tea, *Camellia sinsensis*: Originally from India and China, this plant has been used to make a popular aromatic drink since the third century. Portuguese priests introduced it to Europe in the sixteenth century. The British got so excited by tea, they set up huge plantations in India from the 1700s, becoming globally powerful, quite unpopular and very wealthy.

OLIVE

Opium, *Papaver somniferum*: The milky sap of green poppy seedpods has been used as drug since at least 2000 BC. Its rocky history is peppered with wars and altercations over consumption, addiction and death. Losing the trade of opium to the English led to a 'century of humiliation' for the Chinese. Conversely, the opium trade provided 12 per cent of the budget needed to sustain The British Raj in India. The political consequences of this are still being felt around the world.

Quinine: This bitter substance extracted from the bark of the Andean shrub, *Cinchona officinalis*, is best known as an antimalarial drug and is produced commercially these days. The Peruvians, Andeans and Bolivians kindly shared the indigenous drug with malaria-stricken Spanish invaders in the 1500s. In the days of the British Empire, doctors prescribed quinine to expats in gin and tonic: the tonic contained the quinine dose and gin masked its bitterness. *'Gin and tonic has saved more Englishmen's lives, and minds, than all the doctors in the Empire,'* said Winston Churchill. Today malaria still kills well over half a million people a year.

Chocolate, *Theobroma cacao*: Derived from the seeds of a small evergreen tree of the Malvaceae family that spread from Mexico to the Amazon basin, chocolate has been consumed by humans for many centuries. Olmec pots dating back to 1750 BC depict cocoa preparation. The name of the tree, *Theobroma*, translates from the Greek as 'food of the gods'. This is another Mesoamerican staple that was introduced to Europe by the Spanish.

Grapevine, *Vitis vinifera*: Grapevines have been in cultivation for millennia – Neolithic traces of wine-making include a 7,000-year-old storage jar discovered in modern-day northern Iran. The vines had other uses besides making wine. Among them, the stems were used as fodder, leaves as food for humans and the woody stems from annual pruning dried and used for cooking over. It was my early encounter with vines at my uncle's vineyard that led to me becoming a gardener. The plant demands very little and gives a great deal.

Sugarcane, *Saccharum officinarum*: This highly productive, tall subtropical grass produces some 2,000 million tonnes per annum. There is the pleasure of chewing grass stems for their sweetness, but sugarcane scales that up exponentially with its full 6 metre (19 foot) in height. Human cravings for sweetness have caused centuries of problems: slavery, obesity, diabetes, rotting teeth, corruption and conflict. But the plant itself has good uses, with biogas, ethanol and paper pulp all viable byproducts.

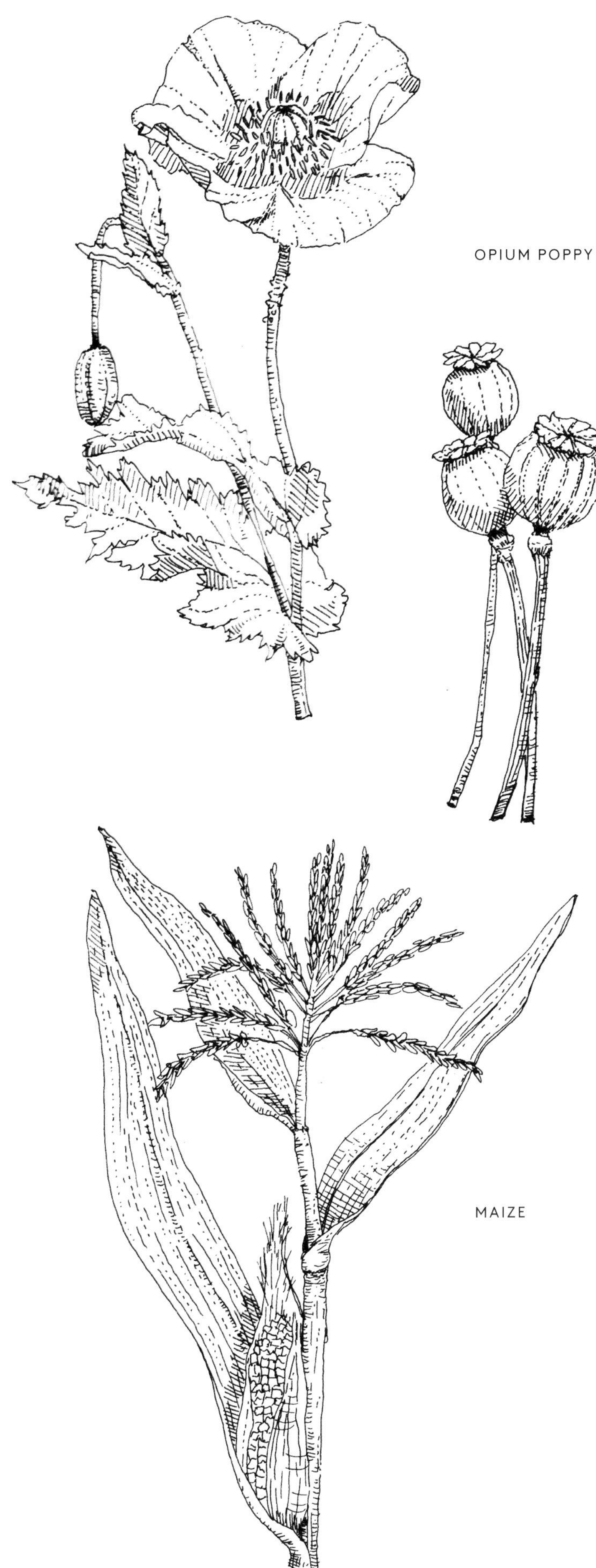

Maize, *Zea mays*: The largest cropping seed grain in the world, producing 1.2 billion tonnes per annum, maize is another grass. A Mesoamerican food plant that probably originated in what is now Mexico, maize is a cultigen, meaning that human intervention is needed in order to propagate it. Maize is widely regarded as humankind's greatest agronomic achievement – testament to the farming skills of great antiquity and fundamental to the cultural philosophies of the early South Americans.

Rice, *Oryza sativa*: A member of the Poaceae grass family, *O. sativa* is the most common form of rice. Roughly 7,000 years ago it was already being cultivated in central and eastern China. Its cultivation today is absolutely vast, as is the acreage it covers; around 510 million tonnes of rice are produced per annum, across 165 million hectares (407 million acres) of the earth's surface. It has also provided some of the most beautiful constructed landscapes in the world.

Olive, *Olea europea*: Grown on a smallish, very long-lived evergreen tree from the Mediterranean basin, Asia and Africa, the olive's origins are prehistoric. In ancient Greece, olive branches were woven into crowns and offered to the gods as symbols of peace and abundance. The oil the fruit produced was used for cooking, lighting, anointing and massaging. The calm countenance of the olive still attempts to unify us. Muhammad is reported to have said: 'Take oil of olive and massage with it – it is a blessed tree.' The first Great Seal of the United States depicts an eagle clutching an olive branch in one of its talons – an indication of the power of peace; in the same vein, the flag of the United Nations is a world map surmounted by two olive branches. It has a lot riding on its slender silvery leaves.

Looking at the list above, it seems we owe a great debt of gratitude to the flora of Mesoamerica that is not, I feel, reflected in how we treat that continent.

Foraged Flavours

Let food be thy medicine and medicine be thy food.

–HIPPOCRATES (460–370 BC)

Wherever possible, I incorporate forage into my gardens. I remember causing havoc early in my career by planting blackcurrant bushes either side of a narrow path in a very large, formal herbaceous border. They are the perfect height, soft to brush against, fruit brilliantly and have that delicious cat-pee smell on hot days. The house was sold and the new incumbent asked me to continue working there. 'I just want to show you something,' he offered, 'what kind of mad person puts currants in a formal border?' We are still good friends.

Richard Mabey's seminal book *Food for Free* (1972), published when I was a child, sent my mother and all her friends into foraging ecstasy. It was the zenith of the 'muck and magic' period and as a result we were all eating the most extraordinary things. At that point no one had any money, so putting kids to work scrabbling through hedgerows for subsistence snacks was considered acceptable and we enjoyed it. Permanently on the kitchen table, I knew the book off by heart. It presented information so beautifully with clear and enticing photographs and spare, informative text. Some recipes incorporated the spoils of a successful forage. Technical information allowed the reader to identify plants accurately, which is pretty important, and there were gems of wit like this, from John Gerard (1545–1612) and his famous *Herball*, concerning the edible tuber of bitter vetch, *Lathyrus montanus*.

> *'The nuts of this Pease being boiled and eaten, are hardlier digested than be either Turneps or Parsneps, yet they do nourish no less than the Parsneps: they are not so windie as they, they do more slowly passe thorowe the belly by reason of their binding qualitie, and being eaten rawe, they be yet harder of digestion, and do hardlier and slowlier descend.'*

It is too brilliant! I love the fact that people persevered with foods that were 'hardlier digested', obviously painfully conscious of the Pease 'slow descent', where everything we eat today is soft and squidgy and full of sugar and carbs.

A forage garden is fairly easy to create and just requires a clear sense of the seasons. I'd add the forage plants into a broader garden structure and mix them companionably with garden plants to make the overall effect more pleasing. I'm not an advocate of the extremely ascetic approach favoured by some eco-fundamentalists. I like things to be attractive. A large number of 'garden' plants can contribute beautifully to the broader sense of forage: rose petals, rosehips, aromatic shrubs such as myrtle, lavender and rosemary, all the herbs. I did once make a 'herb-aceous' border of only edible herbs, medicinal herbs and dye plants. It worked nicely.

Of course, what works best depends on your specific soils, so here I've just recommended plants that are relatively trouble-free in terms of soil. I've not included mushrooms as they really are all about serendipity and studious hunting. Several of these plants are just good old weeds – so eat them up.

FORAGE BY SEASON

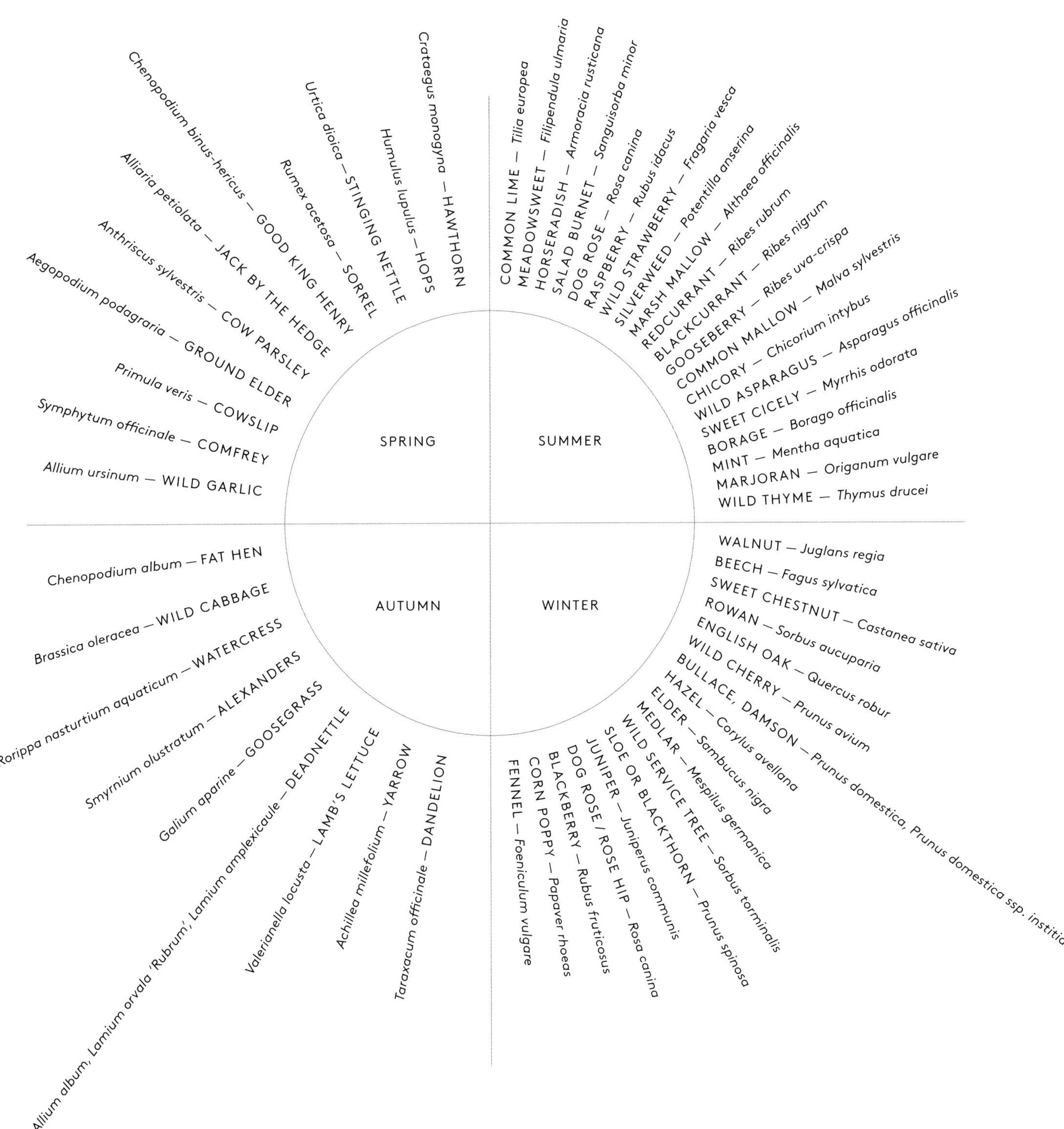

Seasonal Forage Plants of Britain

(Refer to page 59 for each plant's foraging season.)

→ Cowslip, *Primula veris*
The common name comes from 'cow slop', which means cow dung, so not perhaps the most promising sounding forage. However, it does make the most delicious and delicate of country wines.

↗ Hop, *Humulus lupulus* (Spring)
This wild hedgerow climber is best known for its use in brewing and excellent varieties have been cultivated in Kent and Worcestershire in the UK. As forage, the shoots are edible, and the flowers make a tea that has a soporific effect. Hops are sometimes dried and put in pillows to cure insomnia.

↗ Borage, *Borago officinalis*
This bristly, sappy plant has intense blue flowers. Bees love it, but it tears their wings to shreds as they forage for pollen. Its cucumber-flavoured leaves add flavour to summer drinks and it is fun to freeze the flowers in ice cubes. Pliny called borage *Euphrosinum* because of the euphoric effect it bestows on the consumer.

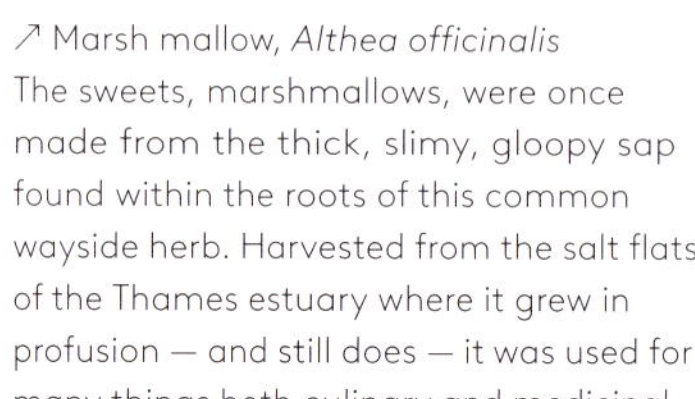

↗ Marsh mallow, *Althea officinalis*
The sweets, marshmallows, were once made from the thick, slimy, gloopy sap found within the roots of this common wayside herb. Harvested from the salt flats of the Thames estuary where it grew in profusion — and still does — it was used for many things both culinary and medicinal.

← Gooseberry, *Ribes uva-crispa*
This beloved culinary fruit originated wild in hedgerows. The origins of the common name are uncertain and are not believed to derive from the bird itself. Ironically, however, gooseberries do make the perfect accompaniment to roasted waterfowl — geese among them — the tartness of the fruit cutting deliciously through the fat.

↗ Bullace, *Prunus domestica* ssp. *insititia*
The bullace was a favourite plum in Europe until we started to cultivate new varieties. It is now a wild plant found in hedges and at orchard edges. Smaller than a damson and larger than a sloe, it's well worth seeking out as the flavour is superb. Use the fruit to make jams, wines and cordials.

↖ Elderberry, *Sambucus nigra*
This bountiful, if stinky, small tree gives us flowers in the spring for making fritters, cordials, ice cream and berries in autumn for syrups and jelly. Judas is said to have hanged himself from an elder bush and it has long been associated with bad luck. Unfortunately, it kills other hedgerow plants, which adds to its unpopularity for me.

← Dog rose, *Rosa canina*
During the Second World War, rosehips proved an invaluable source of vitamin C in the diet, as citrus fruits were unobtainable. I often ate rosehips as a child. You need to wait for the first frost to soften the skin before collecting. It's called dog rose because a member of the Roman praetorian guard managed to cure himself of hydrophobia brought on by a bite from a rabid dog by consuming the roots. That could come in useful.

↗ Hazel, *Corylus avellana*
Everything on a hazel has a use. Once you have availed yourself of divining rods, charcoal, wattles for building, pea sticks, kindling, fishing rods, gunpowder and a potent viagra substitute, there are the nuts. And if these are not enough, hazel also wards off evil.

↗ Medlar, *Mespilus germanica*
Medlar appears in most of my gardens in Europe. The fruit needs to be bletted (left to rot somewhat) before you can consume it. I have yet to find the experience enjoyable, although medlars make a pleasant jelly. They are also said to make an excellent cure for diarrhoea! The tree's other assets include beautiful flowers and a consummately pleasing shape.

Sound

My ears are alive to the sound of music, to paraphrase Rodgers and Hammerstein. I'm married to a musician, have spent a lot of my life in the company of musicians and I sing. The more I explore the senses, the more abstract they become. Sound, in particular, is very hard to describe. Yet without the sounds of the world around us, what could the sensation of life be like? My father-in-law lost his hearing very suddenly in his old age and the isolation he, and we, experienced was devastating. The closest I've got to it is using noise-cancelling headphones but they're too effective. Using them feels like drowning and I find the lack of ability to assess sound behind and around me – a sense so vital to our feeling of security – horrible. I only use them on flights.

The ancient Greek philosopher Aristotle first classified the five senses as we know them. He understood that human knowledge came into us via our senses. Aristotle believed that every physical object has both an essence and a substance; a real bird and a putty model of a bird share similarities, yet their material reality is totally different. Aristotle felt that the psyche is an inherently human instrument that permits us to receive the form of an object without the substance – in much the same way that a seal makes an impression in wax.

I like this interpretation as it allows for the space between physical facts – the bodily construction of the human ear and the science of sound waves and echolocation – and a more subjective, emotional interpretation of how we receive sensory information. The sense of hearing is a key function in how we create relationships and communicate emotionally and cerebrally. Music affects us all differently and powerfully depending on our tastes – here, again, is the manifestation of a visceral emotional reaction to a sense.

Each of us carries a unique series of sonic impressions collected during the course of our lifetime, millions of them. They make us who we are, much more than we realise. They carry, too, what makes us happy, comfortable and uncomfortable. To make a really good garden for someone, I need to try and understand the things that affect them in this way. I had a project in the most beautiful landscape where a new house was to be built. Quite far away was a motorway. I made my peace with traffic noise after living in London for years, but my client couldn't bear it. Even though, at times, we were straining to hear it, for him it was like a red-hot wire pressed into his central nervous system. We had a lot of very technical conversations about it. I designed and modelled a series of huge sculptural sound baffles. It was an intuitive approach based on a mutual understanding of sound waves; it's very hard to counter the Doppler effect created by a car on a motorway. Our answer to the problem was a combination of tree planting with angled baffles set within them.

So often, the sounds around us are processed subliminally while we're fully occupied in another way. While writing this book, I spent time at my home in France. I've been coming to France all my life and recognise the sounds of the place automatically, just as I can identify its aromas – an aural snapshot that is comforting and familiar, loaded with cognitive information. Just sitting working with the windows open on a hot summer's day, I'd hear the buzz of insects that fly in out and the relaxing papery sound of my bare feet on the floorboards. The sounds of people chatting as they walk up the alley or the distant sharp buzzing of a moped might drift in. And there were birds, lots of birds, all busy singing.

Natural Music

Wandering through my garden in England, I'm keenly aware of its sonic elements. Rustling leaves from the poplar tree that sound like water on a shore, the high cry of red kites, burbling noises from wood pigeons, barking, music from next door, the distant drone of traffic. These are all lovely sounds, sounds of home. A garden should protect us from harsh realities and allow freedom to switch off and relax. Like most gardeners, I talk to myself constantly as I potter about. I talk to all the plants. I explain what I'm doing, or plan to do, I mutter about things that aggravate me, like next door's leylandii blocking out the sun or the relentless tide of bindweed emerging through one of the walls. Before our cat died I could pass off my ramblings as 'I'm just talking to Minky'. Yet now, alas, it is obvious that I'm talking out loud to myself. We all do it. Conversation, even one-sided, is necessary for the growth of plants. I'm sure of it. It is something to do with vibration perhaps. Bees communicate by vibrating and drumming – plants definitely respond to it. My friend Stuart tells me he activates pollination of

↱ pp. 64–65: The river Clunie Water is as much a part of the garden at the Fife Arms as the garden of flowers itself. The constant sound of rushing, tumbling, splashing water gives a unique sonic quality to the experience of the place. I was acutely aware of its presence during the design process and even designed a single malt whisky bar to sit precariously along the water's edge. I had dreams of sitting in Scottish mist, under a plaid blanket with midges and a good whisky. My idea of luxury.

↘ A plan for the sound baffles. Of varied length, each was around 3 metres (10 feet) tall, and they were set within a copse planted with silver willow, *Salix alba* var. *sericea*, at the front and white poplar, *Populus alba*, at the back. Both trees have brilliantly silvery leaves that flutter magically in the slightest breeze and contribute wonderfully watery sounds.

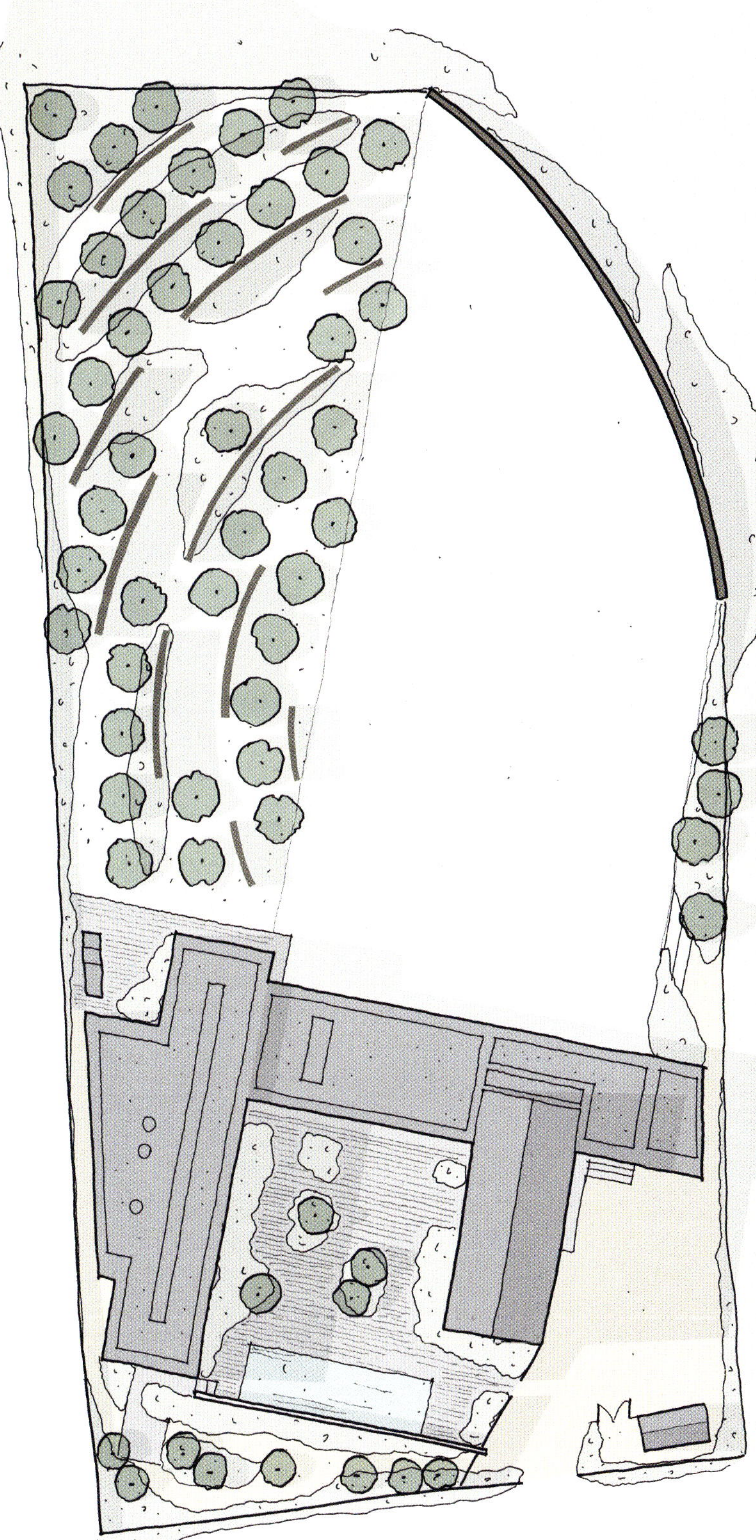

his tomatoes using an electric toothbrush. The vibration assists pollen moving to the stigma and down into the ovary where the bees can come and pollinate. Non-specific humming is another feature of my garden noise production and moves seamlessly to singing as I make up long nonsense songs that last throughout the day's jobs. It is gratifying to think it might be aiding pollination.

Sound, specifically of water, was one of the central pleasures of the Garden of Eden. It is also the feature requested most often in a new garden design. It seems a huge percentage of people value the sound of running water. There is great variety in the sounds water produces: rushing, gurgling, tinkling, splooshing. Often, water is requested in order to disguise another sound, usually traffic noise. However, I approach this with caution. One noise seldom successfully masks another and you run the risk of them combining to make a much bigger noise that becomes more aggravating.

I think we simply love the combined sight and sound of water. Light playing on the rippling surface of the rill at Rousham House, Oxfordshire, is more about movement than noise. The rill eventually falls almost soundlessly into a limpid pool. Atmospherically the water is contributing a huge amount, sonically, less so. Rome's Trevi Fountain is a tremendous feat of water engineering, with much thought given to how the water falls from a central scallop shell and over some low flat stones either side. The sheer weight of water results in a very pleasing sound – in a good waterfall, a large volume of water drops heavily into a basin that is large enough to dissipate it easily.

I was involved in a garden laid out following the classic *pattes d'oie*, or goose foot shape, with two circular, formal stone-edged pools at the end of a pair of quite long avenues. Central to each pool was a fountain with a tall single water jet of about 3 metres (9 feet). Visually they were splendid, yet when both fountains were playing the sound was abominable. For reasons I can't explain they sounded industrial. We rarely used them.

Overall, I'd say that playing with watery sonics is a sophisticated process. It benefits from a very clear understanding of the sound you are looking to create, a clear vision for the water event itself and a significant budget. Technical complexities combined with the adage in landscaping that 'water is liability' leave me much more comfortable with making ponds and lakes.

La Grande Déserte, 1912, Louis Tinayre (1861–1942)

↗ I learned a great deal about the use of colour from the paintings of my great grandfather Louis Tinayre. He was an *artiste reporter* for *Le Monde illustré* as well as being an impressionist painter of some note. He also accompanied his best friend, Albert I of Monaco, on all his naturalist voyages, painting and recording their finds. I'm including this image from his life in Madagascar, which is where my family are from. The colours are sensational. They filled in the gaps in my imagination from when the landscape had first been described to me.

Sight

The eyes are more exact witnesses than the ears.

–HERACLITUS (c. 540–c. 480 BC)

My mother wasn't suited to child-rearing. Her interests lay elsewhere – in architecture, in art, in music, in history, in literature, in travel. She would repeat, with a hint of menace, 'you'll thank me for this one day', as she hauled us through yet another cathedral, through another medieval town, across acres of galleried art. A born teacher, she would demand that we describe the arches, their architectural typology, the variety of stone, the method of carving, what type of wood a pulpit was made from. What was being narrated in the statuary, she'd ask. What was a cantilevered stair? Feel this fabric – what is it? On and on it went until finally she relented. 'OK, now you can go and muck about in the river'. Much later in life, we discussed perception. My mother found beauty in concrete things. I found it in the abstract. She would look at buildings, I would look at the sky. She was right though; thanks are forthcoming for the exhaustive 'look at this' and 'look at that' 'keep your eyes peeled' trials of our childhood. We journeyed a huge amount in her battered old Morris Traveller and looked and looked and looked. It is important to mention that she was partially sighted. She was born in Madagascar and had been accidentally blinded at birth by her father, who delivered her. She had a surgical iridectomy in Paris at the age of two that somewhat recovered her sight and was forever overwhelmingly grateful for her ability to see. I have never known anyone as hungry for visual stimulus as her. All thanks to Ma, I have an extensive visual library stored away. Imprinted indelibly in my mind's eye this comprehensive exposure to art and culture amounts to having been cultivated by my upbringing. It gave me the tools to carry on. My academic education was all but non-existent, yet cultural exposure has compensated and serves as a visual repository that I can readily summon to help with my work.

Heraclitus, the Ionian philosopher from Ephesus, made the observation that eyes and ears are poor witnesses to people if they have uncultured souls. The plastic nature of the psyche and our capacity to stamp so much information into ourselves makes sight an incredible gift. The ability to sense light, focus images, change them into nerve impulses and fire them into our brains, means that eighty per cent of all learning comes in through our eyes. We can distinguish more than ten million colours – how did we end up reducing our colour sense to the seven colours of the rainbow? We have depth perception that allows us to understand the world three-dimensionally and gauge distances between objects, to use perspective. On top of that, we place our own unique value system on visual information. We love things or loathe them, we develop our own sense of visual harmony, we react to colour, we understand proportion and space. Ultimately, we develop our own taste. And it is impossible to unsee something – ask any combat veteran. This ever-evolving focus is added to with freshness and immediacy all our lives. Our bodies may age but I don't think our perceptions do.

Gardens are visual. 'Eye-catchers' only exist in landscape gardening, their sole aim being to draw attention and trigger a change of perception, of scale or circumstance. This useful trick can be used in many different ways in gardens large or small. Pleasurable ruses include forced perspective, employed famously by the baroque architect Francesco Borromini, whose entire vaulted, colonnaded passage at the Palazzo Spada in Rome was an optical illusion, and a moral metaphor: 'the greatness of the things of the world is also just an illusion'. In Japan, near Kyoto, is the retirement villa of an art-obsessed shogun called Ashikaga Yoshimasa. Built in 1482, Ginkakuji, or the Silver Pavilion, has a unique and meticulously maintained dry-sand garden. Known as the Sea of Silver Sand, it has a massive sand cone named Moon Viewing Platform within it. This extraordinary piece has been credited to a famous Japanese painter and landscape gardener of the period, Sōami. At ground level, the cone takes on the form, in miniature, of Mount Fuji. When viewed from above, its flattened circular top represents the full moon. Like most things Japanese, the garden is layered in meaning and visual metaphor, playing with scale and perception. It is almost scientifically modern, and you can't help but wonder how this meticulously shaped pile of sand can have been persevered for the last 540 years, although this point has been clarified by my friend Rosalind, who told me all about it. She says the Japanese have a unique approach to the preservation of antiquities and as long as it looks and feels like the original, it is acceptable to keep remaking it.

Painting is concerned with all the ten attributes of sight, which are: Darkness, Light, Solidity and Colour, Form and Position, Distance and Propinquity, Motion and Rest.

–LEONARDO DA VINCI (1452–1519)

Art: Colour and Stimulation

The tonal character of a garden can be determined, much like a good wine, by its 'terroir'. The land from which it has sprung influences it completely. All areas of Britain can be recognised through their distinctive geological colourations: the creamy golden limestone of the Cotswolds that veers to a darker orange Hornton stone towards Banbury in Oxfordshire; the dark granites of Edinburgh, smooth black lias of Caithness and soft-brown-sugar-coloured limestone of Bath; the grey and white flints and creamy clunch chalk rock of Hampshire; the protected pink pargetted stucco of Suffolk, made of sloe, elderberry, crushed brick, burnt clay and ironstone; the deep, rich grey slate of Snowdonia in Wales that has roofed most of the British Isles. Down in the earth below our feet lies the basis of every new garden and the background hues it will have. Wherever I work in the world, I apply the same principle by which the very first layer of colour in the garden is its rock, whether that be dark volcanic stones, 'red dirt' earth, rich ochre rock, ancient granite or yellow mudstone. That is my canvas, the background wash of colour. Where to go next in building up the layers?

Viewing art is always stimulating. Our creative minds work best when they have a chance to free-associate. Not least, because of the extraordinary colour effects found in paintings. Our literal minds tell us that grass is green and sky is blue. While in the rational planning mindset it is easy not to stray from the path of the literal interpretation, it can be very rewarding to veer off the straight and narrow and allow the mind to wander freely through other people's creative explorations.

Take, for example, Felix Vallotton's paintings. Vallotton occupied an interesting period in art, straddling a succession of movements that included Les Nabis, impressionism and symbolism. His art always looks more modern than that of his contemporaries – to me at least – and has a unique graphic quality. Vallotton chose odd angles of perspective, more like those of a cartoonist, that peered into a subject from a dynamic bird's-eye view. He does this in painting called *Le ballon* (*The Ball*), which swoops us down onto a child playing in a park. There is great movement in the painting, the child separated from her parents by a dramatic change in the foreground colour. Vallotton's colour sense is completely unique. In 1919, he painted *Paysage au coucher du soleil* (*Countryside at Sunset*). The colours: purple sky, bottle green grass, oranges, yellows and turquoise definitely resemble a potent sunset sky, but are they realistic? Do they need to be? Certainly all those colours exist in nature to a degree, yet here they are amplified. Vallotton is giving an emotional rendition of the sunset as much as a representation of the actual event. The colours are vivid and not even especially complementary, yet they work together to convey the power of the dying sun's rays, the wind in the trees, the dark descending over the fields.

How does any of this help in making a garden? I have a Proustian relationship with Hidcote Manor Garden in Gloucestershire. Proust wrote copiously about vividly reliving events from the past through sensory stimuli. Hidcote Manor is where I first understood, at a very minor age, how a garden could be themed by colour. The tonal mood of each part of the garden was subtly different. My feelings changed as I passed through each area and I loved that. The culmination of the route was the Theatre, a vast green lawn surrounded with tall trees and yew hedging. After all the changing colours of the garden, this monumental green space was sobering. I imagine the original concept was that the play itself, the lighting and the actors would bring the movement and colour to this space, though I've never witnessed it. Today, the Theatre is quite challenging, especially now the surrounding trees are at full maturity and huge. The distorted shadows and peculiar scale are entirely reminiscent of the paintings of Giorgio de Chirico, painting in the 1920s. I discovered De Chirico in a book I found at a jumble sale and a link between landscape and art fused in my mind forever.

I've always collected visual images that affect me, either for their composition or colour and often with no direct relationship to garden-making. I can recommend this, as keeping scrapbooks is far more rewarding that digital filing and endless scrolling. Stimuli can come from all over the place. My husband and I love paintings, mainly postwar British and European art. A lot of this work, such as the works of Paul Nash and Eileen Agar, is suffused with landscape references, Agar's becoming more surreal as time went on and Nash's more mystical and introverted. The shapes, colours and moods in paintings by these artists, and others of their time, have always been a rich resource, though not a literal one. Not everything needs to be literal to be relevant.

The Ball (Corner of the park with child playing with a ball), 1899, Félix Vallotton (1865–1925)

Countryside at Sunset, 1919, Félix Vallotton (1865–1925)

↙ These are my paint colours, developed to fill in the spaces where colour needs to be in a garden: gates and railings, planters, walls, drain pipes and hinges. The calm recessive colours blend beautifully with the natural world.

There are no lines in nature, only areas of colour, one against another.

–EDOUARD MANET (1832–83)

Paint

Colour is a particular love of mine. In our work there is a need for good colours that give contextual support to the natural elements of physical materials and planting. Background colours on buildings matter a lot: the colours on ironwork, on doors, on gates; the colour on outdoor furniture, on planters, and if you are as determined as I am, on cars. If you ever want to know where colour is going awry in a garden just take a load of snaps on your phone, it'll jump out immediately. White is the worst. My work is all about context, so nothing escapes notice. I'm reminded of the story about Yves St Laurent who wept inconsolably for days as a child, after his mother went out wearing a mismatching cardigan.

Inevitably, I wanted to develop my own colours – a narrow, yet specific range. There are certain tones I need again and again to support what I'm doing. I worked with the artist Susan Hirsch to develop the colours, and the experience was fascinating. I've always admired her colour sense and knew she would be able, from conversations and mutual experiences, to mix up the right hues for me. Collaboration is an essential part of good holistic work. We worked on a colour range until we were both happy with it and then it sat wrapped up by my desk for six years or so. The process of turning big ideas into reality is a long, hard journey, a mixture of talking to lots of different people, endurance and serendipity. However, the paints have now become a reality thanks to Dominic Myland.

Mylands is a royal warrant-holding, family-run paint-maker. The firm opened in 1884 when 'Honest' John Myland set up his unassuming shop in London's Lambeth. John was absolutely enthralled by the art of the colourman. A colourman is a gifted artist and technician who can gauge how to produce specific colours from a vast array of disparate materials. Honest John insisted on the very best materials that would allow his colourman to create colours that were lustrous, flawless and of unmatched quality. Mylands is the go-to paint-maker for theatre, film and television. You probably see Mylands' colours every day, one way or another, without realising it. They have an exceptional understanding of colour as a mood-altering background, so in that we share a common language. Mylands' colourman took my swatches and hand-mixed them exactly. She did the work by eye: the human eye is the best spectrometer in the world. The results made me want to cry. Seeing something you care about made real is very affecting.

My colours are quiet, neutral tones, yet a unifying thread runs through them. I have one red – every palette needs a unique tone that stands out. Red is so useful outside. I based it on an old, faded red chair I once saw outside a house. It's funny how accurately I remembered the colour, described it to Susan and recognised it again once she had finished mixing. The red will naturally fade over time – apparently it's the hardest colour to 'fix' and make colourfast. It will gradually take on an attractive, slightly dull chalkiness.

We honed down the palette to twelve key colours. They are all named after evocations of British weather and landscape conditions as understood by me after long exposure to them. Three, the darkest, are specifically for ironwork. Murmuration, named after the starlings over Bath, is a deep blue-black ideal for wrought-iron gates and downpipes. Then comes a peaty dark, olive-green black that works beautifully on estate railings, and Woodnight is a soft almost-black, perfect for ironmongery and big strap hinges.

Three mid-toned colours are suitable for garden buildings or building facades – larger expanses of flat block colour that harmonise with natural surroundings. Haar is a mid-brown, mauve-grey – the violet undertone creates a kind of vibration in the colour, a 'now-you-see-it-now-you-don't' hum. Reminiscent of a peculiar grey estuarine mud found at low tide, I created Riverine, a slightly sinister dark-blue green-grey that I associate with the Thames estuary mudflats near Sheerness. I can almost smell them. And Equinox is a colour between other colours, turning from grey to brown, smooth and beautiful.

There are five colours that I use in place of white, depending on the circumstances. White is very difficult to use outside, it is too strong and attention-seeking. It is invariably better to try and tone it down. Natural light is very powerful and bleaches most colours, so don't be afraid of experimenting with tones instead.

The first 'antiwhite' is a minky, minerally, mushroomy pink, a tone somewhere between pale mud, chestnut mushrooms and dirty plaster. It's the most wonderful colour for walls and could be used as a slurry-like limewash on old brickwork or as a flat colour. With hanging strands of Virginia creeper or wisteria it looks soft, inviting and wonderful. Grail – named after freezing fine gritty rain – is a light grey with the slightest whiff of blue; a cool, modern 'white' substitute. Rain, named after heavy summer showers, is a grey-blue with a hint of green, perfect for a wall or for big Versailles planters with strapwork in Murmuration. For a bit more vibrancy, I created Sargasso, a slightly more red-violet tinged grey that will ping out as natural light hits it. Finally in the non-white whites, I made a bright, fresh light green, like the first unfurling of a hazel leaf with piercing spring light through it.

Then the red, a standalone colour in the range, which for now I call Carnelian. The Romans felt that carnelian gave courage to the wearer. Who doesn't need that?

Dyers Colours

For thousands of years, Europeans have used three principal plants to make dyes: woad, weld and madder. Blue, yellow and red respectively, they were the colours of kings, vestal virgins and armies.

Woad, *Isatis tinctoria*, is a biennial member of the brassica family and has been in use as a dye since Neolithic times. Anyone who has cooked purple sprouting brocolli or cavolo nero will have seen a dilution of the colour. Originally from the Middle East, it would most likely have been traded across Europe, such was its usefulness. It is present in almost every historic textile still in existence and is widely used today. Woad stained the ancient Briton's blue, by accident or design, and made them fearsome. Woad is also responsible for the historic riches of my part of France, the Occitanie. The productive area triangulates between Albi, Carcassonne and Toulouse. The wealth made from these small, dried balls of *cocagne* being traded far and wide is still evident in the magnificent woad merchants' mansions in Toulouse, among them Hôtel d'Assézat and Hôtel de Bernuy with its vastly tall hexagonal tower. The thirteen shades of 'Occitan bleu' were codified in the seventeenth century and range from the most intense, kings blue and queens blue, through to very light white-blue and the grey-black of hell blue. Leftover dye from the huge vats was used to decorate shutters and carts and to paint cows' horns as a deterrent to mosquitoes. I immediately want to see a field of cows with blue-painted horns. Thanks to the reuse of waste products from local industry the blue has become synonymous with southern French rustic charm.

Weld, *Reseda luteola*, is a tall, graceful weed with narrow, scented spires of tiny yellow flowers. It produces, and has done since prehistory, a neon-yellow dye that is strong, clear and light-fast. Apparently, the Romans used weld to colour the robes of the six vestal virgins, the keepers of the flame of Rome. I imagine the weld colour was as close to gold as a dye could get and its freshness and vibrancy must have cast a brilliance over proceedings. Roman brides could wear weld yellow robes for their weddings.

Madder, *Rubia tinctorum*, or rose madder as it is also known, was used to dye the linens in Tutankhamen's tomb. Notable for not fading, it is still found in archaeological sites with its colour in unusually good condition. Madder is an unassuming-looking evergreen perennial related to coffee. It produces swollen fleshy roots up to a metre long from which the dye is extracted. Clothes dyed with madder have been found in the tombs of Merovingian queens, Vikings, the works of Pliny the Elder and Dioscorides. Suffice to say, madder was well used, traded hard and of great value. Between the seventeenth and twentieth centuries it was responsible for identifying the Redcoats of the British Army.

My favourite medieval tapestries, *The Lady and the Unicorn* series at the Musée de Cluny, Paris, were produced using predominantly weld, madder and woad. They were created in the style known as *millefleurs*, or 'a thousand flowers', and woven in Flanders from wool and silk. The colours have survived incredibly well over the last five hundred odd years. The designs were drawn in Paris, and each one represents one of our senses. The final tapestry, *A mon seul désir*, is open to myriad translations; the literal translation is 'my only desire'. It is the culminating paradise of the five senses where 'desire' is at peace in a garden. The subject matter is completely engrossing. I've spent hours staring at the flowery mead to see what it's made up of and wondering if it is remotely possible to replicate it using real plants. A kind curator at the museum told me that the tapestries were stitched over very long periods so they were allegorical rather than factual and the flowers, though painstakingly accurate to life, couldn't possibly have flowered simultaneously. As a gardener I could probably have worked that out had I been thinking straight.

Given the rich depth of history in these three simple plants, a dyer's garden seems a lovely thing to make. Again, much like an allotment or a perfumer's garden, a functional garden like this is best laid out in order beds. Children find great pleasure in growing and making dyes, so a small corner of your garden would be excellent for these easily grown plants of magical transformation.

The Lady and the Unicorn, fifteenth century, French School

↗ It's hard to believe two things here. Firstly, that this extraordinary tapestry is more than five hundred years old and still in immaculate condition. Secondly, woven from wool and silk, the tapestry contains only three colours; yellow from weld, red from madder and blue from woad. I urge you to go to the Musée de Cluny in Paris and see for yourself.

Dyers Plants

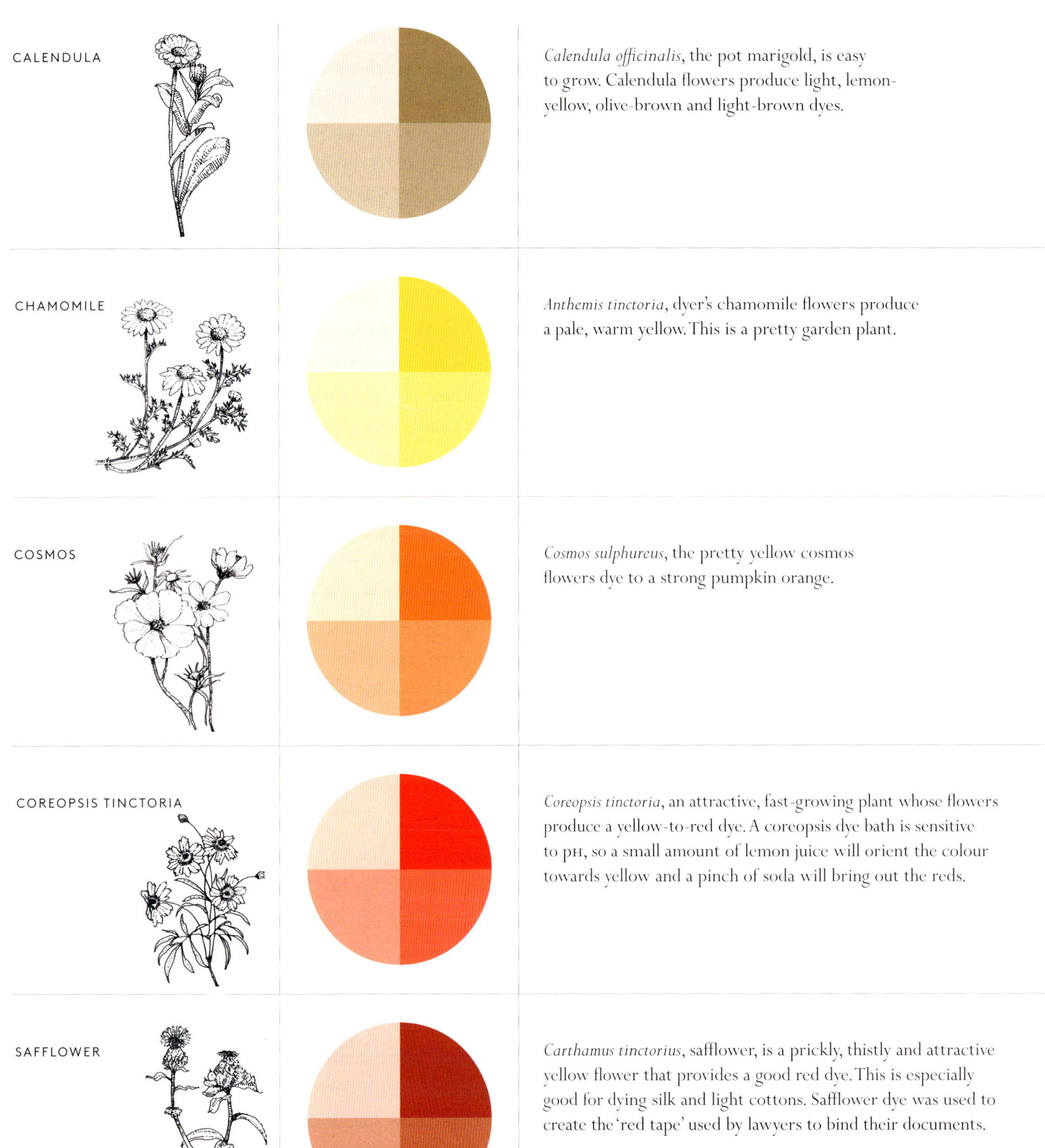

Calendula officinalis, the pot marigold, is easy to grow. Calendula flowers produce light, lemon-yellow, olive-brown and light-brown dyes.

Anthemis tinctoria, dyer's chamomile flowers produce a pale, warm yellow. This is a pretty garden plant.

Cosmos sulphureus, the pretty yellow cosmos flowers dye to a strong pumpkin orange.

Coreopsis tinctoria, an attractive, fast-growing plant whose flowers produce a yellow-to-red dye. A coreopsis dye bath is sensitive to pH, so a small amount of lemon juice will orient the colour towards yellow and a pinch of soda will bring out the reds.

Carthamus tinctorius, safflower, is a prickly, thistly and attractive yellow flower that provides a good red dye. This is especially good for dying silk and light cottons. Safflower dye was used to create the 'red tape' used by lawyers to bind their documents.

ZINNIAS

Zinnia elegans, zinnias are the best annuals going, with huge flashy flowers in mad colours. Flowers yield a yellow dye and the plants are worth growing in abundance to jazz up the dye garden.

FRENCH MARIGOLD

Tagetes patula nana, or French marigold, is such a rewarding plant, flowering beautifully and with many richly coloured cultivars. Fresh or dried flowers produce yellow, gold, old gold, buff and orange colours and combine well with woad to produce some beautiful green shades.

MALLOW

Malva sylvestris, the simple mallow that grows on waste ground has pretty pink flowers. The plant offers a deep green dye.

JAPANESE INDIGO

Persicaria tinctoria is also called Japanese indigo, which describes the deep blue colour the plant offers. The plant looks like bistort and is a member of the buckwheat family.

WOAD

Isatis tinctoria, woad, as we know, is a brassica that yields a strong blue dye. In tandem with the plants that produce yellow dye, many shades of green can be made.

PRISMATIC

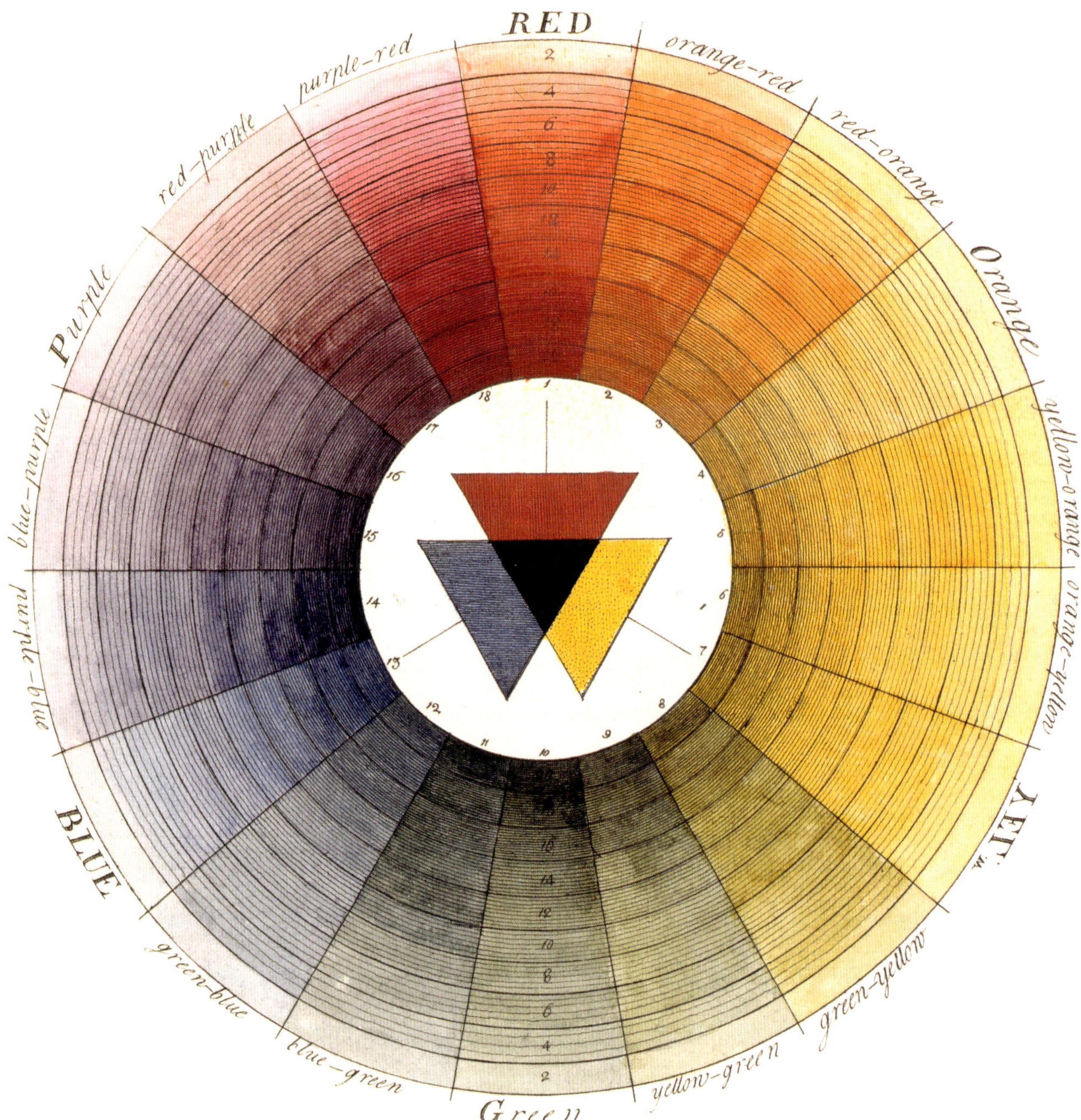

Prismatic Colour Wheel from *The Natural System of Colours*, c. 1785, Moses Harris (1730– c. 1788)

Choosing Colour

Briefs for colour in gardens often come with clear caveats such as 'I loathe reds and yellows' or, on one occasion, 'I only want blue flowers.' While limitations can be stimulating, more often they are stultifying. Choosing colour for a garden is one of the great pleasures of the art. Playing around with it either in the physical structure of the garden or in the planting, or both, gives rise to the atmosphere that makes a place completely unique. I advocate a fearless approach to colour and a strong directive to throw away the imaginary 'good taste' rule book.

Years ago, long before I ever visited the place, I saw a faded old photo of Madame Ganna Walksa's Lunar Garden at Lotusland in Montecito, California. I was hooked. It was mad, visionary stuff! Vast silvery aloes sat against stone-ball-topped columns; huge scallop shells created waterfalls flowing into a cool slate-blue, silvery pond. The colours were incredible and the feat of imagination astonishing. It had a naive, 'outsider art' quality that made it compelling. No one would have dared suggest to Madame that they didn't like orange! In the face of such imaginative abundance, it would have sounded as irrelevant as it is. The woman herself is worth researching. An opera singer, allegedly six unconsummated marriages made her rich enough to pursue her boundless enthusiasm for horticulture. Her vivid imagination has left an enduring mark on 19 hectares (37 acres) of California.

The garden I made using 'only blue flowers' was redeemed by its location and its highly evocative maritime light. Though the effect of a lot of blue is interesting, it lacks any 'ping' and is really quite recessive during the day. The garden in question was in a dark green setting surrounded by evergreen trees, not dark, but unremittingly green. The blues just sank without trace in the wider landscape. It is no surprise that being deeply gloomy is called having the 'blues'. Blues need to be shot through with something brighter and sharper – not much, but enough to lift it, a speck of hot orange will do wonders or even bluish-silvery leaves like an *Amsonia tabernaemontana*. The colours work best at dusk or in low light, when their ultraviolet content seems more at home. It is worth spending some time getting to understand the colour wheel and how it works. The natural opposite of blue is orange – they need each other.

Colour Perception

Everyone perceives colour differently. My husband, as well as being a musician, is a visual artist working in the medium of photography. He has, to my eye, the most extreme metallic-blue colour sense – his colour choices are literally electric. His chosen spectrum is positively extra-terrestrial. I joke that he must be part man, part bee. Bees' eyes are sensitive to the blue end of the light spectrum and into ultraviolet. Flowers reflect large amounts of ultraviolet light and will appear very bright to a bee. Bees are apparently totally red-blind, though how we honestly know this is another mystery.

Is it taste or are we all just seeing the world completely differently? No one can dictate how colour is to someone else. Genetic variations, age, physical differences, language and mood all influence our perception of colour. Perhaps there are cultural norms around colour too – different countries have very different colour palettes, so we must grow up accustomed to certain tonalities. I was struck most by this when visiting New Zealand – so much so, that I collected a lot of commercial paint charts. The colours reflect the landscape, grey-greens and lichen colours that I absolutely associate with the country and its unusual light quality, generated, I imagine, by being surrounded by so much sea. Thinking about colour contrast and the use of complementary colours to increase harmony, the use of neutral colours to increase depth and vibrancy is all part of thinking compositionally when creating a garden.

But what do you do if you are colour-blind? What is colour-blindness? Apparently affecting more men than women, one in twelve men suffer from the most common 'red/green' colour-blindness that causes an inability to easily distinguish these two colours. There are other types of colour-blindness, yet this is the most common. Two landscape gardeners of my acquaintance are both colour-blind. It isn't something they discuss openly. I wasn't aware it carries a stigma, yet perhaps it does. What I can say with confidence is that they both display very good colour sense in their plantings. How much of it they can see, I can't say. How much of the colour choice is intuition or guesswork? All I know is that the end results are harmonic, interesting and widely appreciated. It doesn't seem to be any kind of impediment to good design.

Alchemy

Part 2

INTRODUCTION

Alchemy is a useful metaphor to use when discussing how the making of a garden comes together. When I was a psychology student, we discussed alchemy a great deal. Carl Jung used it as a metaphor for personal transformation – a better understanding of ourselves, our archetypes and our unconscious self. He borrowed from the alchemists of the seventeenth century who were, in effect, early scientists. They sought the transformation of certain base metals into gold via a process of making them soluble. The bottom line in alchemy is about transformation, the result of bringing elements together, mixing them and (hopefully) creating something greater. I see the metaphor alive and well in the process we go through for the transformation of landscapes.

The philosopher's stone is the central symbol and ultimate goal in alchemy. It represents perfection, heavenly bliss and enlightenment. In order to create the philosopher's stone – a garden in this instance – it is necessary to bring together the *prima materia*, or prime matter, the tangible, exoteric, practical materials and sciences, and blend them with the esoteric elements, the *anima mundi*, which connect all living things on the planet. So, in essence we need to combine the practical and the scientific with the natural, the human, the philosophical and the arts. The work of combining these different ways of seeing and expressing the world around us, and the huge effort required to synthesise all the elements required, becomes the great alchemical work: the magnum opus. This is why, in my view, garden-making is possibly the highest manifest form of all the arts and sciences, bringing the mutable and immutable materials of the world together and creating something unique, a living art form.

← My design for this garden included the dry-stone wall, the hand-forged railings in a colour that resembles smalt – the blue crushed glass that used to colour ironwork – and the soft pink rose, *Rosa macrantha* 'Raubritter'. For me, this is a perfect example of the alchemical elements that make up a garden.

↱ pp. 82–83: The image on the following pages shows the same design as a whole and these finer details become almost inconsequential when placed in context. Yet it is so important that everything blends together. With its backdrop of mature trees, the Georgian stable building demands appropriate elements within its new gardens to tie everything together.

4. PRIMA MATERIA

THERE ARE MANY PHYSICAL COMPONENTS to consider when starting the big mix up for a garden. It benefits the end result a great deal if you pan these as you might pan gold and select only what you really need. Gardens don't need a great deal of stuff in them, so having a clear strategy from the start certainly helps the end result.

Immutable Elements

↙ A model for what we called the Sky Garden. Models convey space brilliantly and immediately. This garden is on the top floor of London's Chelsea and Westminster Hospital. Designed for exclusive use by the new state-of-the-art Intensive Care Unit, it has to work on many levels for patients and staff alike. I devised it as a series of rooms all separated by planting and fixed, semi-transparent screens.

↓ This model was made to clarify my approach to a garden with a peculiar orientation. It allows the viewer to look out of the various windows of the house and assess what's happening. It is fun and practical and the object itself is beautiful. Everyone loves a model!

Drawings and Models

Once the ferment of thinking has had a chance to settle down and the particles gently sink to create the first sediment of concrete thought, the tool of choice has to be the pencil. Your ideas must start to become tangible quite quickly, or they can get lost. The first strokes of making a new garden inevitably come from the hand. The only way to feel a plan come to life is to draw it (I say 'feel' advisedly). At the risk of repeating myself, there is no other way to get a good feel for space and proportion than by drawing.

Speaking as a modestly gifted artist I would urge you not to worry too much about what you produce. Making things look good for a presentation comes much later in the process and can be helped along in lots of ways. We use all manner of brilliant software at work. I don't denounce any of it as it is so very useful. However, everyone in my studio is encouraged to draw; each of us has a uniquely different approach, and I love that. A 'house style' is a form of creative suffocation – drawing should be free and expressive and personal. John Ruskin said, broadly, you can make a tool of the man, or a man of the man; it is always more fun to enjoy the complexity of a developing person. I think this is why I've never really liked Humphry Repton, his illustrated 'before and after' books feel too slick. I do like books, though, and we do make hand-bound books of our concept designs, so thanks for that, Humph.

If I'm feeling tense, usually because I've got too much to do, I use charcoal sticks – proper charcoal made of willow. There is a lovely little video on The Metropolitan Museum of Art website that quickly shows some techniques. Big, free gestures in messy charcoal are really liberating – and as a top tip, drawing willow trees with willow charcoal is curiously easy and satisfying. The people we work for love seeing scrappy hand sketches and visual thoughts almost more than a marvellous artist's impression of the end result. Drawing is a form of communication, a language of sharing.

The initial marks are to do with making thoughts tangible – feeling how walls might intersect, the proportion of a space. The turning of a car, for example, is made easier if you draw the space, draw the cars it will hold and the shape of the turning. A lot of plan drawing is concerned with practicality. The structure of a garden is generally quite controlled. It is the planting that subverts and softens it, and it is necessary in garden-making to try and get both sides of the brain involved.

Garden-making is unique in requiring both lobes of the brain to contribute equally. Architects often find it impossible to understand what we do, as we can so readily leave the sphere of the immutable built element and leap into the mutability of nature. Mud is malleable!

For ease, here is a simple table of what each lobe of the brain is arguably covering. I've never been tested, if you can be, but looking at it I reckon I've got an adequate smattering of both. When I was studying, we had a happy day doing brain stuff and were all asked to draw with our less dominant hand. To start with, it was excruciatingly difficult even to pick up a pencil in my left hand. I'd recommend it though. After a short while, the physical peculiarity began to fade, and we all drew like crazy. The results were really interesting – I usually have to think quite hard about where shadows should go, but using my left hand, I just drew the shadows rather than the object.

RIGHT BRAIN	LEFT BRAIN
• Creative	• Logical
• Intuitive	• Analytical
• Artistic	• Linear
• Nonverbal	• Verbal
• Emotional	• Factual
• Musical	• Sequential
• Imaginative	

So, anyway, drawing definitely frees the mind from either side of the left/right tracks, whichever track you are on, and opens up the development of design. When I wrote my first book, *The Thoughtful Gardener*, I had a brilliant aide-de-camp, Laura Diggens, working with me. Laura is 'immensely capable', which in English means she can do anything she turns her hand to. What she didn't do much of at that stage was drawing. However, when we had finished working on the book, she announced she was leaving to go to Florence to study history of art. Now, not very many years later, she has become a quite exceptional artist. She has studied, practised and ultimately set herself free into an unexpected new world. I hope that is an inspiration.

We also make a lot of models. In lockdown, we had a project abroad but couldn't get there, so we modelled the topography. Thanks to good surveys and laser cutting, this is pretty easy to do and extremely accurate. The greenery we enjoy making ourselves, little trees from dried plants, crumbled cork and sphagnum moss and whatever other innovations we come up with – copper-wire trees, tissue paper – anything goes. Having the ability to see the unseen landscape in microcosm made designing relatively simple. This was the first time we had designed only from a model rather than life, so it was very pleasing to see how accurate the design felt when we finally made it out of the country. There was only one area that wasn't fully described by the topography survey, yet that was a quick fix.

Modelling is usually best done after seeing a place and evolving a design. The human eye is staggering in how it can collect, collate and remember complex three-dimensional information. One sweep of looking at a new landscape etches millions of minute details into our memories. It is genuinely extraordinary. How the place feels, unique patterns of light and shade, gloomy sinister bits, inexplicable dips and hollows – they all get hoovered up and stored away in an instant.

Our models are extremely useful for communicating a design. People are not universally able to read plans, so we like to use a combination of techniques, plans, sections, sketch views, words and models. I had one client who had terrible problems with visual information. In the end, we built a very large model of the house and intended garden. We made it big enough to get inside the house so that you could look at the modelled garden from the windows of the relevant rooms. We made it incredibly accurate. It worked a treat. I'm not sure we would ever have managed to build the garden without it.

All this tactile handwork conveys much more than just a visual representation of a design, it is a source of encouragement and commitment. It occurs early in a working relationship and is all everyone has to rely on for quite a long time. Drawings and models become articles of faith.

↗ It can be very useful to make an axonometric sketch for a quick visual description of how a space will look. Once I saw this rendition, I changed the plan quite a bit and loosened everything up.

Tools

We have developed a fetishism for garden tools in recent years. Is it because we lack things to believe in? Almost religious or mystical qualities have been attributed to these inanimate objects – Japanese ladders, sexy secateurs, hand-forged spades, and so on. I'm the proud possessor of a biodynamic hoe. The handle is made from limewood. Apparently limewood, from linden trees, *Tilia* ssp., doesn't give you blisters, and it's true – so far, I've not had any. The head is made of copper with a piece of gold in it. The benefits were explained at length by the Swiss man who made the tool, and are now forgotten. It seemed implausible that a light copper hoe would survive my ground without denting horribly, yet it has and works its way beautifully through it. Emmert Wolf was right: 'A man is only as good as his tools.' Gardening requires a specific group of them and they are rightly to be treasured, if not fetishised.

The benefit of good secateurs was brought home to me years back when I did the grape harvests on my uncle's vineyard in the Languedoc. Light and very sharp, with no bits that can snare and drop off, *ciseaux de vendange* are made for repetitive use and I've never really moved away from them. Scimitar-sharp, curved beaky blades, a simple spring to help them boing open again between cuts, they sit beautifully in the hand, becoming an extension of it.

On the cutting front, it's vital to have a folding pruning saw, a good pair of long-handled loppers and lightweight shears. There are some elegant aluminium shears on the market that are useful for detailed topiary, although tastes differ here. Think of the epic 14-metre-tall (46-foot) yew hedge at Powis Castle in Wales. These days, I believe it is cut mechanically, yet originally it would have been cut using hand-forged topiary shears, the kind with no mechanism, just crossed blades. Imagination suggests the undulating shape that now exists would have been created by the limits of these scissors to get through the tougher wood, gradually allowing the hedge to metamorphose into what it is today. Or maybe it was intentional from the start. There are plenty of ancient garden hedges in Britain that speak of many lives spent diligently cutting and shaping for no really good reason other than the pleasure of the end result. Another example that springs to mind is on Sheep Street in Chipping Campden, that marvellously intact Cotswold village. Go and have a look at it! Good hand tools allow personal eccentricity to stay part of the gardening process, whereas over-mechanising risks losing that.

The current love for long flowery meads gives rise to a number of questions on how best to manage them and tools appropriate to the task. The King has his meadow at Highgrove House scythed and the process is beautiful to watch. We have a small area of long flowery grass, maybe 20 x 12 metres (65 x 40 feet), that we cut towards the end of August once it sets seed. I considered using a scythe, but did not adopt it in the end, as 'Damon the Mower', by the seventeenth-century poet Andrew Marvell is too graphic an evocation of the physical and metaphysical power of this particular blade.

'The edgèd steel by careless chance
Did into his own ankle glance;
And there among the grass fell down,
By his own scythe, the Mower mown.'

Instead we use shears, which are fine for a small space and allow for miniature meadowy haystacks. The stacks are important as they allow the remaining seed time to fall back into the sward. Once the stacks are dried and removed for the horses, we mow using a conventional mower. Larger meadows need something more like a finger-bar mower, which gets through the grass at the base more easily. Always hand-cut a meadow before noon when the stems are moist and fresh. If you have a large area, a tractor-drawn mower of the finger-bar type is best, and tractors can cut after midday, by which time the grass stems have become drier and stiffer and tolerate the machinery better.

Human knees are something of a design failure. Given that they are key to gardening, they are worth considering as part of the tool kit. A basic hinge joint, the knee has a relatively limited range of motion. Gardening, at least my version of it, seems to contain many lunges and squats. Setting out or placing plants prior to planting requires a massive number of one-sided deep lunges. Planting is best done from a squat. Keeping knees healthy is about good muscle strength and having strong thighs is a distinct benefit. Essentially this is about balance and being able to correct your position intuitively. It's well worth practising if you garden a lot. I've been advised to practise standing on alternate legs for as long as possible to enhance strength and flexibility. In any event, our knees clap out pretty quickly – probably quicker than our backs – so, if squatting doesn't work for you, find something soft to kneel on that takes the pressure off this poor benighted joint.

→ I bought this marvellous painting inexpensively in an antique shop. It is a powerful example of Second World War propaganda. A good-looking couple strides out beneath an English summer sky, farming tools slung over their shoulders. The man's ominous scythe can only mean one thing and the woman has a broken hay rake with half its teeth missing. I feel the storm clouds are gathering.

Untitled, c. 1940, Leopold le Grys (1876–1961)

The Vintner's Costume, c. seventeenth to eighteenth century, Bonnart (family of engravers)

↑ This gardener's costume is brilliant. He wears all the tools of his trade: sickle and hoe, a bucket for collecting fruits and vegetables and breeches made of vines. He's ready for a fancy-dress ball or a day at work.

↘ This is a beautifully romantic evocation of what is, in fact, back-breaking work. Armed only with an adze, the man in question is laying a hedge as the sap rises in spring. The razor-sharp adze 'cuts to the quick' of the thorn and hazel, leaving a small, living hinge of bark. He can then gently lay, without tearing the fragile hinge, the long pliable stems around his vertical palings. Thus forming the warp and weft of the woven hedge.

The Hedger, 1858, John Brett (1831–1902)

↙ The Fondazione Museo Ettore Guatelli near Parma, Italy, is a museum of the everyday. Signore Guatelli was fascinated by objects from 'the age of bread' — that is to say, items of no special historic value but that supported our lives. He arranged them in these wonderful displays to create something quite unique — a reverent memory to lives hard lived and not forgotten.

↱ pp. 92—93: I have a soft spot for tractors. Not only are they required for creating most gardens of size, they are also the most brilliant workhorses. My father became a tractor designer at a young age and designed the Massey Ferguson 135, 165 and 175. That shade of MF red is burned into me!

Ladders are essential in a garden of any size, and without doubt Japanese tripod stepladders are the best. Their wide legs might seem a bit unwieldy to start with, but anyone who has teetered horribly up a conventional ladder or stepladder will marvel at their solidity. It is a precarious business wrestling with big climbers such as wisteria or roses that fight back. To do jobs at high level successfully, you need to lean and stretch and generally writhe about. Stability is everything. I doubt there are many people without a first-hand ladder accident anecdote.

Digging tools are the stout boots of gardening and so many of them are an absolute waste of money – they look like tools but don't actually work. When I was small there was a potato fork in the garage. It was vast, made of unbelievably heavy forged steel with wide flat prongs and in a beautiful shade of War Office green that I still hunt for. The border fork was similarly made but lighter. Both had nice wooden handles that were cleft at the top with the hand bar inserted. Solid, strong and long-lasting, they'd probably been handed down from a relative. A border spade, a shovel, a trowel and a kind of hand claw for riddling and weeding all shared the same characteristics and that was it, a very simple set of digging tools that could cope with any ground conditions and never, ever broke. Each was cleaned and oiled after use and hung on a peg in the garage. This is what I strongly recommend. There are excellent handmade, hand-forged tools available and its worth investing in a proper set once only. Handmade things tend to be more comfortable to work with.

Rakes are due a design overhaul, particularly lawn rakes. Either I'm very heavy-handed or they're mostly junk, as they seem to break as soon as any pressure is exerted. Having discussed this with a lot of fellow gardeners, I think there's a consensus on this. Consider the amount of pressure required to rake up leaves or dead grass properly. It's probably to do with the advent of detestable noise-polluting leaf blowers. Give up gym membership and get a lawn rake. Cultivate an admirable six pack and cut down on energy consumption.

Watering requires a lot of thought in terms of equipment. The bottom line is to invest in a very good set of properly made watering cans in different sizes and with excellent roses, and a proper hose with brass joints and fittings. Plastic is just landfill waiting to happen; it breaks all the time and is completely infuriating.

I really can't cope with irrigation systems, yet they certainly have their place in a big garden scheme. We try and install a minimal system and only use it for the period needed to establish larger trees and shrubs, usually about three years. On the subject of trees, I regularly receive less than positive 'feedback', the contemporary word of choice for criticism, on the scale of trees we plant and have no trouble defending it. Neither I nor my clients are going to live long enough to see trees mature and we want the impact now. There are excellent industries set up for the production of large trees and they deserve to be supported as they have a unique skill set. Choice is part of democratic life. Choice also goes hand in hand with responsibility. We minimise road haulage by shipping full loads. Writing a good methodology of how to dispose of all the irrigation plastics in due course is also essential.

At home, I am trying to devise a system that relies completely on the rainwater from our vast roof. The roof has a surface area of 460 square metres (5,000 square feet). The calculation is that roughly 4 centimetres (1½ inches) of rain falls per square metre (10¾ square feet) per annum, making 18,400 litres (4,000 gallons) of free water. I don't want to use underground tanks as they support no life, plus the impact of digging for huge underground cisterns is prohibitive in terms of cost and space. The hope is to build a gravity-fed sequence of pools for the birds and the frogs and a New York style water tower as the principal hopper. I've always thought the water towers of New York very impressive – a low-tech solution in such a seemingly high-tech city. All methods of water-saving and recycling should be part of any new garden or house-building infrastructure. Inevitably, it only springs to mind in times of drought, by which time it's too late. The easiest thing, if there is space, is to build a pond.

Fundamental Elements

The tangible aspects of a garden have remained broadly unchanged since the dawn of garden-making. Wood, stone and metal are our principal building materials. Combined with the elements, earth, air, fire and water, we can make almost anything we like. The following ingredients form the skeletal structure of every garden and landscape. The 'chord' structure is different for each one, though we will leave the subject of style until later. For now, let's focus on the Roman architect Marcus Vitruvius Pollio's assertion that structures must exhibit three qualities; *firmitas*, *utilitas*, *venustas* – that is, to be solid, useful and beautiful.

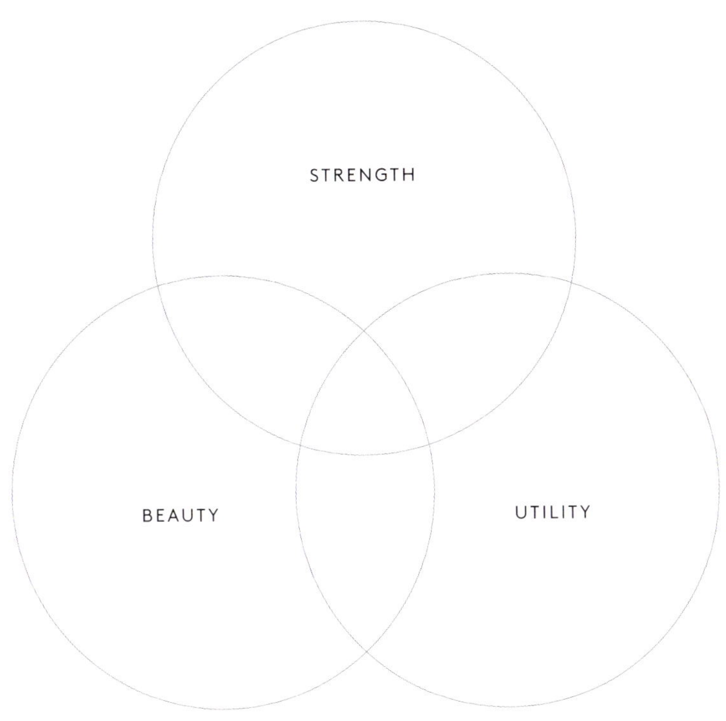

← In this garden, I wanted all the separations between the garden rooms to be different and to follow a hierarchy. On the whole, it is a garden of new stone walls yet here, separating the herbaceous walks, I used a fence. Fences are lighter and more transparent – this one is a handmade oak picket that is silvering down nicely.

↑ I made this fence from locally cut cleft timber. It stands around 1.8 metres (6 feet) tall and protects against deer, rabbits and porcupines. This method of fence-making exists in most cultures and hasn't changed for centuries. It suits its purpose to protect a vegetable and flower garden in a rustic area.

Walls

The English word 'wall' is derived from the Latin *vallus*. However, it wasn't the Romans who invented the wall, it was the Pre-Pottery Neolithic hunter-gatherers, the earliest of the Neolithic people, who created possibly the oldest extant walls in the world at Göbekli Tepe, or 'Belly Hill', near Urfa in southeast Turkey. The walls are roughly 11,500 to 12,000 years old. This level of architecture is a staggering achievement for a nonstatic culture and is unique to this period of history. The wall was born, and we haven't looked back.

Historically, walls were built for defence. Typically, they encircled towns or villages for privacy and to protect the population from danger, either from other local cultures or from the wild animals that predated most settlements until we managed to extinguish them all so comprehensively.

There are some wonderfully famous walls in the world. Here are my favourites, in no particular order: the great Cyclopean Lion Gate and its walls at the Bronze Age citadel at Mycenae, where the massive stones are coursed. How on earth did they do that and why? Next is the megalithic temple of Mnajdra in Malta. The scale and precision of the stonework is breathtaking. The Great Wall of China deserves a mention for sheer dedication. We should remain quite impressed by a nation that, more than 2,240 years ago, pursued an idea with absolute devotion over a staggering distance (more than 13,000 miles/20,000 kilometres). The Great Wall was mainly built of rammed earth, wood and stones, a building technique used far and wide.

I have always wanted to visit the thousand-year-old Great Enclosure in Zimbabwe. I watched a documentary about the wall years ago and realised that the breadth and depth of African history has been disappointingly underplayed. The dry-stone walls are exquisitely worked and coursed with decorative motifs at the top. There is a beautiful, sculptural quality to the whole structure, curving both upwards and on the radius of the outer wall, which is well over 10 metres (33 feet) tall.

The wall of Ston, in Croatia, is another mad escapade in stone. It traverses some very complex terrain and is entirely stone built. In fact, in Croatia, I've seen some of the most beautiful stone walling ever. I am an absolute devotee, and it is fair to say, if you do it once, do it properly and it won't disappoint.

Frequent trips to North Africa have brought me into contact with mud-walled towns such as Taroudant, which remains largely as it was when built by the Saadians in the 1500s. The city within the walls feels protected and holds secrets within secrets with beautiful, secluded gardens tucked away.

Walls are the mainstay of my gardens. I love building them. The deftest way to create a sequence of spaces is through walling. Walls can in turn give way to hedging and fencing, including these softer styles of division within them, yet nothing beats the permanence of a confident wall.

With the aid of structural walls, hills can be shaped – think of terracing in Greece and the south of France. The added dynamism of ascending and descending a hill with level land at your disposal is seductive. Walls can be straight or curved. Think of the marvellous crinkle-crankle brick walls of Suffolk, built to deflect the bitter east wind and protect ripening fruit. Many parts of the world have dry-stone walling. We built a wall in America made of an intractable, hard grey limestone. The wallers were Guatemalan and the walling they produce is refined with tiny joints and a beautiful pattern, random yet considered, across its face. Without thinking, I blurted out: 'It looks as beautiful as the Mayan stonework. You guys must be Mayan.' 'We probably are,' they replied.

My love of stone walling is well known. I'll build as much of it as anyone will allow. Not only does it represent phenomenal skill, it is also completely carbon neutral. The only carbon consumed is that of transportation from the quarry and the walling team's vehicles. Stone walls last forever. They require no concrete. Most dry-stone walls require no foundations as they are usually built on ground that is already very stony and hard. They create the perfect environment for plants such as stonecrop and erigeron. They become little vertical gardens. Dry-stone walls are a citadel of crevices perfect for insects, lizards, toads and, later in life as they age, holes big enough for small birds.

Brick comes a hot second to stone. Many places aren't suited to dry-stone or mortared stone walls. Brick is beautiful. The trick to good brick walling is to use handmade bricks with lime mortar. With a lime mortar there is no need for the expansion joints used with cement mortar as the cement mortar is stronger than the brick and can crack, whereas lime is flexible and porous and

↘ Given the superabundance of dry-stone walls in this garden, I decided to plant them all up. These are very thick retaining walls, so their backs stay cool while their fronts bake in the sun. The depth of the spaces between the stones allowed us to push soil in quite deep for anchoring the plants. We squished in caper seeds planted inside ripe figs to give them some traction. These images are from a few months later. The experiment worked.

moves complicitly with the bricks. Cement mortar is death to brick. How many walls have you seen where the cement pointing is intact, but the brick has shrivelled away? It is usual for a structural engineer to recommend lots of lovely reputation-saving concrete. It is vital to go and learn about alternative methods of building so you can hold your ground, literally, and stave off this monstrous substance. My reference is always the medieval brick-built cathedral in Albi, France. It has no expansion joints.

Brick lends itself readily to decoration, either in form such as the crinkle-crankle wall, or in the endless permutations of piers, copes, drip lines and so on. We have a bricklayer's apprenticeship manual in the studio that is getting on for a hundred years old and we refer to it frequently for ideas and also for terminology. As with all special skills, bricklaying has its own language. Brick also provides structural integrity for less stable materials such as flint and clunch, creating beautifully varied textured walls. Some of the most sophisticated I've seen are in the Somme region of France.

I also like to build stuccoed walls over a brick base, just like the ancient Romans did. Roman walls are a revelation, especially those of Herculaneum and Pompeii, where the construction method is exposed. The substructure for circular columns takes shape as tiny bricks cast on a radius to allow for the cylinder to be built and then rendered with lime plaster and decorated to look like expensive stone. For the walls, the Romans used 'tufo', a very light pumice stone that they cut into bars and laid as a diamond pattern, points up, and then rendered again with lime plaster. So taken with the method, I've imported some tufo bars, still produced in Italy in the same way to this day, and have designed a garden around them.

The ha ha is the best British landscape invention. It allows an infinity edge to a lawn so it can segue out into the landscape without visual interruption. Essentially it is a walled ditch. The parkland can be grazed without ingress of animals into the garden. I've adapted them successfully for different types of animal in different countries – it just needs a bit of analysis to establish how high the ha ha needs to be to keep animals out. Sheep and cows are managed easily at 1.4 metres (4 feet) whereas elephants need closer to 2.5 metres (8 feet) for effective control. A ha ha doesn't suit every landscape, so apply with care.

Fences

Depending on where you are in the world, and your circumstances, walls may not be relevant. Some places are resolutely rural, and a built structure could look anachronistic. Enter the fence. Remember *vallus*? The Roman for 'wall'? It actually translates as a wooden post or a spike. Since time immemorial, timber has been the fastest, easiest and most accessible material for a quick boundary.

Spike-topped cleft-stick fencing can be seen in agricultural locations the world over; every country has its own variant. Some of the most beautiful I've seen are in Transylvania. In England, we have our own styles of cleft fencing that change from county to county. At some point, these rough agricultural fences became gentrified and the picket fence was born, redolent of cottage gardens in certain parts of Britain, a simple yet appealing boundary device.

Far away on the other side of the world, the Americans opted for white-painted, machine-sawn picket and made it a central statement of middle-class suburban life, ensuring order and conformity, safe children and pets, peace and stability. It is interesting how the white picket is a transmutation from the tall, pole-fortified stockades of not that many years earlier, known to most of us only through westerns. A fear of attack was possibly much more alive in the psyche of such freshly settled pioneers.

The indigenous population of America also used pole-fenced corrals to surround their villages. They were beautifully made. I've seen a number of paintings of them showing fascinating woven chicken coops and other structures within them. Rather than signalling a fear of imminent attack, they were more likely farming structures designed to keep predator animals at bay during the night. They remind me of the corrals I've seen on the high plateau of the Rift Valley in Kenya that serve the same purpose.

In Charleston, Carolina, there are the most beautiful pickets. Tall, slender, sophisticated and elegant timberwork with equally beautiful ironmongery. The posts are all made from joinery and have a dazzling array of styles. They contribute enormously to the sense of genteel prosperity. It is hard to condone the source of this wealth yet the craftsmanship, if it can be separated from the fact, is second to none.

The new Americans made another world-altering fencing invention. In the 1880s, barbed wire was introduced. Used by ranchers in the Wild West to keep new settlers from encroaching on pastureland, it then spread all around the world. It became synonymous with the First World War defences featured in art from the period, such as *In the Trenches* (1917), by C.R.W. Nevinson.

All these systems for creating fences are very much in use today in the gardens and landscapes that we build. We work often with 'woodmen' who still produce cleft-wood products from oak and sweet chestnut. We use copious amounts of hazel. Hurdles are woven from the smaller, more flexible trees such as hazel and willow and have been used for myriad purposes over time. Willow associates better with water and we mend banks of ponds with little hurdles or 'spiles' as they're called. These help shore up eroding banks very effectively. Willow woven in situ is very popular and there are many specialist weavers around to help.

Hazel hurdles make perfect windbreaks to protect young planting or to screen views while waiting for planting to grow. They last about five to seven years, and because they contain no pollutants, they break down and can be composted or just left to rot away.

A type of fence that belongs only to our era is the acoustic barrier. These have been developed mainly to control traffic noise in areas where the population is dense and space is needed for housing. In Brixton, London, there is an entire apartment block that was designed as an acoustic barrier to a main road that was never built. However, acoustic barriers are interesting, if not especially attractive, and can be incorporated usefully within domestic settings with a bit of care and attention to detail.

The Agony in the Garden, c. 1500, Sandro Botticelli (c.1445–1510)

↗ It is gratifying to see Sandro Botticelli using a fence just like mine in this painting. I'm drawn more to the flora and garden structures in paintings than to their intended themes. Aren't the pollards lovely?

← To accommodate a huge change in level in this garden, I decided to make a feature of the steps. At the top they form a small balcony with a view out over the garden and as they descend they turn, creating an alcove for a substantial lead fountain. The railings are very light and simple and will, in due course, host a white wisteria that will wrap itself through and over them.

Iron Railings

Nothing beats iron railings, properly made by someone who knows what they are doing. There is so much to know about the metal, proportion, style and colour that it is a source of constant fascination. I studied metalwork at school. It was my favourite subject bar none and I would love to have pursued it. The fact that metal can be extracted from rock is alone astonishing. Then, the malleability and strength of the material itself is like magic. Members of my family, the Kenricks, were originally iron founders who set up large businesses in Birmingham. Perhaps it is in my blood. I often work with my good friend Brian Hall, a sculptor, master blacksmith and superb metal conservator. Brian is from the Black Country, so we have a shared understanding of that part of the world and all the immense activity that went on there, turning raw materials into the pinnacle crafts of the Industrial Revolution. Brian is steeped in metalwork and we collaborate often on designs for many other items than railings.

Growing up in a purpose-built Georgian spa town exposed me to a huge amount of exceptional wrought ironwork. The town was embellished with the best balconies, verandas, railings, gates, lanterns, lantern overthrows, hinges, door escutcheons and door knockers that you could possibly imagine. As a small child, I found them engrossing. Not least because a good family friend, Daniel Roth, was a notable architect. He made an exhaustive study published in a small book, still referenced today as the best work on Georgian wrought iron. He took great pleasure in discussing all this with me and I am forever indebted. I can, if nothing else, tell the good from the bad and the ugly.

So, to the basics. Wrought iron is 'worked' using heat in a furnace to soften it, and then hammered out either mechanically or by hand on an anvil. 'Wrought' supposes all the decoration is also hand-worked and then applied to the finished product. Cast iron, a generic term covering a number of alloys, is produced in a foundry. Ingots are melted down in furnaces and the molten metal poured into casts. There are numerous ways of casting, depending on the scale and end result required. Casting allows for a great deal of detail that would be unavailable by forging. It also allows for mass production. The majority of heavy railings made by the Victorians were cast – cast-iron railings.

In the studio, we tend to use wrought iron for railings with cast finials for the verticals. They have a lightness and beauty that is unparalleled. For a run of railings, important decisions rest in the weight of the vertical bars and the style of finial. Having backstays is also a sign that they have been made properly, and dog bars if you need to keep animals in or out. We invariably lead-wipe the rails into the stone coping in the traditional manner. This involves coring the stone coping so it can receive each upright, placing a railing in each hole, and then pouring molten lead into the holes to seal the junctions. It is very satisfying. Feeling the workings of the blacksmith in the metal in your hands is part of the beauty of the end result. An imperfect surface feels good and refracts light differently.

Finally, the paint colour is really important. Railings were never black. I believe that came during the reign of Queen Victoria. When her consort Prince Albert died, she went into deep mourning and asked that all railings reflected the mood. That became the mood of the nation, and we never went back. As far back as the Renaissance, and certainly the practice for a long time after, early metalwork was often finished with smalt, a silicate of potassium and cobalt that after much grinding, purifying and cooking was used as a vitreous blue finish on metalwork. I still love seeing dark blue on wrought iron. Victorian ironwork was, more often than not, a deep green or stone colour. The choice is yours.

Another firm favourite are the estate railings that make the marvellously genteel perimeters of country estates, keeping animals where they need to be without obscuring views. I don't know when they were first introduced, but it seems likely to have been in the eighteenth century. We use mile upon mile of them for the very reasons just stated. It is vitally important to get estate railings made to your specification by someone who understands the need for onsite welding and running lengths that follow the contours of the land. Nothing looks more atrocious than cheap, jet-black, powder-coated railings made in panels that step horribly across a beautifully undulating landscape. Estate railings must always be painted in situ too, unless you like the look of it rusty, and some do.

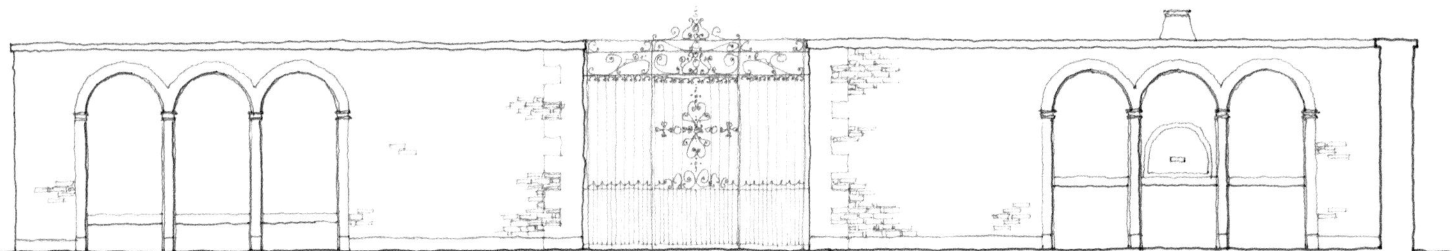

Gates and Doors

Boundaries need gates. The first thing to do with gates is establish the hierarchy of them across a site. For example, for one garden, we made simple and elegant wrought-iron gates for the main entrance. These had a *clair voyer*, a fixed panel of tall railing with matching motifs, set into tall the stone walling either side of the gate. *Clairs voyers* make an entrance took larger and lighter – the term literally translates as 'clear view'. To the side of the main house, we installed panelled oak gates with oak overthrows. Across the lawn, we had a walled garden, for one side of which we made little wrought-iron gates that gave onto a staircase; for the other side we made a pair of wrought-iron doors leading into the walled garden. Beyond the walled garden, with a solid oak door in its wall, was a lawn devoted to football with estate railing leading to a meadow, with single and double gates made to match the estate railing. Around a corner was a working yard for which we made metal estate railing field gates. At the bottom of the meadow was a wooden field gate. That makes nine different styles of gate and door on one property, yet they are all coherent and signal the nature of the area you are in.

It is necessary to build up a very good lexicon of door and gate styles and to know how and when to apply them. Decide on the level of decoration you might want. A farmhouse will require something very different to a big country house or a bungalow or a townhouse. For an old Tudor farmhouse in Kent, we made absolutely everything from cleft oak, every gate within the hierarchy was handmade in the same way. The research into this was, in itself, very interesting and added to the resources we had in the studio. Nothing is ever wasted.

Much of the work is dictated by the architectural style we are working with. So, while creating unique modern doors and gates is exciting, the application for them is limited. My own house is a unique example of English modernism from the late 1960s. I am hopeful that I can cook up something exciting with Brian Hall as we share the same interests in that regard. I fancy a Brutalist pergola. Brutalism hasn't seen the light of day for a while.

↖ Gardens tend to have to accommodate tennis courts, which have unnaturally long, straight lines. This sketch was for a tennis court wall with a difference. On one side there is a little niche of three arches with a bench; on the other side the arches house a pizza oven and worktop. Aligning with the centre line of the tennis court, I designed pretty wrought-iron gates with fixed side panels to give some light and air to proceedings.

→ I'm immensely proud of these gates. They are the result of a long and happy collaboration with my client. The gate piers belong to a Grade 2 listed William and Mary house, so the research had to be thorough. Hampton Court Palace is the same period and has a screen made by the French master blacksmith Jean Tijou. I wondered if the fashion for Tijou might have inspired a blacksmith in this area. To my delight, I discovered that the smith in this village had made the gates at Blenheim Palace. So, our country blacksmith had the skills and could easily have made the original gates to this house. Armed with the relevant research and corroboration we obtained listed building consent and off we went. The results are quietly magnificent.

↖ I once booked an advance visit to the Palazzo Querini Stampalia in Venice just to see these steps, which are famously part of an intervention by the great Professor Carlo Scarpa. Having made the epic voyage, I was told the Fondazione was closed. I made a very un-English fuss and was grudgingly let in. The thinking, design and execution is remarkable. This seemingly simple set of steps, and the writings of Carlo Scarpa, have changed the way I look at design ever since.

Steps

There are records of steps in existence going back more than 12,000 years. Most likely built to suit the human gait, they allowed bipeds to traverse complex terrain with ease. Humans have always needed to carry heavy loads, often on their heads. Steps would have made balancing much easier as they evened out our pace, making each step reasonably predictable. Steps were revolutionary. Much has been written about steps leading to the tops of temples and pyramids for acts of worship, yet I wonder if the more prosaic need was one of trading. They are much more like early roads to me. Take, for example, the famous 'stairs of death' at Machu Pichu. They must have been built to get materials and crops up and down from the high town. They remind me of steps carved by workers in the limestone quarries of Menorca, impossibly steep and narrow steps that allowed the quarrymen to get in and out of their extraordinary workplace.

Think also of the great stepwells of India. They are the most exquisite things. Roughly two thousand of them remain, now protected as the feats of engineering and building that they are. Not only do they display incredible ingenuity, they are also humane. There are places to sit and rest in the air cooled by the water; they are convivial. Chand Baori – *baori* meaning 'stepwell' in Hindi – is one of Rajasthan's most spectacular, apparently built by King Chand, a local Rajput ruler, in the ninth century. Rajasthan was the world's epicentre of mathematics at that time, so perhaps that explains it. Were there plans? How did they do it?

The Italians embraced steps in gardens in a big way during the Renaissance, making the best use of their topography to display their landscape architectural skills. The Villa Aldobrandini, set on a steep hillside at Frascati, being a case in point. The landscape has been built out with astonishing, if somewhat overbearing, results. The steep hillside leading up to the villa has been stepped and terraced in its entirety, and then continues on up behind the villa to the summit of the hill. The optical illusion is as splendid as the mathematics. The villa that appears vast on approaching is only two storeys at the back. A master Italian stepmaker was, of course, Carlo Scarpa, whose steps for the Querini Stampalia in Venice displayed ingenious lateral thinking, allowing the waters of the Venetian lagoon to flow inside the building while keeping the inhabitants dry in a cleverly conceived causeway. Another master of the stair is Charles Jenks, whose Garden of Cosmic Speculation at his home, Portrack House, is a symphony of level changes. His landforms are honestly second to none, and the complex ziggurat steps he designed down to the water are reminiscent of the Indian stepwells.

My favourite set of landscape steps was created by the Italian architect Gae Aulenti for Villa Pucci in 1968. She set the villa on a series of exquisite plateaux, each only a few centimetres high. Doing so, she evened out the terrain with such subtlety that she elevated the house both figuratively and literally to a new plane. Her intervention, the tiny tufo steps holding a simple grass sward, is beautiful.

Steps are a predictable feature in any garden. Inevitably, there needs to be a transition between levels or there needs to be a levelling of an area to create a garden in the first place. At this point, I urge you to start getting excited about the possibilities. Steps make a place beautiful. Harold Peto, the great Suffolk-born landscape architect and garden-maker, had a deft touch with steps. Iford Manor, his home in Wiltshire, uses steps and level changes beautifully to manage the hillside, creating a series of lateral, classical Italianate terraces that are invisible from the front of the house. He was a master of his art, and many technical lessons can be learned from his gardens, even if the style isn't to your taste.

Steps are to gardens what punctuation is to language. They alter the tempo, create pauses and full stops and amplify mood. They are also mathematical. Outside, they should be no more than 12–15 centimetres (5–6 inches) high. Other things to consider are how the 'going' works – for example, if steps are too deep, they are uncomfortable to climb, necessitating a one-and-a-half step skippity-skip that is very aggravating. Tape them out on the floor and test them until you have a good sense of what is comfortable. Landscape steps can be virtually any style you like: formal, built-in stone, cast concrete, steel, ramped and turfed, brick or creasing tiles, like the lovely Lutyens ones at Great Dixter – anything you like. Bear in mind handrails and landings for steep and narrow stairs or long runs of them. Good flights of steps and interesting changes in level make the voyage through a garden comfortable, interesting, dramatic and revealing.

↗ I took this photo during a walk through the landscape of Mount Desert Island in Hancock County, Maine. This is such an enjoyable way to experience a wild landscape, traversing all the creeks and boulders yet being part of it all at the same time. The simple timber paths are no different to those that Neolithic man would have made: simple, attractive, sustainable and quick.

Routes

Key to the skeletal structure of a landscape garden are its routes, which need to have a clear hierarchy as they are the subliminal indicators of how you are expected to navigate a place. They tell you why you are here and where you hope to go next. They ensure the visitor and the dustman appreciate their respective points of access. The main drive or entrance path needs to signal its status emphatically. Studying the stately homes of the British Isles makes the point clearly. Gatehouses signal whether you are entering the main drive or a secondary or even tertiary drive. The principal drive will lead you through the best of the landscape, offering sweeping views to lakes with ornamental 'rustic' bridges, clumps of trees in the parkland and peaceful herds of grazing deer. Wide arcs of the tree-flanked drive will conceal the house until the moment is right for the big reveal, at which point you, humble visitor, will gasp with appreciation, envy and astonishment.

Of course, not many of us live quite like this nowadays, but the principles are absolutely correct and transferrable to any sized plot. The main arrival point must be clearly signalled. The route to utilities needs to be functional and discreet. The passage to and through the pleasurable parts of the garden should by turn be broad, accommodating and easy to walk on, transforming into smaller more imaginative and whimsical paths as the design dictates.

Roman legions laid down the first roads in Britain. They brought their exceptional road-building skills with them. Anyone who has seen original Roman roads in Italy will appreciate what Italians are capable of creating. Besides being practical they are beautiful acts of craftsmanship in which interlocking, broadly hexagonal stones of significant size are laid in tight patterns. In towns Roman roads were almost like canals, with high pavements each side and stepping stones strategically placed as crossings for pedestrians. Given their depth, you can imagine they were used much like an open sewer, with slops and domestic water thrown out into them to be minced down by the endlessly passing cartwheels. In the countryside the principles remained similar, only with drainage ditches either side and the road itself built on an embankment of material generated by digging the ditches. The method for building a drive or path is exactly the same now as it was then. First, the ground was cleared and large rocks laid in the bottom then compacted. Over this went another layer of smaller crushed rock, again compacted. The final finish depended on the material found locally. This could be stone or gravel, with sand as a binding course. As anyone wishing to conquer new territory knows, dependable routes make communication between parts of your new empire easy. It is no different in a garden. The principles of the early conquerors are entirely reliable.

There are older roads in Britain, such as the Ridgeway, which is estimated to be more than 5,000 years old. As its name suggests, it is high up on a chalk crest. The chalk is naturally warm and dry to walk on and the views afforded safety to early users of this great droving and trading route from the stone circle at Avebury, in Wiltshire, to London. There are many other early traces of routes and pathways, and each has its local character that can still be used today. If we are really keen on saving carbon, many of these are worthy of further exploration and exploitation. Across wetlands are vestiges of Neolithic routes made using alder logs. Alder, *Alnus glutinosa*, is a waterside tree and has been used for centuries for work in wetlands as it doesn't rot. Much of Venice is built on alder piles. Various styles of path were made, including wide roads that had mattresses of alder brash laid down as a base to spread the load and were then topped with a weave of alder logs running widthways to take traffic. Not unlike modern decking, only flexible and squashy, such paths might possibly have been topped up with rush as a wearing course. This is virtually the same method the Irish navvies used to take the West Highland Line, the railway that first penetrated the remote west highlands of Scotland, across Rannoch Moor. The notoriously squishy moor is almost impassable, so the usual stone construction techniques failed, and the labourers resorted to laying huge mattresses of birch brash instead. The anaerobic peaty water ensures the timber never really rots down but mummifies instead. Paths across bogs and wetlands have remained unchanged since our predecessors first started building them. Short stakes with split-log walkways are still found across all parts of the world.

In a commission that saw us restoring a very ancient site and reopening its historic flood channels from a river that ran through the land, we reintroduced Lonk sheep, a breed that can cope with high rainfall and wet feet. Similarly predisposed to a damp life, old English Longhorn cattle were especially useful for managing a species-rich grassland that we redeveloped with the help of nature, replanting large areas of alder and willow as they would have been historically. The cattle naturally brash their own areas of willow into matts to stand on. We made a lot of elevated alder walkways to traverse the land in flood. People, like most livestock, also hate having wet feet. Interestingly, all the domestic routes around the very old house, from courtyards to tracks to paths, were cobbled, in part due to the local ground conditions, but also because they work well in areas of high rainfall. The cobblestones are water-worn pebbles, readily sourced from the nearby river.

There are a few rules for comfortable routes and pathways. A drive needs to be somewhere between 2.75–4.6 metres (9–15 feet) wide. On a longish drive, I tend to settle on about 3 metres (10 feet) and have passing places as necessary. Paths for tractors, quad bikes and such need to be between 1.65–2 metres (5–6½ feet) wide. Principal paths in gardens can be 1.5–2 metres (5–6 feet) wide, a width that allows people to walk and chat convivially. Then they can start to narrow down considerably. A width of 1.2 metres (4 feet) makes a pleasant subsidiary path around a lawn, next to a border. In a vegetable garden 90 centimetres (3 feet) is wide enough for a barrow and also makes a nice sized mown path. A 60 centimetre (2 foot) path is perfect for running through a more relaxed area, such as a deep shrubbery, where kids can play hide and seek.

On a final point regarding the hierarchy of routes, it is worth noting that classical design from André Le Nôtre to the Arts and Crafts Movement has always incorporated ordered formality around a house leading outwards towards a more ornamented interpretation of nature where lines soften, planting billows and we can get lost in thought. Both the texture and the design of paths are key to making these transitions feel inviting. Somewhere deep in our minds we know we are not being led anywhere provocative or dangerous. The peaceful routes of the garden are safe and protective. The garden is transporting us, literally, to another realm.

Surfaces

New roads; new ruts.

–G. K. CHESTERTON (1874–1936)

The structure of every landscape needs an array of different surfaces. Drives are the introduction to a new place. Courtyards invite us in. Terraces offer us places of sociability and repose. Paths encourage us on new journeys. Vegetable gardens are free draining and practical. Utility areas are robust. Open ground is soft and green. As humans have expanded, so has our need to evolve beyond the gentle muddiness of a green lane to the serious surfacing of a multi-lane motorway and a heavy stone pavement. These are all our daily surfaces and they all need some sort of covering.

These surfaces, at their most basic, are needed to prevent erosion. We have developed them to also enhance performance and to support all our varied activities. Each surface we create is a visual message conveying much about the style and purpose of a place. They have become creative expressions of our moods and desires as much as our practical needs. By no means an exhaustive list, the following are the main contenders.

↖ When looking for paving inspiration, it is a good idea to drive around the area to see what has been used locally. When restoring the *castello* in Italy, I found inspiration in this image of an old hilltop village. The photo to the left is my interpretation of the same. Using vast slabs of very thick stone from a local quarry, I paved the whole place in this way.

Stone Paving

Stone is used extensively in landscaping: the majority of terraces are laid in stone, most steps are made of stone, and walls are coped in stone. In Britain there are numerous different types to choose from, depending on where you are in the country. Not all of them do what you need, so it takes time to get to know the available sizes, attributes and finishes.

York stone is by far the most popular choice both for colour and wear. I'd recommend properly investigating and choosing the quarry of origin if your investment is going to be significant, and making sure that the seam currently being extracted has what you are looking for in terms of figuring. It can be a shock when, having looked at a 10 x 10-centimetre (4 x 4-inch) sample, the stone that actually turns up is completely different. It's not like choosing carpet. I like York stone when it is plain and unfigured. Often, it has great swirly swathes of iron running through it. This is very enjoyable from a geological point of view but can make you feel a bit seasick on a terrace. Beware reclaimed York stone. The majority of the good stuff is gone and often all that's left is stone from old factory floors back in the day when oil was liberally sloshed all over it. Once saturated, it can never be cleaned.

Limestone, such as Portland, is beautiful. I use it sparingly as a landscape surface because it goes green very easily in shaded areas. I think it is better used as an architectural stone.

Imported stone, such as travertine, Chinese granite and Indian Kota stone, always look as if they have come from elsewhere. Stone should ideally stay where it is quarried. I extend this mantra to projects abroad. For a project in Kenya, all the stone we used was local, creating a place that looks complicit with the surrounding landscape. Foreign or imported stone doesn't belong in a country garden, though it can be used successfully in a town garden where a wider context is less limiting.

Laying stone over a porous base and leaving the joints open, or filled with gravel, is very attractive. It is also practical as it retains water permeability, unlike a concrete slab. And it allows for the surface to settle over time, giving an authentic feel. Things growing in the cracks unbidden is a matter of personal preference.

Patterned Stone Floors

I love patterned stone floors and make them often, like carpets, for town gardens or internal courtyards. The very finest examples I've ever seen are in Venice and Pompeii. The floors of Pompeii are absolutely engrossing – tiny tesserae less than a centimetre square are laid over huge floors. Even the predations of volcanic eruption and 2,000 years under ash haven't really damaged them. The precision is astonishing considering every piece was hand-cut. Floors also exist made of rare, coloured marbles in tiny triangular form. These decorated floors have been used time and again throughout European history. There is a particular stretch of pavement outside the Duomo in Siena, Italy, that I marvel at every time I go. It's not large yet it has so many different styles and patterns going on in it. It makes you wonder who made it and why. I enjoy designing floors, or rather plagiarising those of others, as someone long ago devised almost every pattern you can think of. Working with a stonemason is a fascinating eye-opener on the whole process of choosing the stone and cutting, fixing and finishing it.

Cobbles

Cobblestone is another favourite of mine. We tend to get cobbles made from whatever walling stone we are using as that's how they were made originally. The walling stone is laid on edge so that the lie of the grain is visible. The stone absorbs more water this way and as the stone delaminates, it tends to lock itself into position with its fellows. Cobbles are hard work to lay as they are of uneven depth and need deep bedding. We tend to sweep the joints with fine-crushed gravel and stone dust and let nature and time do the rest.

The most beautiful cobbles I've ever seen are the tiny whinstone slips in Edinburgh's New Town. They must have been leftovers from the mile upon mile of cobble paving laid during the Georgian build of this beautiful neighbourhood. Around the little central garden in Moray Place is a ring of parking and next to this are the exquisite little slips. I've tried to replicate them but they are a by-product of a bigger process and so can't be made as such. I did hear a rumour that people complain about the noise of cars on cobbles and that they might be ripped up and replaced with tarmac. I thought we were all sick of the destruction of beauty.

Gravel

Gravel is, of course, crushed stone, though several waterworn pebbles and shingles also get classed as gravel. It is one of the most useful substances in the landscaping lexicon. Stone crushes into a functional waste or decorative material, depending on what it is to start with. Once the blocks are quarried, the remaining bits are put through a screener and crushed to different sizes for a range of purposes.

Big lumps are known as 'crusher run' stone, or hardcore, a mix of coarse natural stone graded in size from larger pieces of crushed rock or gravel down to stone dust. It is used as a subbase for concrete slabs, foundations and drives – in fact anywhere a good, solid free-draining base is required. It is also called MOT Type 1, and can be made up of many different materials including limestone, crushed concrete and granite. The MOT stands for Ministry of Transport, the organisation that approved the material for road-building. We often hire a crusher on bigger jobs and recycle as much as we can from demolition; old 'demo'ed' brick and concrete can be crushed to 40 millimetre (1½ inch) and used as a subbase. I hate taking material to landfill and we are, on the whole, very proactive recyclers. Truth be told most 'muck' has value.

Decorative gravels can be any type of stone crushed to fairly standard sizes – here are the basics: 20 millimetre (¾ inch) is used on drives, 10–14 millimetre (½ inch) is used on paths and 6 millimetre (¼ inch) – dust – is the superfine compacted stuff you fine in smart gardens and public parks. This is what lines The Mall, in London, as it approaches Buckingham Palace. The man who laid it told me it's so durable the Queen could have landed a MiG fighter on it as required. However, I'm not sure Her Majesty piloted fighter planes back then … and aren't MIGS Russian? I'm barely going to dignify resin bound gravel with a sentence of its own. Don't use it.

Terrazzo

As far as fabricated stone goes, terrazzo is the best for paving and I recommend making up your own to suit the project. Literally everything can be made if you are prepared to hunt for the right people to do it for you. That is the best part of this work – there is someone out there for everything,

Terrazzo is made of stone chips bound in a cementitious base, levelled and then ground back to polish the surface, exposing the colour of the stone chips at the same time. It is available as a 'single pour' or as tiles in different formats. For the sake of it, I'll also mention those fabulous 1960s exposed aggregate slabs. They are made of cast ballast (pebbly cement) that is then washed back to expose the stone. For years, they were everywhere but now you can't find them for love nor money. So, my loathing of concrete, like all good prejudices, is patchy. As I said before, locally quarried stone is a low carbon choice so apart from local appropriateness, there is a strong eco-conscious reason for choosing it. Act local where possible.

← Top left: A paving design I came up with, based on a fragment of a very old floor – now happily installed in a beautiful secret garden.

Top right: The ubiquitous 20 millimetre (¾ inch) crushed limestone I use for drives. It stays put. I use angled gravel because I loathe gravel that squeaks about and forms tracks.

Bottom left: Basalt paving in Naples, which inspired a design for a garden I made in a city far away.

Bottom right: An amazing floor I saw in Pompeii, made of chips of different Italian marbles. The Pompeiians were master floor builders.

Architecture starts when you carefully put two bricks together, there it begins.

–MIES VAN DE ROHE (1886–1969)

Brick and Clay Pavers

We get through an awful lot of bricks. Brick is a very good invention. Again, only use it where it is appropriate to the location as local clays look best in their natural environment. I'll spare you the history of the brick, other than to say that, as long as mud has been sun-baked, there has been brick.

Brick pavers are excellent for paths and terraces, especially in places where it rains a lot or under trees. The slightly abraded surface takes on a lovely patina with time, with mosses and tiny plants colonising the cracks. Brick, with its small unit size, settles very attractively, taking on undulations that enhance its beauty. Bricks are soft to look at, gentle. They grip well in the wet. They are attractively rustic if laid in patterns like herringbone or basketweave, giving a cottagey appearance. They can also be modern – at my house, which is a modernist barn conversion from the 1960s, we have stack-bonded bricks in the manner of that period.

There are handsome, wood-fired and handmade brick pavers on the market and they are worth paying for. I usually lay them on edge; they look refined with all their firing marks visible, adding to the overall effect. In some areas they are traditionally laid flat, so decide what looks best for you, the larger or smaller format.

Stable pavers are also very good to work with. These are generally much harder than a brick paver, having been fired hard to withstand metal horseshoes. Called 'Staffordshire blues', after their place of origin, they are often a very dark grey-blue clay and have a diamond pattern or a 'chocolate block' pattern cast into them. Stable pavers were a Victorian invention at a time when industry was growing incredible fast, and horses were very much part of daily working life. These sturdy pavers withstood everything that was thrown at them or deposited on them! They drain and scrub up well.

Recently, Dutch and Belgium road bricks have had their moment in the sun. These small, dark, engineered bricks are used extensively in northern Europe as road finishes. I used them in my own London garden, laying them in a running bond over a series of terraces. I went off them quite quickly once they were laid. On balance, I wish I'd used an English brick paver – they just looked too 'designer' and foreign next to my standard-issue Victorian brick semi.

The final brilliant thing about brick is its natural permeability. It is best laid over a flexible base of compacted stone and a weak 'dry mix' bedding of cement and sand. This means the whole paved area drains beautifully and the bricks breathe. Avoid laying a big concrete slab when using clay; they don't like each other.

Clay also makes very good tiles. Tiles look great outside if you like the particular aesthetic – I have put some 1970s black quarry tiles in our porch to mirror similar ones inside the house. The Victorians used encaustic tiles a lot and we think of them in association with that period, yet they were a medieval invention. The encaustic process allows complex patterns in up to six different coloured clays to be burned or fired into the tile. The tiles are very hard and strong. Almost every Victorian town house had encaustic-tiled garden paths and porches, sculleries and outside lavs. The Victorian enthusiasm for all things medieval knew few bounds.

I have used beautiful, long slim bars of Italian *cotto* just like those in Piazza del Campo in Siena in some projects. Being handmade and not super hard-fired, the tiles are of variable strength, yet bonded together in situ with their sand joints, the strength becomes mutual. A soft delamination with age only adds to their beauty over time. And look at the piazza – it has the Corsa del Palio, a mad horse race, thundering over it twice a year. Any material that can withstand that is worth having.

↱ pp. 114–15: This close-up shows a surface I put into a newly made Italian garden. The site is ancient and I didn't want to make everything too new looking. Gravel was the perfect way to blend paving back into the natural surroundings. I planted it very heavily and left all the different types of thyme to fight it out.

→ The path to my front door. Brick always blends so well with its circumstances, making it an enjoyable garden paver. In summer this path all but vanishes, subsumed by plants, and in my case, weeds. It was laid stack bond in the late 1960s as part of the Modernist conversion of our sixteenth-century barn. Giving such an ancient material a modern pattern signals a new interpretation.

Lesser Evils

There are other, less decorative yet helpfully practical, surface treatments that deserve an honourable mention.

Tarmacadam

I'm proud to reveal, given the substantial volume of Gallic blood coursing through my veins, it was a Frenchman, engineer Pierre-Marie-Jérôme Trésaguet, who took road construction to new scientific levels hitherto unexplored since the Romans, in the 1790s. Having engineered the roads of Limoges – no doubt important to the good burghers of that town and their need to transport pieces of the finest porcelain without smashing them to bits – he was offered the greater opportunity of paving the roads of Paris. In essence, he altered the build-up to a three-layered compacted stone with a fine finish and created the 'cross camber'. This cambering sloughed off water into ditches, so preserving the road surface for longer. It also allowed increasingly speedy traffic to take corners more safely. I might be missing something, but it doesn't sound especially revolutionary. It was cheaper and quicker to build, though, so that must accord him a place in history.

Despite his efforts, Pierre-Marie-Jérôme wasn't lucky enough to have his name perpetually associated with road building. Instead, that honour lies with John Loudon McAdam who is forever associated with macadam (though not, I may say, tarmacadam). In the 1820s, John McAdam decided that the road surface could be saved from distortion and rutting by greater compaction followed, after rolling, by adding a bitumen or concrete covering. The process created a bound surface and it was a revolution. It was Welshman Edgar Purnell Hooley who ultimately patented 'tarmacadam', a crushed stone, sand and tar road build up, in 1902. Methinks he might lose that patent in a modern court of law. Thanks to the collective combined good offices of Messrs Tresaguet, McAdam and Hooley, not to mention the legions of legionaries from Rome, we are to this day able to offer our customers exceptionally well-detailed and high-functioning drives.

Concrete and Cement

By mixing crushed sand and gravel with cement and water, we end up with concrete. Cements are finely ground powders that, when mixed with water, set to a hard mass. The ancient Babylonians and Assyrians used clay as a bonding material, the Egyptians refined this into something more familiar to us today, using lime derived from crushed limestone and gypsum, which is crushed chalk rock. They also used crushed oyster shells. This combination is also known as pozzolana. The mixture remained the basis of concrete until the 1820s, when Englishman Joseph Aspdin ground together clay and, presumably, Portland stone from Portland Bill in Dorset, and created what we still call Portland cement.

Pozzolanas were used in the eastern Mediterranean from around 400 BC. The mix had been around for many years, but the Romans, with their empire-building need to expand, eventually developed the latent abilities of lime pozzolan. Specifically, they discovered its unique ability to become stronger under water as it cures. *Opus caementicium* is especially durable, thanks to the unique properties of pozzolanic, or volcanic ash, which prevents cracks from spreading. It's quite hard to stop going on and on about Roman concrete – it's still standing, after 2,100 years, in the Roman Tuscan port town of Cosa, along with some exceptionally high-quality dry-stone walling; two birds, one (volcanic) stone.

I love using concrete as a specific material and have, in the past, made gardens entirely from in-situ fair-faced concrete. We designed an impressive, Brutalist-inspired, in-situ concrete 'rockery' for Lord Rothschild at Waddesdon Manor. Putting all the framing or shuttering together to make giant moulds is exciting. The pouring is a very skilled job. I worked with the man who poured all the in-situ concrete for the Channel Tunnel, which is exceptional. He also made the marvellous concrete facade decoration for Arne Jacobsen's Royal Danish Embassy in Sloane Street, London – perhaps even more exceptional, as this was his first professional job working in this way.

So, for surfaces, concrete is useful to make simple 'tank track' drives, like the one my friend and collaborator Piers Von Westenholz has at his home. However, I am strongly opposed to using concrete anywhere near natural materials and I refuse to countenance any cementitious pointing on either stone or brick walls. It kills them. Literally. Over time, the brick or stone shrinks and disintegrates leaving just the rock-hard cement pointing. For this application it can only ever be lime mortar. I dug all the cement out of our house, which is made of coral stone, and replaced it with lime. If it was good enough for the Romans . . .

Play Surfaces

Play areas for kids are often nicest on grass, though for areas with lots of children using them, it's better to have a purpose-made material. For a fairly long time, crumb rubber was considered a good option. It is made from used minced tyres bound together with resin. It is flexible, bouncy, drains well and is neat to lay. It is a reassuring surface for kids. However, there has been controversy around its potential toxicity and many learned reports have been published on the subject. Because tyres are exposed to a long life of road wear, they are in contact with a lot of nasty stuff and it is unclear whether this is still in the rubber matting in particulate form or not. So far, reports have proved crumb rubber safe. It is certainly a very useful material and is also used a great deal on tennis courts, where there seems to be no fuss about them. There is also a resin bound mulch that incorporates bark and has a more natural look, although it is still predominantly made of minced tyres. Warm and bouncy – I like these surfaces and so do children.

↙ This is a photomontage we made in the studio, in order to establish the tiering and massing for our Brutalist-inspired concrete rockery at Waddesdon Manor. Obviously, it would be planted differently in reality. This version wouldn't look out of place in the tropics!

Naturals

Several natural surfaces find regular use in gardens. The juxtaposition of a hard surface to a soft surface is one of the ways of differentiating the spaces and changing the atmosphere. A hard surface seems complicit with action – a drive, a terrace or a courtyard – whereas soft surfaces are relaxed and less formal.

Lawn

The best natural surface covering available for landscaping that gets little wear is lawn. It looks lovely, it is relatively easy to care for, it is useful for parties and games, and shows you have full control over your domain. Short grass has been popular for a long time. Traditionally, it was maintained by grazing – by sheep, rabbits or geese (who are really good at it, as anyone with a lake will tell you) – or scything. It was the English, in the early 1830s, who mechanised lawn care. Admittedly, André le Nôtre introduced a *tapis vert* at Versailles a hundred years earlier, but it didn't catch on. Instead, it is to Stroud engineer Edwin Beard Budding that we owe a huge debt of gratitude. With his ingenious transference of thought from watching a cutting reel on a loom, he revolutionised life for the aspiring British middle classes. Through a combination of the perfect grass-growing climate and the rotary mower, a new world of gardening was born. Every man loves a machine and here was a domestic contraption offering the utmost in domestic pleasure. Not only did it cut grass, but it also required care, oiling, cleaning and storing. Within thirty years, it had become the equivalent of a good Swiss watch, an indispensable domestic fetish item and a consumer durable that every home required – the ultimate progenitor of suburbanisation. And it was what the rest of the world wanted too. Along with the picket fence, the Americans took to lawn like ducks to water, followed swiftly by the Australians.

Lawns definitely have a place and in the new world of wilderness and I can't imagine a closely mown sward will ever really disappear. How we treat them may well change – fewer or no chemicals, no irrigation and being less fussy about them browning off in drought, for example. Given the speed grass greens up again after a rain shower, the lawn has to be the least complaining part of any garden.

Its main strength for me is erosion and weed control. Earth should never be left bare – to me it feels raw and exposed, like a grazed knee from falling off a bike. Weeds are best controlled by mowing over spraying: simply make areas fallow, overseed them and mow until the problem is gone. It is a slow yet effective process.

Bark

One of the simplest ground coverings is bark mulch. My top tip is not to use the huge chunky stuff. It looks terrible and won't rot down in your lifetime. Always use a well-produced, dark, composted bark in medium-to-fine size – say 10–20 millimetres (⅜–¾ inches). Dark, warm and mysterious, it makes marvellous paths through woodland, protecting the roots of trees and other plants. It smells good too. Just top it up annually. Do not, under any circumstances, use a geotextile underneath it. Geotextile is plastic and always rises to the surface like some long-supressed family secret.

Decking

Decking has been around for a long time. Roughly planked wood kept feet out of mud or muck, helped people work on wet land without destroying soil structure and made passage possible where it was otherwise difficult. The etymology is simple – it is a Middle Dutch word meaning a 'covering' on a boat, *dekke*, that hopped over the channel to become *dec* in Middle English. It wasn't invented in the 1980s by gardening programmes. My own feeling about decking is that it certainly has its place in the lexicon of landscaping tools. I know where I would and wouldn't use it, but I'm not here to dictate. My own preference is to use reclaimed hardwoods until they run out, by which time, we might have got our forestry continuum sorted out. By all means use recycled plastics if you like them.

↗ An incomprehensible moment of English daftness. This is London Zoo's own camel lawn mower, ridden by gardener Fred Perry in 1913. It all seems quite civilised.

Drains

I'm a drain bore! No landscape or garden on earth can exist without good drainage. All surfaces will carry or hold water to a lesser or greater extent. It is very important indeed to make sure they do it easily, efficiently, attractively and comprehensively.

'Capability' Brown was an excellent drainage engineer. All I can see in his landscapes are the workings of a very practical mind. He made a huge contribution to eighteenth-century landscape civil engineering, earthworks, dams, pumps, lakes, roads and huge volumes of relatively straightforward tree-planting over graciously undulating parkland. We would have got on well I think, especially as he was partial to a glass of red wine. As well as understanding what his clients wanted in terms of pomp and circumstance, Brown also understood the needs of the vast new houses they were building, their water consumption, the need for fish and fowl for the kitchens, amply supplied by the lakes.

On our projects, we spend a lot of time assessing and designing the drainage. It needs to speak to the place. If the project is large, there will be a specific drainage engineer associated with it. Their job is essential to understanding the volume, behaviour and management of water. These days, this is critical as hundred-year storms are now more frequent and unpredictable. However, it is in the hands of the landscape designer to take the technical information and make it visually appropriate to the space that is being created. The visible hardware of drainage needs to be chosen with care, whether that be cast-iron or stainless-steel drain covers, open ditches, brick-lined drainage channels, proper ceramic drains or more drastic landscape solutions, including lakes and wetlands for water storage.

On one site, we built a comprehensive series of interconnecting culverts in rockwork with stone-lined bases. They were conceived as seasonal streams, following a newly imagined and built 'lie of the land'. They were beautiful landscape features in their own right, with ferns tucked into the crevices and other native plants colonising them. And they were absolutely necessary for managing the colossal downpours in that part of the world, combined with the enormous leaf fall from the surrounding woods in autumn. The rain and the leaves alone would be far too much for piped culverts to manage and would be at risk of clogging. Looking at the local environment is very important when studying drainage. I like surface drainage to be 'daylighted' wherever possible. This means easily visible, so you can see where it is getting clogged and can clear debris out of the way. This technique is relevant in more places that you might imagine. I use the same principle, in miniature, in urban locations – simple edge drains that stay open are far better than a 10 millimetre (3⁄8 inch) slot drain that fills with moss and fag ends and no one ever clears.

Embellishments

Having covered the essential skeletal structure of the garden, it's time to think of the innumerable flourishes that personalise the place. Here we have a hierarchy of 'stuff' that we all interpret in highly individual ways. The originality of every garden is the province of the maker, so while the list of enjoyable things is encyclopaedic, so too is the enormous breadth of interpretation of style. I have no desire to steer people's choices. *A chacun son gout*!

↘ We designed this building, called the Cherry House, to sit at the centre of a large scheme for Waddesdon Manor, Buckinghamshire. It occupies the site of a now demolished Victorian glasshouse known as Paradise where Walter Rothschild used to drive his lunch guests around in a zebra-drawn carriage. Ours is a glasshouse for growing cherries, a restaurant and an exhibition space. I owe a debt of gratitude to architect Louis Kahn – the central brick cylinder was certainly inspired by him.

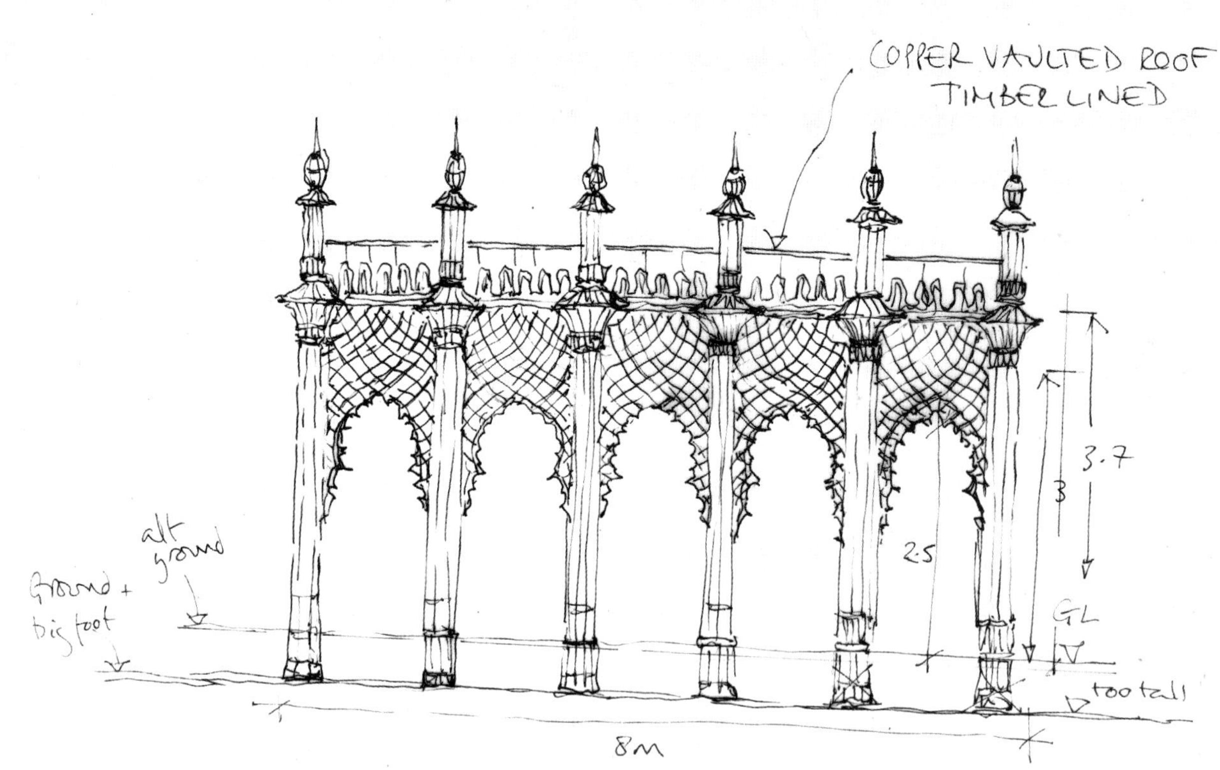

SIDE ELEVATION

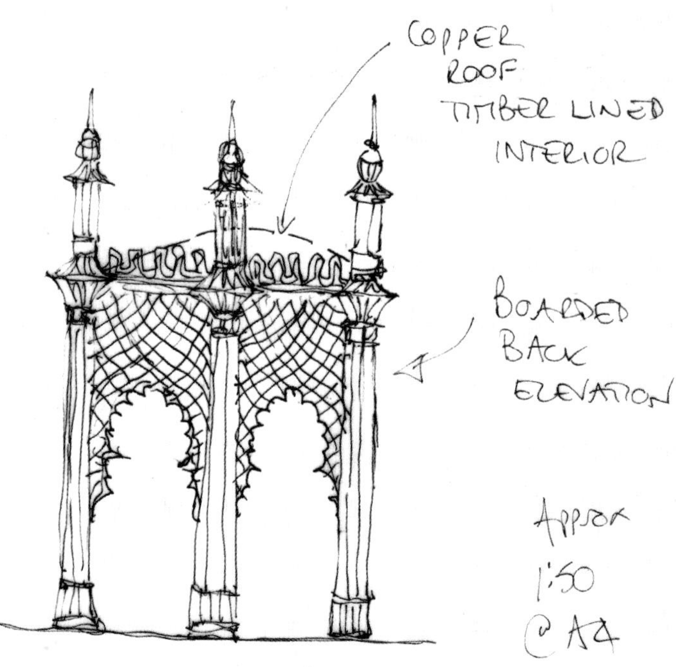

Little Buildings

Most gardens need some kind of building in them. We usually end up designing a suite of buildings to accommodate all the necessary equipment, from lawn mowers and tools to the pleasures of being outside in nature. Greenhouses don't require designing as they are utilitarian – they need to work properly and that is best left to the professionals. Yet greenhouses do require careful siting in order to function properly. The style is also important. I've used everything from commercial aluminium greenhouses with wood burners inside, to swanky, traditional, cedar-built ones, and all stations in between. For myself, I am having a black one. I like the recessive nature of it. My godfather had a marvellous summerhouse made of wood that was set on a steel track and could be rotated to make the most of the sun. It was a magnet to us as kids as we tried to turn it on its slightly ceased-up wheel. The pleasure of having a little house in a garden stimulates even the most jaded imagination. We have a kit house in our garden that we use as an office. It's lovely to work in as it feels like a completely different environment to that of the main house. It has a holiday atmosphere, somewhere to bunk off to and relax. My husband works out there all summer long with the doors open so that he can enjoy the proximity to the garden and the birdsong and the horse periodically greeting him over the wall. Most commonly, we design pool houses or collaborate with an architect to design them. A good pool house is a beneficial luxury too, especially if it has facilities like a shower, a kitchen and a fireplace. Increasingly, homes are multigenerational, and the more facilities there are, the more coherent they are to live in. I tend to consider the bigger gardens we design more like hamlets or small villages, allowing everyone space to live and do their thing. When considered like this, the cost of doing the work feels more pragmatic. I also enjoy placing buildings in gardens so that there is a purpose to exploring, making destinations and vantage points where views can be reversed and you can look back to the house or out to a view. Even in small gardens – my own is a relatively small third of an acre – there is scope to apply this way of thinking.

- Pool houses
- Book room
- Garden office
- Follies
- Gazebos
- Sheds
- Greenhouses
- Glasshouses
- Tree houses
- Saunas

← For a Regency country house I wanted an eye-catcher at the end of a wide central avenue — somewhere to meander to through flowering shrubberies after a good lunch. The inspiration came from Brighton's Royal Pavilion, with its light and playful nods to other cultures. This one, as yet unrealised, has a vaulted copper roof and would have been painted in good Recency colours — bright blue verditer, yellowy pink, peach blossom — with gilding on the points.

Art and Decoration

Generally, I like to design everything in the garden myself so that the end product has a clear harmony to it. It is so enjoyable finding people with unique skills to work with. We set up the principle of the design direction and then evolve the finished product with the specialists who know what they are doing. I am a Brother of the Art Workers' Guild in London, where more than sixty creative disciplines are in action among the members. It is invariably an easy process to find someone who can specialise in a field of interest that we need. I often work with stone carvers to make bespoke fountains and furniture. We collaborate a great deal with conservation iron workers either to create gates from scratch or to repair and conserve old ones. Trellis is as old as time, yet needs a skilled mind to make it from scratch. The opportunity for creating bespoke decorative items is endless. I love designing lanterns, too, as there isn't much to choose from in landscape lighting. Art and sculpture can take us on some interesting journeys. Beauty is very much in the eye of the beholder and the interesting part for me lies not so much the choosing of an item, but in the proper placement of it within a landscape setting.

- Gates and railings
- Furniture
- Rockeries
- Stumperies
- Art/Sculpture
- Lanterns
- Planters and pots
- Bird tables
- Aviaries
- Labyrinths
- Trellis
- Pergolas
- Eyecatchers
- Obelisks

It's easy to have an idea. It's quite another matter to make that idea a reality. In this instance the stars aligned and my friend and fellow Brother of the Art Workers' Guild, Paul Jakeman, said he could carve these table legs for me. The process is completely fascinating. It feels good to be leaving them to posterity.

↱ pp. 126–127: *Weeping Girl*, 2009, Laura Ford. This bronze weeping girl, shown here at Pilane, Sweden, is by one of my favourite sculptors. Her work is always surprising and affecting. Placing sculpture in a garden needs care. My golden rule is that you don't want to see any more than one piece at a time.

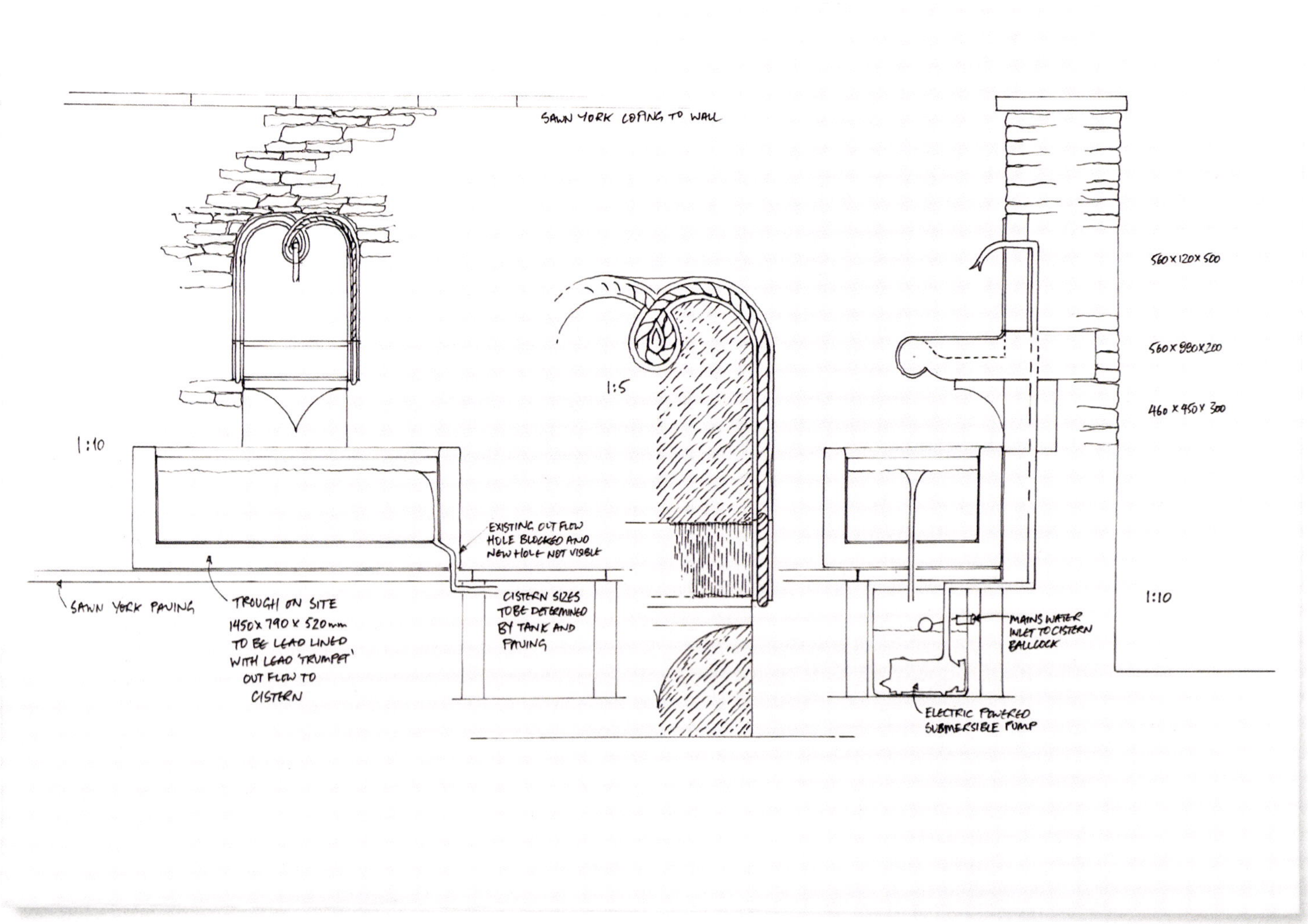

↗ I sometimes pull ideas together from all over the place, and this fountain was one of those hybrids. Richard Podd, who was to carve all the stone elements, produced this lovely shop drawing so we could check all the aesthetic and technical elements were working together.

→ I like making spouts with snake heads — simply bent copper pipe with two rivets for eyes and a shaped slit for the mouth. It helps the pipe pour nicely.

↱ This is the origin of my fountain design pictured above. It's a hand basin beside a pool in France that both my clients and I know very well. It's our homage to many happy times.

Water

All gardens need to have some water in them, even if it's nothing more than a birdbath. If you have naturally flowing water, then that is the supreme luxury – be sure to monitor it to keep it free of pollutants. Next best is a pond or, if space permits, a lake. I'm reliably informed that the definition of a lake is if a swan can land on it. Swimming ponds defy logic for me. If a pond is big enough and deep enough to swim in, then surely it's a swimming pond? I always make a big pond 3.5 metres (11½ feet) deep at the centre, to keep the water cool and to avoid too much evaporation. For a smaller garden pond, a minimum depth of 60 centimetres (2 feet) works well, with the planting scaled suitably. Formal water is also very useful as a focal point, particularly if you need to keep eyes within a garden rather than wandering off to a far horizon or eyesore. Then there is fun water: swimming pools, outdoor showers, hot tubs and Jacuzzis. An outdoor shower is invaluable and is used far more than you might imagine.

- Ponds
- Lake
- Streams
- Swimming ponds
- Bird bath
- Canals
- Fountains
- Swimming pools
- Hot tubs
- Showers
- Bridges
- Walkways over water – duckboards

Play

Gardens are all about play. From the pinnacle of playhouses right down to the most basic homemade den, opportunities for play can be as complex or as easy as you like. In my experience, children prefer making up their own imaginative games and finding their own places to play in the garden. Their fertile little minds need neither encouragement nor much in the way of material goods. That said, trampolines are hugely popular and I've not found it necessary to dig them into the ground. Jungle gyms are brilliant if you have an area of trees that can be pressed into service. Equipment placed in trees has other benefits besides being more for the kids, including shade and camouflaging of the equipment. Gardens are rarely enhanced by having a play frame front and centre of the view. For older kids, we routinely put cricket nets alongside tennis courts as the dimensions are similar, whereas croquet lawns and petanque courts are the reserve of the garden proper. Petanque is best closer to the house, while croquet needs a large, flat and perfectly kept lawn. Outdoor kitchens are becoming more popular in the United Kingdom, although they are better suited to less volatile weather patterns where they can be used year round. The more there is to do outside, the more a garden will be used, and designing all of these things into the scheme will allow it all to be beautifully presented.

- Playhouses
- Swings
- Climbing frames
- Jungle gyms
- Trampolines
- Bike trails
- Dens
- Exercise trails
- Tennis courts
- Cricket nets
- Croquet
- Petanque
- Yoga platforms
- Fire pits
- Outdoor kitchens
- BBQS

Utilities

There are many utilitarian requirements in most gardens. Don't avoid them, but try to work them into your design because you'll be glad you did. I like making drying grounds hidden behind high hedges, for example – a place to hang out all the sheets and washing without them being an eyesore. Storage is a constant thorny topic. No one wants to give over precious space to it but a garden can't function properly without it. I fight a losing battle at home. My shed is far too small, and I can't decide where to put a bigger one. Anyway, it needs sorting out. I always try and allow for lavish storage that is nicely designed – it is needed and it should be practical and aesthetically pleasing.

- Compost bins
- Bike stores
- Bin stores
- Log Stores
- Washing lines
- Dog washes
- Car chargers
- Fruit cages

5. ANIMA MUNDI

IN ALCHEMY, after the *prima materia* – all that is tangible, practical and easily accessible to everyone, comes the *anima mundi* or the *psychè kósmou* in Greek, the 'soul of the world', the unspoken connection between all living things. To make the perfect paradisical garden, we need to combine the immutable with the mutable, the inanimate with the animate. So, the next aspect of putting a landscape together concerns all living beings and their place within the structure.

← The success of a garden is when, after a build, the animals and birds return. We are building for them as much as for ourselves. Allow for soggy ditches, crevices in walls, deep undergrowth and other places in which creatures can have lives of their own. That, for me, is a sign of a well-considered and executed plan.

↙ Give much thought to your meadow and long grass mixes. They need to be as site specific as possible. Read about microclimates, soil types and locally endangered species as your actions might make a difference. In the United Kingdom, our wildlife is under terrible threat due to habitat loss. Even small interventions could save lives.

↓ Hand paintings like these exist in caves all around the world. All are stencilled by what looks like a method of blowing a fine spray of earth pigment over the hand as it is held against the rock. In Chauvet, France, the hands were created using red oxide. In Cuevas de las Manos, in Argentina, the paintings were executed using natural mineral pigments. Iron oxides create red and purple, kaolin makes white. Natrojarosite contains sulphur and dries to a yellow, and manganese oxide turns black. Not much has changed — we have been grinding the earth's minerals to make paint for millennia.

Soil

In Sickness and in Health

The base ingredient of all gardens is the ground we walk on. There is skill involved in determining whether your soil is healthy or not. Feeling it and smelling it tells you a great deal. Looking at the sward it is supporting reveals more still. Having a bit of a dig around allows you to learn more about its structure. A lot of gardening is the physical combined with common sense.

Roughly 12,000 years of farming and food self-sufficiency have conditioned humans to react instinctively to soil. It is a substance that can sustain or starve us. These days vast numbers of us are completely dislocated from soil and have virtually nothing to do with it in our day-to-day lives. Gardeners choose to have direct contact with the earth and love it deeply. Any gathering of garden lovers, be they of a practical or aesthetic bent, rapidly sees them falling into detailed descriptions of their soil conditions. 'A nation that destroys its soil destroys itself,' said a prescient Franklin D. Roosevelt – a sentiment that was presaged by Karl Marx when he pronounced, 'Capitalist production, therefore, develops technology, and the combining together of various processes into a social whole, only by sapping the original sources of all wealth – the soil and the labourer.' I'd like to hear the two men discussing this together today.

Soil regeneration could completely reverse global warming if tackled on as large a scale as modern industrial farming. Even the American Midwestern dust bowl could be reversed and the land made viable again with the right attention. It was once completely healthy, deep-rooted prairie, brimming with many of the plants we love to grow in our gardens, such as echinacea, veronicastrum and asclepias. As human populations have exploded, so too has our misuse and abuse of soil. Driven by the need to produce huge crops for global markets, industrialisation of farming and fiscal imperatives have overtaken basic good practice. This has caused a desperate degeneration of the soil, resulting in decreasing crops and climatic irregularity that have struck panic into farmers' hearts. It is not possible to chemically fertilise the way to success – the ground rejects it. The truth is much simpler, and is explained brilliantly, simply and graphically in the American documentary film *Kiss the Ground*, which explores the core ideas of regenerative agriculture. The film shows how responsible management of land can be achieved by any farmer willing to make the change. By reducing ploughing, limiting nitrogen fertilisers, using green manure crops and prioritising animal and plant diversity, the turnaround is incredibly fast. The symbiosis of running grazing animals over land is well known. Their excrement fertilises and feeds microorganisms and their urine softens the soil. As their feet firm the surface, they tread in seed, making it easier for it to germinate. Mimicking this cycle is also useful in gardens, especially when trying to establish wildflower areas or areas of lowered intervention.

Though this is a book about what makes a garden, the soil health story is integral to the ways in which we manage our earth in even the smallest spaces. I often make large gardens from scratch. This involves a great deal of soil disturbance, removing trees and old buildings, reusing spoil from building projects on site, creating new contours, creating new buildings and features, developing watercourses, ponds and wetlands. The process involves heavy machinery and lots of feet. Frequently, we work around builders and the impact on soils can be colossal, even with all the good practices of soil protection in place. We are also, increasingly, converting old commercial arable crop land back into 'garden' or more accurately, low management landscape. This is not a simple task. Land saturated with decades of chemical fertilisers and compacted by ploughing is very miserable, intractable stuff. The interface between good gardening practice and regenerative agriculture is a fast-closing gap. In my practice, we are learning how to build up soil health through experimentation, research and lots of discussion with colleagues across the disciplines of farming, arboriculture and ecology. There is a huge proliferation of specialists in all forms of compost-making. Compost is the new sourdough!

In the not too distant past we all had chamber pots until the advent of domestic plumbing in the nineteenth century. In rural areas without flushing lavatories they persisted much longer. Night soil was invariably used in the garden or on the vegetable plots. Rather than being disgusted by this, consider that most diets were vegetable based with small quantities of meat and wholly organic. The night soil biodegraded easily, the uric acid offering a rich source of nitrogen, potassium and phosphorus – all much needed for plant growth and soil health. It was probably unavailable in any other form so the simple logic of this is clear. Ultimately this simple home-produced fertiliser was replaced by increasing use of modern chemicals. Persuasion, in the form of aggressive advertising, overwhelmed smallholders and farmers alike. Over the years, countries across the world have adopted farming methods of all kinds that have not been in the best interests of the land and its soil. Globally, we need to join up our thinking and act in a more coherent way. Gardens, in microcosm, are part of the seismic shift towards better sustainable husbandry. We can be revolutionaries in our own plots and effect the changes we believe in. I also believe land, however little of it you have, is of infinitely higher value than gold. As the saying goes, they aren't making any more of it.

Dung

Let's stay with matters scatological for a while, as excrement is considered the cornerstone of good garden soil. I don't doubt for a minute that the contents of urban chamber pots have found their way into domestic vegetable gardens in the past. When I first moved to London in the 1980s, people in my area kept pigeons, rabbits and chickens in their back gardens – a domestic food supply unchanged since the Middle Ages, if not longer. The creatures were bred as a continuum of fresh meat and eaten as required. Their 'scat' and soiled straw was essential for the garden, used as composted mulch or manure. The urban garden might have consisted of lawn, roses – huge lovers of manure – fruit trees and currant and gooseberry bushes alongside a small vegetable plot. In London, my elderly neighbour Rose bemoaned the fact that milk floats were no longer horse-drawn, because people used to run out with shovels to collect any fresh manure. And the 'totters', or rag and bone men, the original street-cleaning rubbish collectors, had also automated to flatbed trucks by then. I was fascinated that central London had been so full of manure until that time. It supported huge flocks of sparrows that have all but vanished now. London was a lateral city of many small streets with cottage-sized workers' houses and their yards and gardens rather than a place of high-rises, so it stands to reason that it was a very productive place with cocks crowing at dawn. It made complete sense. People depended on their scraps of gardens to bolster their diets, and for a good diet you need a well-fed soil. This 'needs must' type of living had a strong communal element as people would barter their gluts. There was no waste.

My design studio is near the meat market of Smithfield in the City of London. On our website, we have an old street map of the area dating from the late 1700s that names the plots of land. Many are referred to as 'garden' – although it is not clear what that meant in reality – others as 'pasture', places where the animals would have been held before being taken to slaughter. On the corner of our road is a plot called a 'laystall', which was specifically where all the dung would be collected – huge steaming dung heaps right in the middle of the city. Imagine how useful that could be to us now. Just think how much life they supported.

I'm captivated by the thought of communal urban dung heaps. It would be the best start to any compost heap, piling riches upon our gardens. In a rather idealistic way, I think of these laystalls as welcome meeting places alive with chatter, not unlike the multi-seater Roman latrines that were considered to be a place of convivial conversation and 'hail fellow, well met' bonhomie. Animal dung is an excellent adjunct to soil, provided it is thoroughly rotted down to remove weed seeds. I once had a terrible experience of a well-meaning gardener spreading fresh cow manure over a large, newly completed garden and infesting it with a crop of creeping buttercup. It took years to remove it and the borders never really took off. In 2022, author and environmental campaigner George Monbiot wrote a persuasive book, *Regenesis*, on how we can turn the current Armageddon of farming into something more enduring. He points out that animal manure, even if organic, is not what it once was, but is filled with antibiotics and other gubbins. In fact the term 'organic' is convoluted, full of loopholes and contradictions – organic farmers are not obliged to use organic manures, for example, which rather makes a mockery of the whole thing.

So, it would seem the safest route to making soil happier in a garden is through traditional, composted green waste, and lots of it. Ideally, it should be home produced so that you can know what's going into it. I am in favour of minimal digging as the destruction of worm holes has always upset me. I have a soft spot for these tireless feeders and aerators of the soil and like to give them as tranquil a life as possible. Worms pull astonishing quantities of organic material and oxygen down into the deep, creating wonderfully rich friable soil as they go. They are the easily visible tip of the iceberg of creatures that live in our soil and make it better.

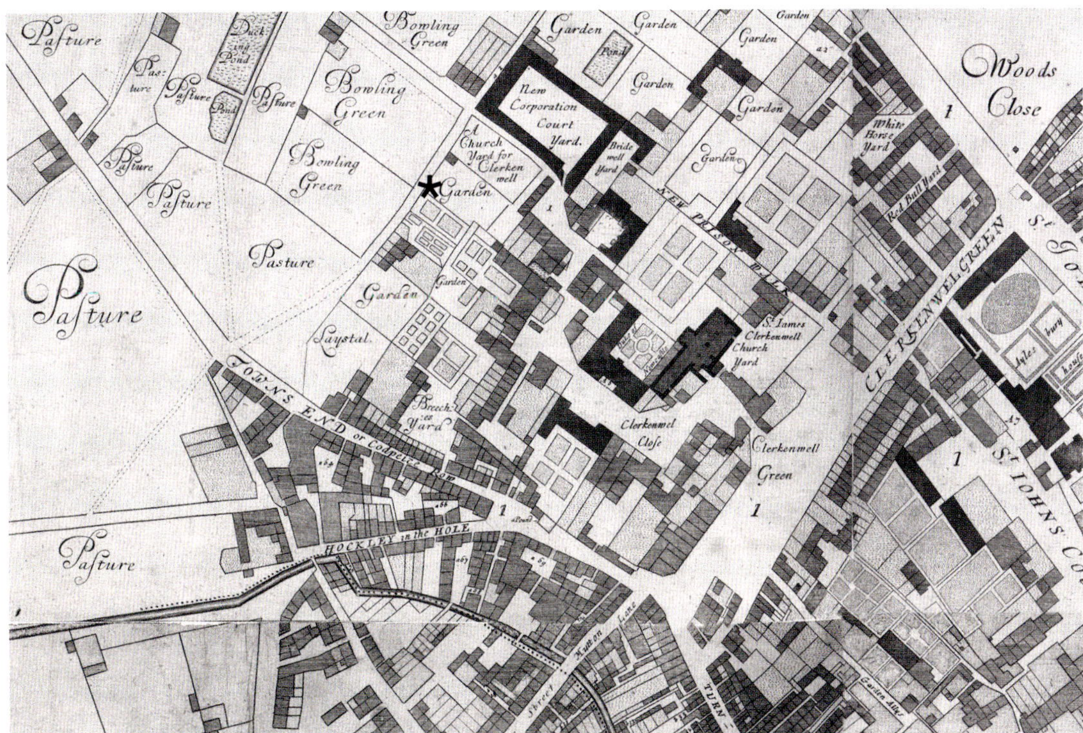

↗ This map from the 1700s shows the area of London where my studio is today. I love looking at maps as snapshots of times gone by. The noise and stench here must have been tremendous as animals were driven through these streets to be slaughtered at Smithfield Market. Curious, then, that between all the pens and laystalls were so many bowling greens on which the game of *pallemaille* was played – known as pall-mall – in which you clout balls with a mallet, like croquet. Our own studio is on the site of a garden. How apt.

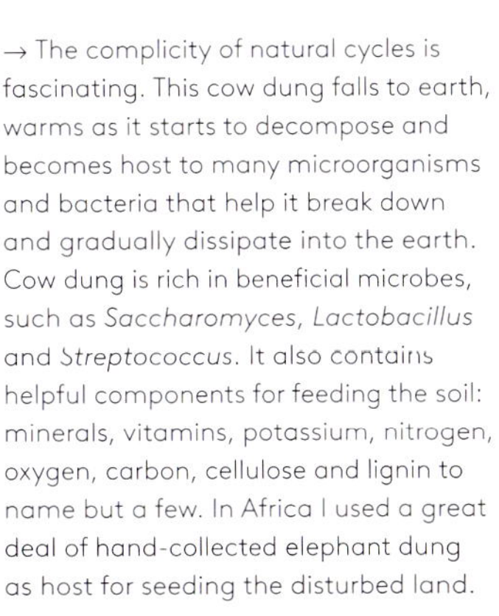

→ The complicity of natural cycles is fascinating. This cow dung falls to earth, warms as it starts to decompose and becomes host to many microorganisms and bacteria that help it break down and gradually dissipate into the earth. Cow dung is rich in beneficial microbes, such as *Saccharomyces*, *Lactobacillus* and *Streptococcus*. It also contains helpful components for feeding the soil: minerals, vitamins, potassium, nitrogen, oxygen, carbon, cellulose and lignin to name but a few. In Africa I used a great deal of hand-collected elephant dung as host for seeding the disturbed land.

Soil by Nature

The most fundamental element of creating a new garden is understanding the physical make up of your resident soil. Soil is one of the most precious materials on earth and deserves the same, or greater, level of care and attention you might lavish on a shiny new material object. Establishing its specifics and how much of it you have will strongly influence the structure, the planting, the character and the final result of your garden.

Thorough investigation from the outset is what drives the ultimate comfort and longevity of a garden. Not many years ago, advice focused on digging and mulching. Now, digging has been exposed as being bad for soil structure and much discussion rages about how to make compost, how to care for soil and how to sequester carbon in the process. We all need to be amateur microbiologists these days. The microbiome of your soil describes a collection of microscopic life forms. These include bacteria, archaea, viruses and fungi. Together these microscopic elements create a healthy, functioning soil. Bacteria are possibly the most valuable of the life forms in soil. They help drive the nutrient cycles, allowing nitrogen and minerals to be taken up easily by the roots of plants. I tried using mycorrhizal fungi when planting a native shelterbelt – you can buy it in sachets at garden centres. I was sceptical, yet the root development of the new plants was much better than I expected and I am converted by the logic of how it works.

Soil science is becoming a much sexier topic nowadays and deserves to have its own dedicated branch of study. I have read that soil sequesters carbon at a far better rate than trees do. This is not to say that we should stop planting trees. It just makes sense to check that the area that is about to be wooded should be, and isn't naturally better disposed to being open grassland. Wherever you are, the countryside will originally have been made up of mixtures of woodland or forest, naturally open grasslands, savannas and steppes. We can look at our little plots to see what they used to be before we turned up and built on them. That's a pathway to a potentially interesting new garden. Every little thought helps.

First, it is important to grasp the pH of the soil – pH refers to the 'power of hydrogen' measure and tells you how acid or alkaline the water content of the soil is and, in turn, the acidity and alkalinity of the soil. This is the best way of determining what you can plant. Inexpensive tests are readily available and it's fun probing the ground to see it change, sometimes in a matter of paces, from one reading to another. Classified according to their pH value, soils are as follows:

- *6.5 to 7.5:* neutral
- *over 7.5:* alkaline
- *less than 6.5:* acidic
- *less than 5.5:* strongly acidic

A simple 'by eye' test of the soil type and its pH is to look at what is growing locally, as plants are easy indicators of acidity and alkalinity. For example, camelias, rhododendrons, conifers and heathers are a pretty sure way of telling you the soil is acidic. Alkaline soils host lilacs, honeysuckles and wild clematis scrambling through hedges. Leaf texture is another aide, with acidic plants having a harder, shinier, more leathery leaf than the softer leafed ones that appear on an alkaline soil. This is a good way to develop your horticultural knowledge.

Plants, specifically weeds, can also help you understand the quality of your soil. Do you have a deep rich loam or a weak and undernourished soil? Is it soggy and anaerobic or light and crusty? Before you clear the weeds away, make an audit of all that has chosen to live there. Great mats of tap-rooting dandelion and burdock – traditional bedfellows and regulars in many old recipes – indicate densely compacted soil that is lacking in moisture and nutrients. Tap roots have the power to smash through, then collect and store anything that can be siphoned from the soil in their fleshy root. They also help by busting up the ground and are an indicator that you'll need strength and determination toachieve good results.

Another sign of a compacted soil is broadleaf plantain, *Plantago major*. Often found on heavily compacted green lanes, paths and trackways, this is an ancient indicator of human routes. As often happens in history, a culture gets stereotyped (and this is true of the Anglo Saxons who have become synonymous with never travelling abroad, living in narrow-minded tribes and wearing hairy boots in a sodden, muddy country). By contrast, the spread of *Plantago major* across the world could only have emanated from the British Isles – seeds trapped in the aforementioned hairy boots were tramped far across the continent and beyond over many centuries. Aboriginal Australians call the plant 'Englishman's foot', and not by accident. The wonderful sympathetic magic of herbs proves it is also a widely used as a healing plant – the leaves have a cooling effect on skin and frequently lined the shoes of weary travellers with blistered feet. Tall spires of mullein indicate acidic soil with little fertility – docks and goldenrod love damp and poorly drained soil. Oxeye daisy likes weak acidic soil.

Another simple visual test is to look at local historic building materials. Are you in an area where old houses are built of brick? This indicates that there are likely to be clay beds in the region as, until relatively recently, transportation of large quantities of heavy materials was difficult. People tend to use what they have to hand. London, as built by the Victorians, benefitted from yellow clay beds below the city. Everywhere, brickworks churned out the ubiquitous London Yellow Stocks. A conservative estimate suggests there are more than sixty billion bricks in London buildings – an excellent use of local natural resources. Paris is built of luminous, pale Lutetian limestone, which has been quarried locally since the Romans and gives rise to the name 'city of light'. *Lutum*, from which Lutetian is derived, is Latin for 'mud' or 'marsh'. Paris is also built on a swamp – a working knowledge of Latin is very helpful in gardening. These are just swift illustrations that give a clear indicator of the ground conditions in either place.

Soil is sensory. It can best be understood by feel and scent. Getting your hands dirty and your nose engaged is essential in assessing the quality of the earth. Sometimes it's so revoltingly slimy, anaerobic and emitting of foul odours as to make it untouchable. I had one project in which soil that looked fine on the surface revealed the most disgusting, reeking, grey-green clay a few inches down. As we cut the new garden levels the clay, turgid with the stench of long-trapped water, sat in a vast morose pile. Weeks passed and virtually nothing would grow in the soil. Eventually we gave up hope and sent it all away to be industrially reconstructed as loam. The malignant odour lingered for weeks.

↗ Amblecote, England, c. 1930. Imagine this job. These women and others like them across the country probably supplied the labour that created the bricks that built your house. Not only did they make the bricks, they then hauled, day in and day out, these hefty wooden barrows with their 135-kilo (300-pound) loads. They were the finest-quality bricks and the pride in them is clear.

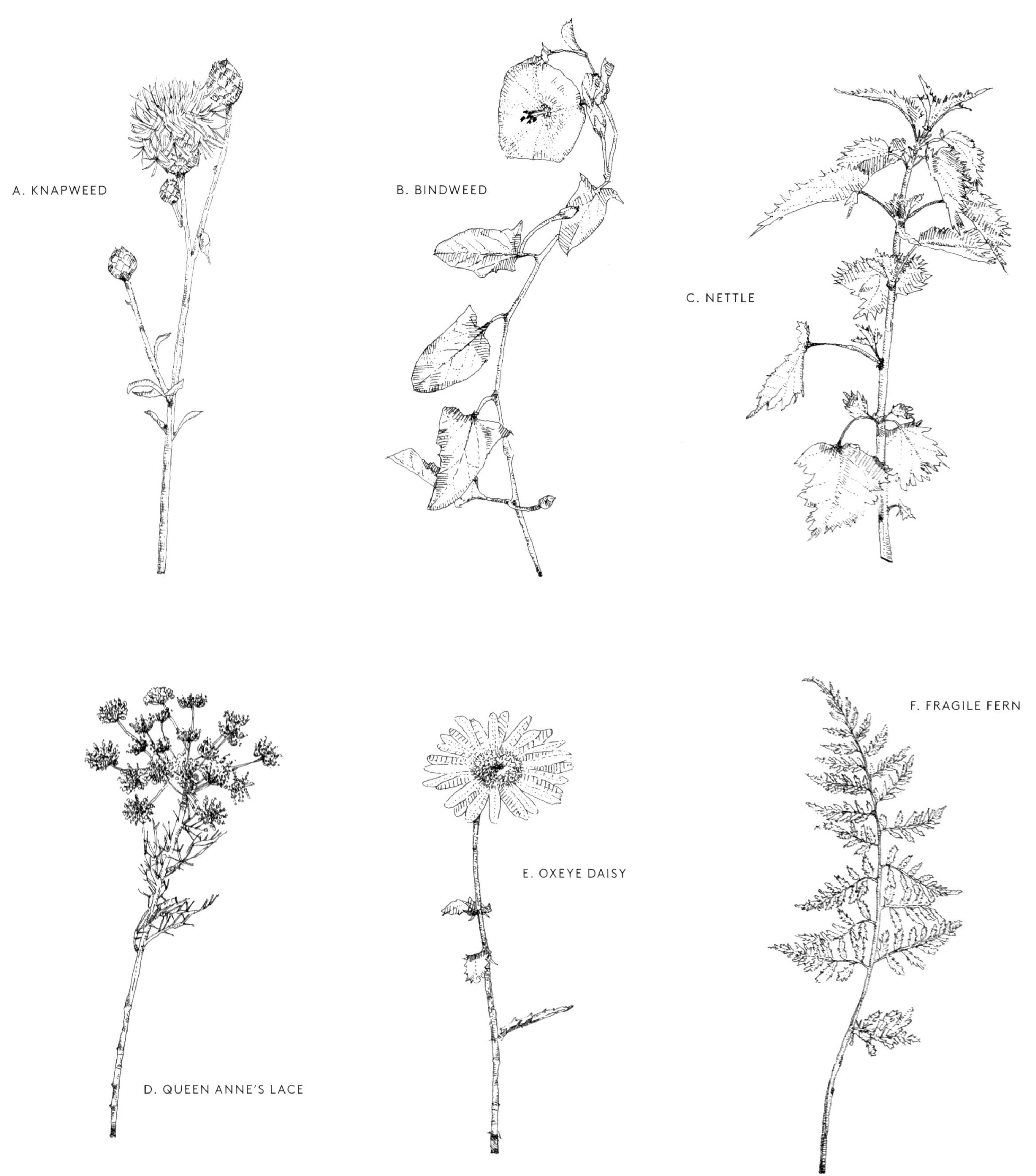
A. KNAPWEED
B. BINDWEED
C. NETTLE
D. QUEEN ANNE'S LACE
E. OXEYE DAISY
F. FRAGILE FERN

Weeds and Their Indications

A	RICH	GROUNDSEL, indicates rich soil	*Senecio vulgaris*
		CHICORY, prefers rich soil	*Cichorium intybus*
		PURSLANE, enjoys a rich soil with lots of phosphorus	*Portulaca oleacea*
		LAMBS QUARTERS, grows in rich soil with high nitrogen levels	*Chenopodium album*
		KNAPWEED, grows in rich soil with lots of potassium	*Centaurea nigra*
		HENBIT, prefers soil with high nitrogen levels	*Lamium amplexicaule*
B	POOR	BINDWEED, grows in compacted soil	*Calystegia sepium*
		YARROW, thrives in poor, dry, sandy soil	*Achillea millefolium*
		CRABGRASS, grows in soil depleted of nutrients	*Digitaria*
		DANDELION, grows in poor soil	*Taraxacum officinale*
C	ACIDIC	NETTLE, likes rich acidic soil	*Urtica dioica*
		SHEEP SORREL, enjoys acidic soil	*Rumex acetosella*
		OXALIS, prefers acidic soil with lots of magnesium	*Oxalis corniculate*
D	ALKALINE	QUEEN ANNE'S LACE, likes 'sweet' soil – that is, a good alkaline soil around 7.5 pH	*Daucus carrota*
		CHICKWEED, grows in compacted alkaline soil	*Stellaria media*
		BROADLEAF PLANTAIN, favours heavy, compacted, anaerobic soil	*Plantago major*
E	WET	OXEYE DAISY, enjoys acidic soil with low fertility and often soggy conditions	*Leucanthemum vulgare*
		MOSS, likes soggy and boggy acidic ground with low nutrient levels	*Bryophyta*
		DOCK, likes heavy, sodden, poorly drained soil	*Rumex ssp.*
F	DRY	MUSTARD, likes dry, phosphorous-rich sandy soil	*Brassicaceae*
		FRAGILE FERN, indicates dry conditions	*Cystopteris fragilis*

There are broadly six different soil types. I've encountered regional variations as I've roamed the world, but the following are the bulwarks of most gardens:

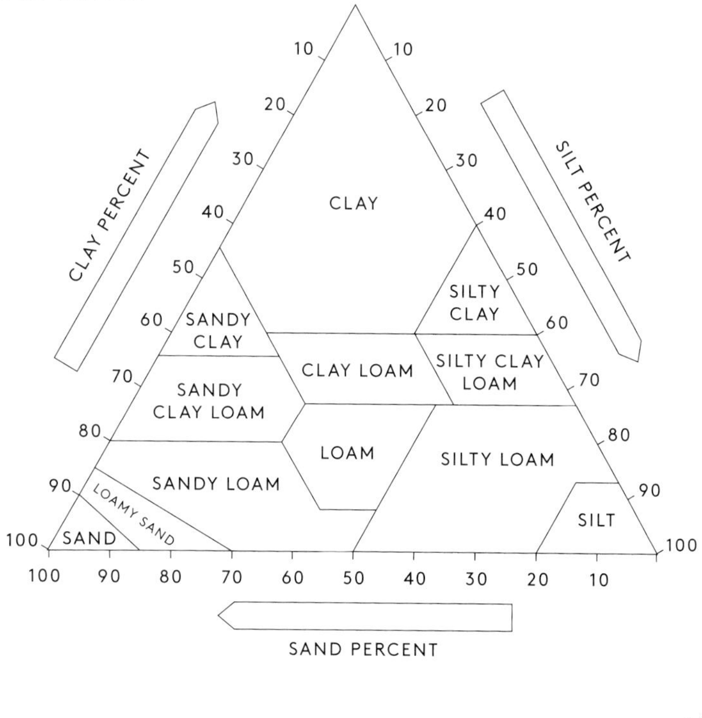

Clay Soils

Easy to roll into a ball, clay soil has great flexibility and can be manipulated just like potter's clay, for that is what it is. This smooth, heavy, sticky soil tends to be fertile. Nutrients are held in as they bind to the fine texture of the clay minerals that make up around 25 per cent of its composition. Clay also holds water – think of puddled clay used traditionally to line farm ponds: 'puddled' daily by the feet of drinking animals, the soil is literally trodden on repeatedly, sealing cracks and fissures to keep it compacted and watertight. This lack of porosity means that clay tends to hold moisture and stay colder for longer in spring. Its ease of compaction is both a blessing and a curse and you need to beware of walking on it too much for fear that decompaction becomes impossible. It is better to walk on boards and use designated routes when creating a garden on clay and especially when working on flower beds. Clay hardens like a brick in summer and can develop alarming cracks. I learned all about clay the hard way. My house in London stands on solid brick clay. One year the combined effects of a serious drought and a thirsty 100-year-old black poplar caused my house to crack in half as the clay dried out. One summer's morning, I found myself looking straight through my bathroom wall into the bathroom of my neighbour! Clay has extraordinary strength. It is also brutal to garden on, especially if you are not possessed of primeval strength. Take the slow route, heavily mulching each year with large volumes of organic matter and grit and try to avoid digging. The results will be rewarding as the heft and fertility suits so many good plants. Clay is a substance to respect, understand and indulge. It can be challenging to build on and I strongly advise using a structural engineer if you plan to.

CHART FOR CLASSIFYING SOIL TEXTURE

CLAY PERCENT
SILT PERCENT
SAND PERCENT
CLAY
SILTY CLAY
SANDY CLAY
CLAY LOAM
SILTY CLAY LOAM
SANDY CLAY LOAM
LOAM
SILTY LOAM
SANDY LOAM
LOAMY SAND
SAND
SILT

Loam

This is the soil that dreams are made of. In soil terms, loams are like the carefree summers of youth. Languid memories of sweet, gentle loam are to be enjoyed and reminisced over. Soils can be clay loam or sandy loam depending on their predominant composition. They tend to have a good core structure that can veer off into heavier clay loam or, at the other extreme, be sandier and lighter. Fertile, warm, well-draining and easily worked they are what all gardeners fantasise about. An extraordinarily rich and famous garden-loving pop star once told me he hated his clay soil, to which I tactlessly suggested he had the wherewithal to move to a soil he liked! I know I would. Loam still needs careful management to give of its best and should have regular influxes of organic matter. It is typically called a 'fine tilth', a term that describes a spongy, delectable soil ready for anything, and it is perfect for planting. Plunge your arms into it up to the elbow and feel the warm humus-y richness suspending air and nutrients. These soils support superhighways of friendly bacteria, and worms and roots simply glide into their new milieu. In most landscape construction projects, we like to try and make our own loam on site rather than buy in denaturised screened soil, devoid of life and structure. We use 'as dug' soil and set about ameliorating it with whatever the base material needs – we add more organic matter, sand and grit to make clays less dense or, conversely, we make lighter soils heavier. A good digger driver should be able to pull this together with ease, saving money and effort in doing so. On a smaller scale, a clean cement mixer is great for mixing up homemade batches of loam. The exercise can become as addictive as finding the ultimate coffee bean.

Sandy Soils

Much as the name suggests, sandy soils are made up of very light, free-draining sand particles. There can be a great deficit of organic matter in them and very little clay to bind them. Sand doesn't only occur at the beach, so a little amateur geology can be interesting. My own garden is on sand and a bit of a poke into prehistory shows that our village was once a coral reef. Around 160 million years ago, during the Late Jurassic period, England was located further south and was submerged beneath a subtropical sea. Imagine the size of the squid! Warm conditions meant that coral reefs flourished in the shallow waters. When the coral died, it was buried under successive layers of sediment and other debris. After millions of years, this became fossilised. Our local stone is coraline limestone – basically lots of dead sea creatures glued together by calcium – and the subsequent soil is very sandy, yet we are resolutely inland, in fact at as far as you can be from the sea in Britain. Sandy soils drain quickly after rain or watering. To my glee, after years of gardening on London brick clay, I discovered that sandy soils are very easy to cultivate and work. They also warm up quickly in spring, so everything gets off to a flying start. The downside is that they can deplete very quickly, dry out in a flash and are low in nutrients that rapidly wash out in rain. High summer, the zenith of the British gardening year, can be extremely challenging on sand. Winters need to be spent mulching and summers require intelligent planting to inhibit the need for constant watering. Sandy soils are often acidic and support an unusual range of planting. Trees love an acid sandy soil with a high water table, which is why the flat, reclaimed lands of northern Germany, Belgium and Holland have such wonderful tree nurseries.

These are the typical soils of Europe. I have a fanciful notion that the soils also shape the characters of the people who live on them.

Silt Soils

Silts are laid down by particles washing off rocks and minerals over extremely long periods of time and collecting in areas where they rarely move again. They occur near rivers, or at the base of hills and mountains, or beneath glaciers – anywhere that could have trapped fine particles over time. Silts change landscapes, so it's worth doing some background on the location if you think your soil is silty. The local area could be part of a long-disappeared river delta or flood plain. Most silts are fertile, fairly well drained and hold more moisture than sandy soils. They can, just by the nature of their fine-grain make-up, become easily compacted and very slippery when wet. I once built a large garden on chalk silt that had washed down steep chalky hillsides since time began. It was such a weird substance, an eerie, pale greyish-white, and it hardly drained at all. It wasn't clay. It was simply so fine-grained that, once we started working, compacted so badly that we had to stop work and think hard about how to manage it, how to traverse it and how to drain it. Soils are living matter, and it makes me uncomfortable to see them becoming damaged. A challenging experience like this can honestly confirm why thinking before you act is so beneficial.

Chalky Soils

These are largely made up of calcium carbonate and are very alkaline. Chalk is strikingly light in colour – a pure, soft white – and warm to touch. Chalk soils can be a clay or rock, known in Britain as clunch, or a light, thin soil with many flint nodules in it. Chalky lands have given rise to some beautiful architecture, notably Marsh Court in Hampshire by Edwin Lutyens, a masterpiece of building with clunch. The historic towns and villages in the Somme area of Normandy, such as Montreuil-sur-Mer, show the subtlety of building using chalk, brick and flint. On chalk there is sometimes a thin scraping of a more brownish soil on top that might have accumulated over years of grasses rotting down and accumulated organic matter trapped on the surface. Chalk is challenging to work with in a garden, yet it supports some of the most beautiful plants, so perseverance and diligent research are amply rewarded. It has a characteristic delicate winsomeness – in nature it hosts gentle swards of wild grasses punctuated with harebells and wild roses set against big skies.

Peat Soils

Peat is rarely found in gardens as it is a natural phenomenon of bogs and marshlands on which you cannot easily build. Bogs are large, often deep accumulations of purely organic rotted matter that ultimately becomes the dark brown spongy material we call 'peat'. Peat is acidic, very fertile and holds lots of water due to a very high sphagnum moss content. It is valuable in gardens and has been instrumental in ameliorating garden soils for centuries. Increasing industrial extraction levels have been a cause of significant alarm to ecologists. We have learned that peat bogs are essential as carbon sinks and do much to manage climate control. The UK banned peat extraction, starting in 2024. Peat is a phenomenal substance. Being almost totally anaerobic, things don't rot in peat in the way they do in mineral-based soils. Hence, in Denmark, the survival of prehistoric bodies such as Tollund Man found in peat bogs. In Ireland and Scotland, the phenomenon of 'bog wood' is where trees fell into the brown waters of the peat bogs thousands of years ago, yet are preserved intact and still workable. It is illegal to extract this timber, though I did manage to buy some taken from an Irish bog where a service pipeline was being cut through. I made a stumpery with it, confident that the ancient pine stumps will never rot down.

↗ Sand dunes are interesting for the symbiosis of what grows on them. In this image it is possible to see the dune-binding marram grass, *Ammophila arenaria*, doing its thing. This tough, waxy grass spreads stoloniferously, trapping sand particles as it goes and gradually stabilising the ever-shifting surface, thus making land.

→ Peat bogs are exciting places. They have an atmosphere unlike any other soil type. They are host to peat moss, or sphagnum, which is one of the principal components of peatification. Other than the plants, peat develops via the availability of nutrients to support bacterial life and of oxygen, acidity, and temperature. Peat often feels warm.

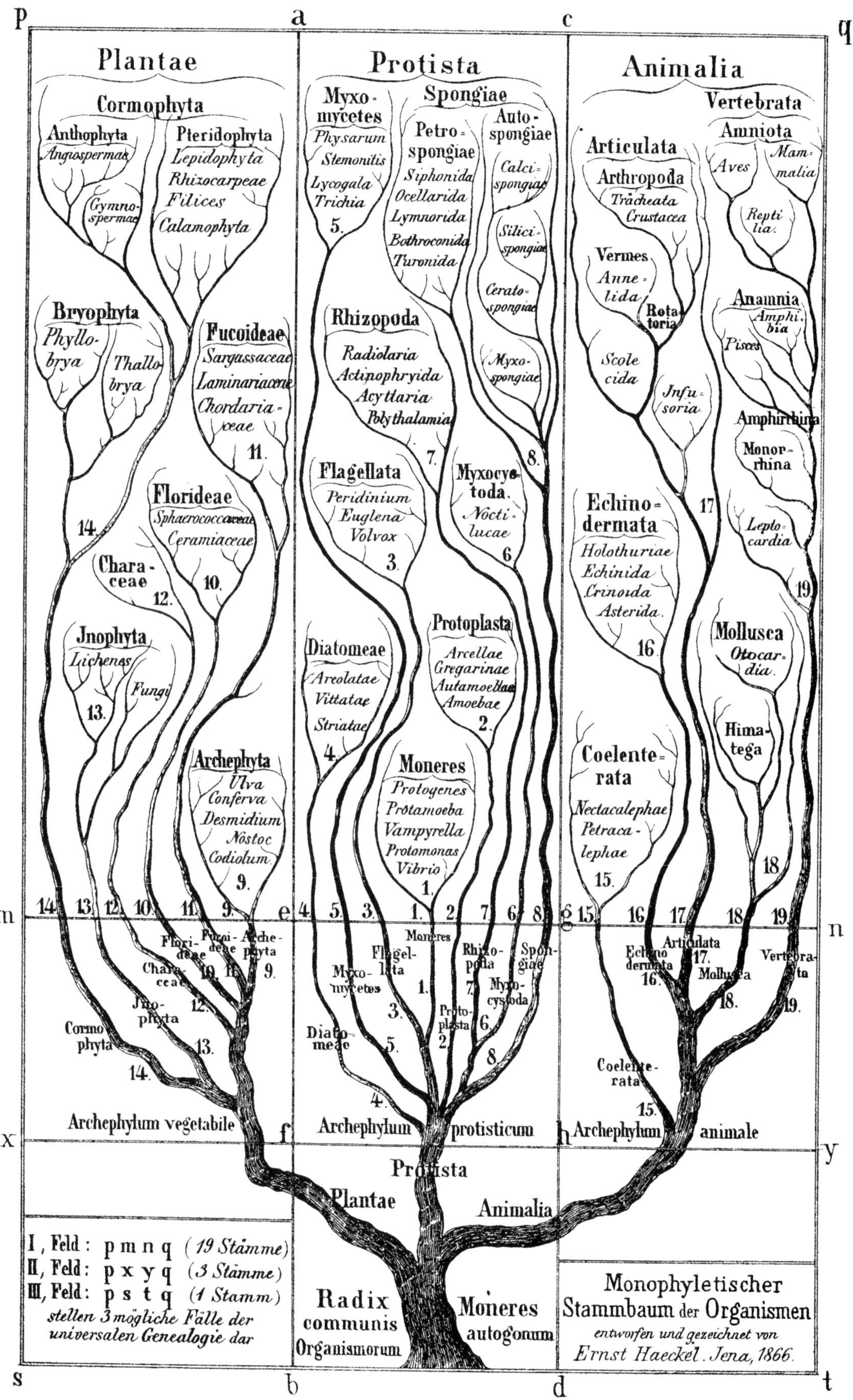

Illustration of the Tree of Life from *Generelle Morphologie der Organismen*, 1866, Ernst Haeckel (1834–1919)

The Six Kingdoms

Carl Linnaeus, the 'father of modern taxonomy' was a Swedish botanist, zoologist, taxonomist and physician. In 1735 he formalised what is still used as the ranking of organisms in biology. The highest rank was given the name 'kingdom' and was followed by six other main, or principal, ranks: phylum, class, order, family, genus and species. The last two ranks in Linnaeus's classification, genus and species, are how we recognise the scientific names of all organisms, including plants. It is helpful to develop a rudimentary grasp of Latin and to know plants by their Latin names. The naming conventions that Linnaeus developed assist in understanding the nature and needs of a plant, its family or genus, and then its individual type. For example, the species term *sylvestris* means 'of the woods' – think of sylvan or sylviculture. *Palustris* means 'of the marshes and wet places', *alpinus* is 'of the high mountains', and so on. So, at a glance, the Latin names help you find your way around the plant world speedily and efficiently.

Within the rank of kingdom are six groups, all with Latin names: Animalia, Plantae, Fungi, Protista, Archaea and Bacteria. When it comes to garden-making, the main kingdoms we think of are Plantae and Animalia. The bee is possibly our best-loved insect. We have all grasped the elementary fact that, without bees and the ramifications of their complex interactions with plants, we would probably not be here. But what do we know beyond this? Given this book is concerned with the interconnectivity of everything, it's worth having a quick whiz through the six kingdoms. Each is entirely relevant to what we do and are interested in, and none must be ignored. In the landscapes we design, we consider all six kingdoms as part of the initial plan. In simple terms we make as many different habitat possibilities as we can. We limit spaces between trees and shrub groups to 200 metres (650 feet) as that is as far as many small birds can fly without needing to rest or take cover. In a world covered in vast arable fields, it's not difficult to see why small bird numbers are diminishing – they literally have nowhere to go, nowhere to rest.

Water is essential. I'm pro ponds, however tiny, as they support such an extraordinarily huge range of life. As a child I found ponds and streams mesmerising. Children don't seem to be particularly squeamish about slimy snails, worms, frogs and so on. Curiosity is greater than revulsion which, I imagine, is often learned from adults. Kids are natural information sponges and are fully sensory, touching, tasting and smelling the things they pick up irrespective of what they are. Kids are also closer to the ground, so everything is magnified – the smell of fresh earth, cut grass, stinky pond water – all delicious scents to be snuffled up and remembered. When we were kids, some friends had a rockery with a 'frog pond' in it. The pond itself was a cleverly concealed yellow plastic washing-up bowl set into a rockery of old Victorian furnace clinker. It was covered in mosses and lichens, baby's tears *Solleirolia solleirolii,* and for all the world looked like a beautiful natural outcrop of rock with a secret pond at its heart. To see the frogs with their golden eyes and quivering nostrils poking through the duck weed was one of the central reasons for visiting.

> *As our mother earth is a mere speck in the sunbeam in the illimitable universe, so man himself is but a tiny grain of protoplasm in the perishable framework of organic nature. This clearly indicates the true place of man in nature, but it dissipates the prevalent illusion of man's supreme importance and the arrogance with which he sets himself apart from the illimitable universe and exalts himself to the position of its most valuable element.*
>
> –ERNST HAECKEL (1834–1919)

Animalia

Animals are the first kingdom of living things, the top of the pyramid. Animals are principally 'eukaryotes', meaning organisms whose cells have a nucleus. They eat organic material, reproduce via sexual activity and can move around under their own steam. There are more than seven million known animal species, of which roughly one million are insects. There are complex ecological interactions between animals that we humans, as we are animals too, don't understand as well as we like to think we do. Animals form complicated 'food webs' that are fascinating to explore and offer great insight into the intricacies of interaction between living things. No animal is an island.

→ Here are some of the more mysterious things growing on earth. Mushrooms belong in the kingdom of fungi. According to the *Encyclopaedia Britannica*, there are about 99,000 distinct varieties of fungi, including mushrooms and yeasts. Lichens are another matter altogether, and can belong to up to three different kingdoms. Conventionally they are listed with fungi, yet they are also found in protista and archaea. Not to be confused with mosses, lichens are some of the oldest life forms on earth. They are part algae and crept up out of the oceans. Mosses, so often found living in a happy harmony with fungi and lichens are, quite simply, plants.

Plantae

Plantae includes trees, shrubs, vines and climbers, flowering plants, grasses, herbs, ferns and mosses. Plants are 'the second kingdom of living things. They are autotrophic eukaryotes, which means they have complex cells and make their own food. As they are rooted, they cannot move. Plants get most of their energy via photosynthesis. Taking energy from sunlight through their leaves, they reproduce sexually, though some are asexual. There are around 320,000 known species of plant and many of these distribute seed as a means of propagation.

Fungi

Simply put, these are the mushrooms. Linnaeus originally grouped fungi within Plantae, but it became apparent to German polymath Ernst Haeckel, probably best known to us for his marvellous illustrations of living things, that these mushrooms were a separate entity – a fact confirmed in the 1960s by American ecologist Robert Harding Whittaker. Whittaker thus created a sixth kingdom from Linnaeus's initial five. He also found that fungi are closer in their make-up to animals than plants. That is the basis for a very good B-movie.

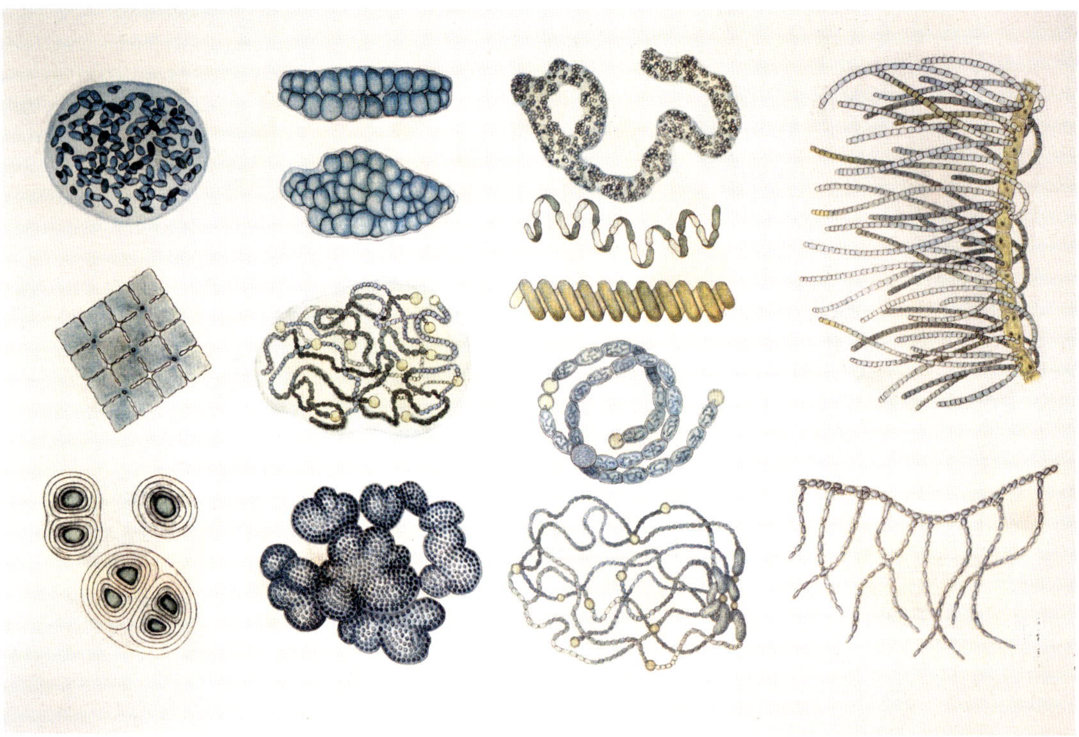

↗ A selection of bacteria in close-up

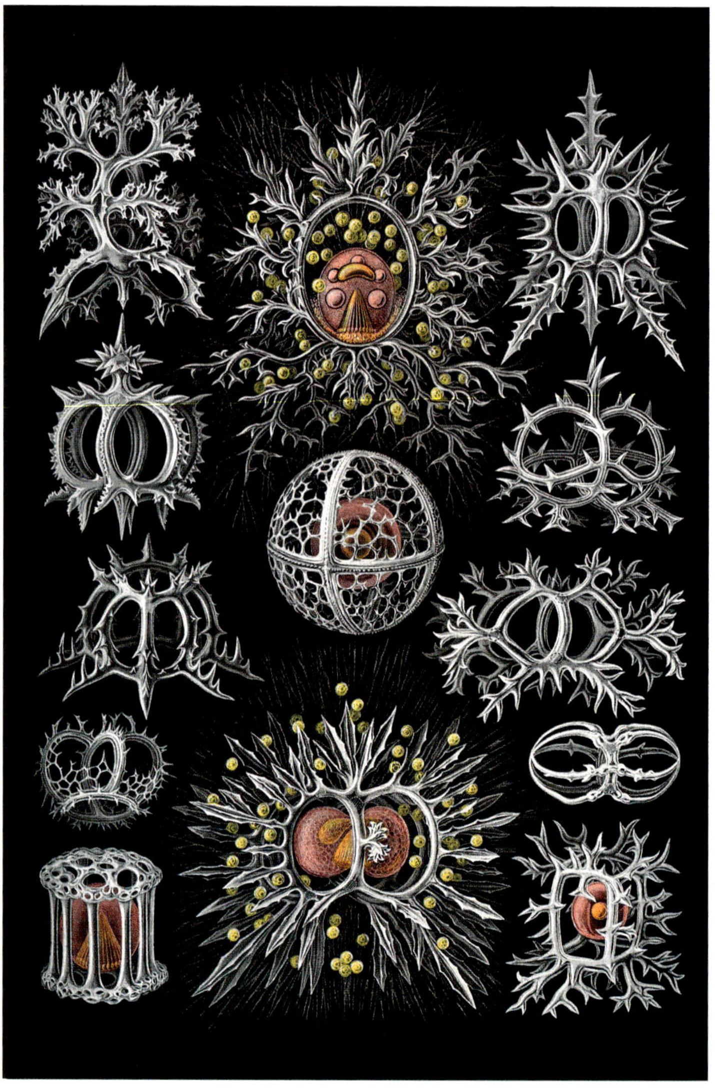

Illustration of Stephoidea from *Kunstformen der Natur*, 1904, Ernst Haeckel (1834–1919)

Protista

Now we are heading into organisms whose type and function are harder for a lay person to describe, so forgive the laborious description. We could not occupy earth without protista. These are single-celled organisms, the majority of which live in watery or moist places. They tend to have pseudopodia – that is, 'fake' (*pseudo*) protruding 'feet' (*podia*), that help to propel them towards food. Some protists have flagella to enable movement, others have cilia (fringy hairs) that allow them to push themselves through water. Examples of protists include slime moulds, kelp, algae and amoebas. Ernst Haeckel called Protista the kingdom of primitive forms; other biologists have been known to call it the kingdom of odds and ends. It has been estimated that protists produce half of the oxygen in the world through photosynthesis. They seem to be both good and bad, working positively and also parasitically. They play an important role in nutrient recycling, fulfilling the essential function of returning inorganic nutrients to soil and water. This process allows for new plant growth, which in turn generates fuel for other organisms along the food chain. Protista can also be parasitic in plants and animals, causing diseases and destroying crops.

Archaea/Archaebacteria

Earth has its limits and it is the microorganisms Archaea that define them. These microorganisms exist in extreme environments – hot springs, hydrothermal vents, very salty or acidic or anaerobic conditions, such as our reeking subsoils or bogland. They do something unique in that they produce biological methane gas. Equally important are Archaebacteria, one of the oldest forms of life on earth. Both groups produce and consume organic matter in areas of very great heat and hostility, such as geysers or natural oil wells. Research suggests they form as much as 40 per cent of the microbial cells in the ocean as well as living in swamps, sewage, acid and alkaline waters, the guts of animals and humans and, of course, in soils.

Bacteria/Eubacteria

Finally, there are bacteria and eubacteria, microorganisms that exist in almost every environment in the world. Bacteria play several vitally important roles within our ecosystem. They are decomposers – they take dead matter and recycle it for energy. Without bacteria breaking down organic matter and recycling, soil couldn't function, and plants couldn't grow. We are all familiar with 'good bacteria' from the numerous adverts promoting life-changing yogurts that 'aid digestion'. They basically biodegrade our food to make it available to our bodies as fuel. In soil, bacteria 'fix' nitrogen, converting into a form the plants can absorb. Some plants, including peas, clover and beans have a symbiotic relationship with such bacteria, which live on their roots.

Eubacteria are especially useful as they transform oxygen, carbon, nitrogen and phosphorus. None of these nutrients would be available for use by animals and plants without the transformation occasioned by the eubacteria.

Without a working knowledge of the six kingdoms, we cannot fully understand the complex ecological make-up of our own little paradisical enclaves, let alone the wider world. The interconnectivity of these diverse biological structures ensures that everything from healthy soil to snuffling hedgehogs to stunning planting is working in happy symbiosis. Invisible living things are working tirelessly to support our ecosystems and sustain them in balance. Gardeners, I tend to think, are supportive of any life forms unknown to them and instinctively caring towards them. It is impossible to calculate the number of gardens that exist on earth, yet it is safe to say there must be tens of millions. Each is a tiny ark.

↱ pp. 150–51: The organic world has pulled together the most complex sequences of events to offer us humble gardeners a palette of beauty to use in our schemes. I like giving individual plants space to shine, and none more so than this marvellous *Papaver orientale* 'Patty's Plum'. The colour is beguiling to even the hardest-hearted observer. Use lavishly.

Copper engraving of Doctor Schnabel (Dr Beak), a plague doctor in seventeenth-century Italy, c. 1656, artist unknown

↗ The colloquialism of referring to a doctor as the 'beak' stems from the plague in Venice in the seventeenth century. The beak-like mask was stuffed with lavender as a prophylactic.

Plagues

Ring, a-ring, o'rosies, (a redrash on the skin)
A pocket full of posies (herbs and flowers to ward off the stench)
Atishoo, atishoo (tell-tale symptoms)
We all fall down. (death)

The six kingdoms are not under our control. They never have been. Humans have so far experienced three recorded plague events caused by the bacteria *Yersinia pestis*. These bacterial plagues have altered the structure of our society. Remember the sixth kingdom? Bacteria have no morality; they work for good or ill. The Justinian plague of 541–544, a bubonic plague, killed more than 100 million people worldwide and predicated an eight-year famine. The staggering loss of life changed the system of farming as there simply weren't enough people to work the land. The economic consequences and social disruption marked the end of Roman rule, in turn leading towards the cultural shifts that formed the nations of medieval Europe and the birth of the Dark Ages.

A bacterium did that. And no one found out what it was until the late 1800s.

Since I wrote my last book, *The Thoughtful Gardener*, another plague has wrought devastation and yet I am shocked by how little discussion there is about it. A scourge of the Sino-Korean moth *Cydalima perspectalis* has swept through wild box forests, *Buxus sempervirens*, defoliating millions upon millions of acres of ancient trees. Contrary to popular myth, this isn't a plague caused by dirty nursery trades, but by moth larvae transported on commercial shipping crates. Box forests have been around for millennia and are very slow growing. In my part of France, they are the natural understory to the scrubby oak forest. Although the Occitanie is a hot region, the *Buxus* keep the landscape cool and green. Not anymore. The box forests – and with them their enchanting hanging fairy moss, woodland floor of sweet pulmonaria, ferns and alpine aquilegia – are all gone. In the space of four breeding seasons – less than two years in our case – these moths have deprived Russia, Turkey, Bulgaria, Germany, Italy, France, Spain, the Caucasus, the Black Sea coast and many more of their natural evergreen *Buxus* forests. This is a total deforestation of one of our most loved and best used trees. In the gardening world, unfortunately, most people see box as a decorative garden trinket that is met with an 'oh well, what shall we use now?', yet for me, this feels like the death of a dear relative. It is the death of music – without box there will be no oboes, no clarinets, no recorders. When I look out of my window, instead of a green box-covered hillside I see a ravaged, brown and crispy land. It looks lovely to the untrained eye, all rocky and exposed like Provence, but it shouldn't look like that. It should be a deep, rich green even in the blistering heat of a southern French summer.

As much as I read around the subject of this moth invasion – and there is precious little – I cannot find an explanation of how insect plagues work. Where do the creatures go? What happens next? Will there be a slow recovery of a few vestigial trees? Is that what happened after the bubonic plague – we limped along and gradually multiplied again? When we were kids there was a plague of Colorado beetle, *Leptinotarsa decemlineata*, in France and we spent all summer picking them off my aunt's potatoes. After the initial onslaught the subject faded away and the spuds remained. This is different.

We are in the grip of some deadly serious horticultural plagues. Since I was a child, all the English elms have died. Now we have ash dieback on *Fraxinus excelsior*, the sad skeletons of which pepper the English landscape. In France, the mighty plane trees that line the roads, *Platanus* x *acerifolia*, made famous by numerous painters, are being decimated by the fungus *Ceratocystis platani*, which causes a disease known in France as *le chancre coloré* (the canker stain). In a single summer, it killed all of the plane trees in our market square – pruned over time into a mighty umbrella that was well over 100 years old. *Aesculus hippocastanum* also have canker, *Quercus robur* is under threat from climate change. An arboriculturist we work with told me there would be no more oak in England within our lifetime – the English oak, a mainstay of folk songs and legends, a living metaphor for age, wisdom and stability; the physical structure of our old houses, our ships, our furniture. The sturdy oak. Gone.

Try as I might, I can't find much to be positive about in the short term. The pathogens and infestations causing these issues are not restricted to the countries discussed here, but are happening worldwide. The threat of the bacteria *Xylella fastidiosa* hangs over us, threatening to finish off gardening as we know it. A bacterium with a symbiotic relationship with a sap-sucking insect, it is a plague-in-waiting. It isn't hard to imagine that Covid-19 was a taster for something rather more effective at managing the population, at which point I believe the world we live on will self-regulate, much as it has done for millions of years, without us, or certainly with far fewer of us. As English economist Thomas Robert Malthus said, 'The power of population is indefinitely greater than the power in the earth to produce subsistence for man.' He believed, with some justification, that populations level themselves out. While waiting for your seeds to germinate I can recommend reading his *An Essay on the Principle of Population*, published anonymously in 1798.

Remember the plants from Mesoamerica that changed the world? Those Mesoamericans understood the fragility of crops. They cultivated and ate tubers across a huge number, I believe more than two hundred, of varied Solanaceae species rather than just one or two. When people are intimately involved in their own and each other's survival great care is manifested in every action. The profit being health, not wealth.

Pests

Let's keep this simple. Not every fluffy animal is cute. A huge amount of damage is done each year to gardens and natural landscapes due to the increasing volume of introduced pests. These animals, many of them insects, are settling into a comfortable new way of life, often without natural predators other than busy roads and occasional human intervention. If our lives depended on it, we would definitely have controlled their inexorable rise. I am all for eating more wild meat. We routinely shoot and eat muntjac and other deer in season. Wild meat is lean and low in cholesterol. My byline is 'Fit food for fit people'! Here is my list of edible species.

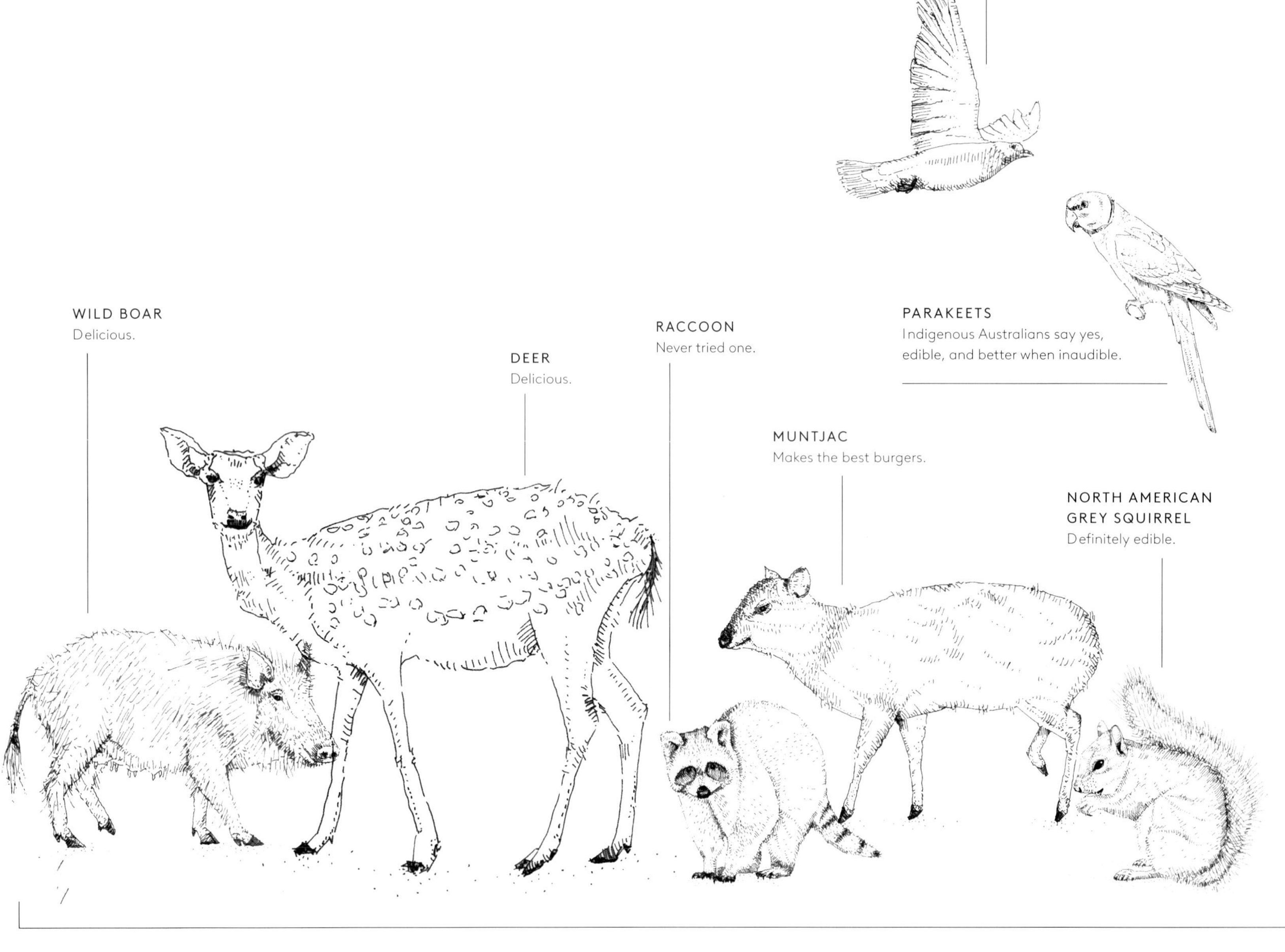

THE CUTE ONES

Cuteness is the enemy of reason

–BIRDLIFE INTERNATIONAL

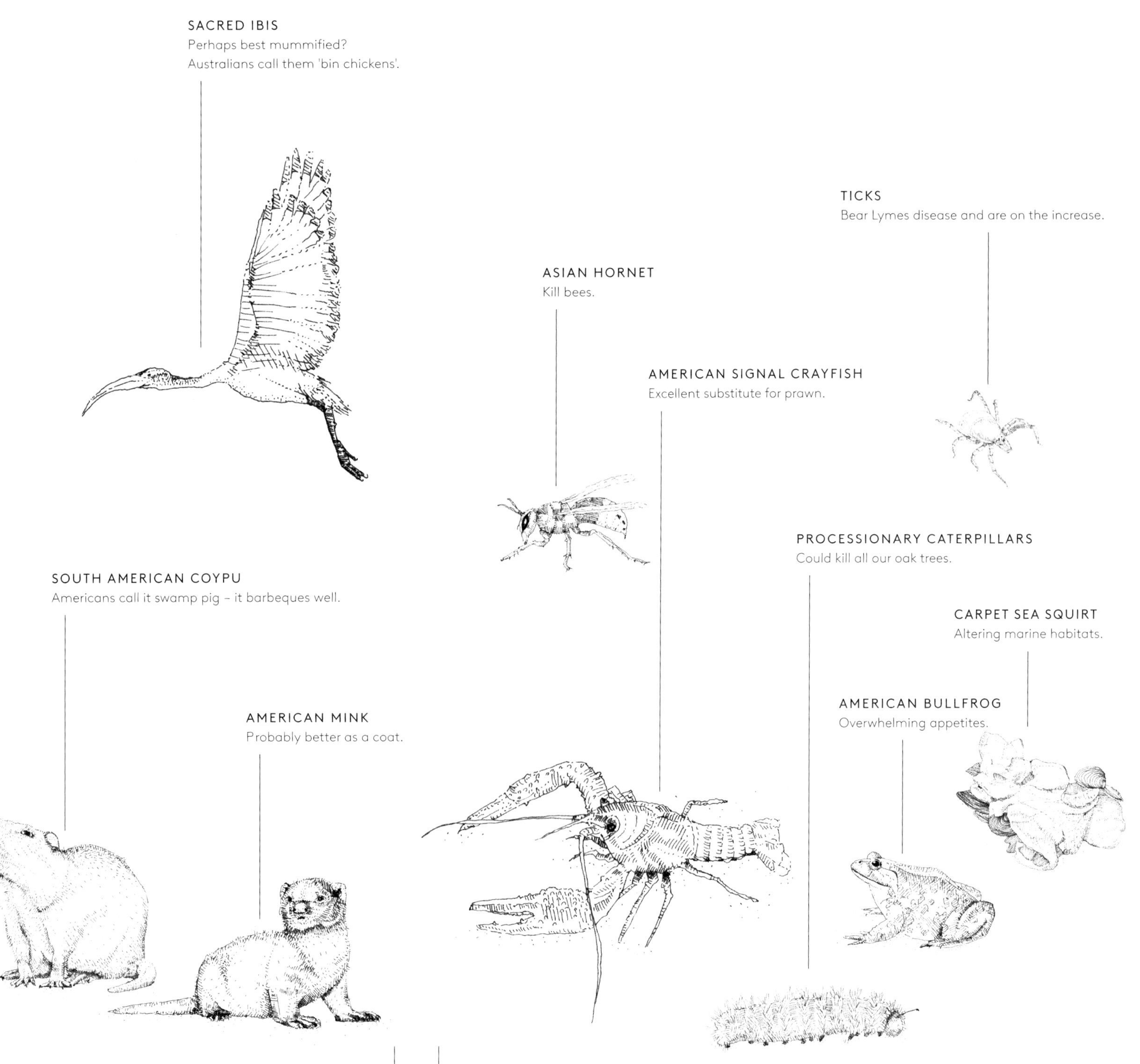

The Genesis of Urban Gardens

In the end, gardens are all about life. Our lives. The lives of plants. They are about the sudden, miraculous return of an ecosystem of the creatures, insects, birds and bees that depart during construction. They are about the planting combinations, the layout of trees, shrubs and hedging that brings the softness to the forms and sucks us all in. The artful fusion of all the elements creates the magical gardens that we are all so obsessed with.

It was the Romans who made gardens as horticultural oases, purely for the love of plants. Being farmers, they had an innate affection for the land. Through their burgeoning wealth, they were able to build smart new houses, acquire property and own the requisite quantity of slaves to manage it all. The Roman garden revolution lay in their recognition of the beautiful range of ornamental plants that could be grown. They also attached the garden to the house, a hugely significant yet seemingly obvious innovation, making it an inseparable extension of it. This is how the vast majority of us appreciate our gardens to this day. They are immediately accessible, making domestic life immensely pleasurable, thanks to the proximity of a private flowery playground. The Romans didn't stop at their own front door either, but carried on up the streets, twining roses around columns, sowing grassy areas for sitting around on (the origin, perhaps, of our urban parks). They planted fragrant shrubs along the roadsides for all to enjoy. This freedom to adorn shared urban spaces with planting has a lot to commend it. I say let's subvert the urban sprawl and see who comes and tells us off.

We must cultivate our own garden. When man was put in the garden of Eden he was put there so that he should work, which proves that man was not born to rest.

–VOLTAIRE (1694–1778)

↗ This is a good example of a balanced meadow mix several years after sowing. Meadow plants can be very frisky for the first few years, with explosions of oxeye daisy one year, followed by yarrow the next. Then, miraculously, the plants settle.

Guerrilla Gardening

I remember the term 'guerrilla gardening' coming into use in the early 1970s, when some New Yorkers got together and transformed a plot of waste land into a garden. I was completely gripped by that. When I moved to London in the early 1980s, a lot of it was derelict and there were still empty bomb plots on street corners where houses had been. We had three alone on the road where I worked in Brixton. Hoarded off and brimming with self-sown buddleia, they smelt good yet were inaccessible. We itched to get our hands on them, but it proved impossible. The late 70s and early 80s were a time of 'direct action' when there was still a fantastic sense of possibility. Everyone was skint, the political and social landscape was undergoing a period of huge upheaval and we all felt anything was achievable if we made it happen. It was a very liberating time to be alive – none of us had cars, houses, holidays or even new clothes. I can't remember anyone feeling hard done by – we had a riotous time, all living in squats, setting up co-ops, building adventure playgrounds on waste land, gardening anywhere we could. It was summed up by *Citizen Smith*, a BBC 1 sitcom starring 'Woolfie' Smith from Tooting, who believed he was a Marxist urban guerrilla emulating his hero Che Guevara. BBC sitcoms are definitely not about anarchy anymore.

In 1996, in Denmark, that hotbed of civic rightmindedness, the Organic Starters, Økologiske Igangsættere, joined by 1,000 members of the public, made 'A garden in a night' on empty land outside Copenhagen. Now that would have been fun to get involved in. The garden persisted briefly but was eventually cleared to make way for housing. This is the great shame that came later in the 80s, when every scrap of land became prey to building developers and its value changed irrevocably.

These days, guerrilla gardening has been marketed into polite and prettily designed seed packets you can sprinkle uncontroversially (and possibly unsuccessfully) onto grass verges, while feeling vaguely rebellious and plainly virtuous. But there is a practical response to this is: don't go throwing seed into the wild unless you know what it contains. I recently bought a 'wildflower mix' on impulse from a garden centre to overseed our grass verges after some emergency gas works along the lane. We are in the countryside. Just prior to sowing, I read the list of ingredients. I was shocked – these weren't 'wildflowers' at all, but a strange mix of echinacea, California poppy, a cultivated vetch, penstemon and lupins. It was too extraordinary. They must have been the sweepings from a commercial seed company being put to good commercial use. I did a controlled experiment. Only the vetch grew.

In conclusion, absolutely do set about making gardens where there aren't any and be prepared to fight hard for them. If you think about it, the High Line in New York is probably the most famous guerrilla garden. Yes, it's been formalised into a public park owned by the city, but the seed of the idea was definitely sown by determined social reformers and revolutionaries.

Cutting Gardens

People love cutting their own flowers from a garden and it's better to have a dedicated area rather suffer the predations in the borders. A cutting garden is designed in much the same way as a vegetable, herb, dye or perfume garden. You need a series of long, slender straight beds, preferably well edged with timber or stone. I made a cutting garden in Italy, using tufo as the edge restraint. Tufo, a pumice stone, has the added benefit of holding water. The first thing to think about is space – a good cutting garden needs quite a lot of it. And water – ideally lots of rainwater stored in big tanks as the plants need plenty in order to keep going and stay in peak condition.

Plant a 'hedge' of flowering shrubs, sometimes in multiples, as you'll need lots. Shrubs like buddleia, guelder rose and lilac all work well. For smaller posies, and if you have a warm, sheltered garden, myrtle and rosemary are good. Wild roses give lots of hips in autumn, as do many of the garden roses such as *Rosa glauca* and *R. moyesii* 'Geranium'. The beds can be dedicated to the plants you like most: dahlias, chrysanthemums, phlox ... No, I'm not making a list. There are just far too many and the fun comes in doing the research, seeing how much space you have and your personal level of mania for it.

I recommend looking up Becky Crowley, who I met briefly when she was running the cutting garden at Chatsworth House. Becky is an artist in every sense of the word. Her flowers, her colour sense, her photography – all of it is stunning. Then there is the marvellous flower farm Green and Gorgeous in Oxfordshire, that produces flowers for the wholesale market on a huge scale and with very good taste. Volume doesn't need to mean a reduction of quality or style. To my eye, cut flowers seem to flourish best when grown in this kind of cropping way. The farm welcomes visitors and that would be my starting point – go and find a place growing flowers in this way and see how they do it.

One of my personal inspirations in the world of plants and gardens is Christin Geall. Christin has a very long history working with plants, herbs, people, ecofeminism, and cutting flowers. Her book *Cultivated: The Elements of Floral Style* (2020), is well worth a read. The marvellous thing about gardening people is their generosity. They are human mycelia, spreading their hyphae over distances and subjects that are beyond encapsulation.

My favourite cutting garden ever was in the Powell and Pressburger film *Black Narcissus* (1947). Watch the original version and keep an eye on Flora Robson.

↘ I have Becky Crowley to thank for this backstage image of her work in progress, composing flower photos. Becky is an amazing gardener with an artist's eye and is following her star to combine the two skills with beautiful results.

A garden is a grand teacher. It teaches patience and careful watchfulness; it teaches industry and thrift; above all it teaches entire trust.

–GERTRUDE JEKYLL (1843–1932)

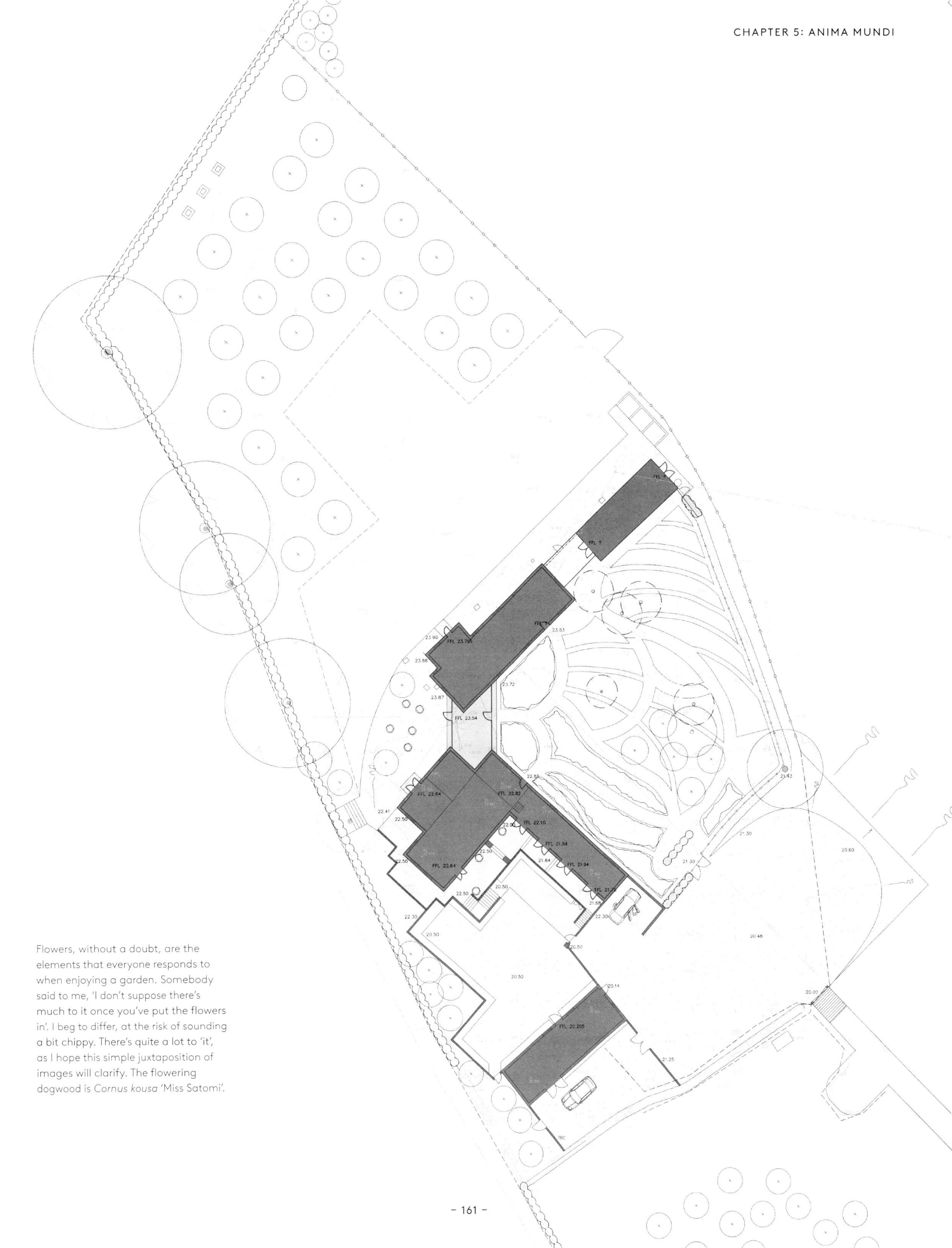

Flowers, without a doubt, are the elements that everyone responds to when enjoying a garden. Somebody said to me, 'I don't suppose there's much to it once you've put the flowers in'. I beg to differ, at the risk of sounding a bit chippy. There's quite a lot to 'it', as I hope this simple juxtaposition of images will clarify. The flowering dogwood is *Cornus kousa* 'Miss Satomi'.

Plantsmen

Much like artists having a favourite paintmaker, we gardeners have our favourite nurserymen. Without these dedicated souls, our palettes shrivel away and desiccate. Large commercial nurseries sell only the 'top sellers' in increasingly reductionist form. We go to them for bulk buys but for couture outfits one needs proper fabrics.

Graham Gough of Marchants Hardy Plants is one such couturier. He started life as a classical singer – I always think it's a good sign if people have done other things before plants and gardens win them over. I met Graham through our mutual friend John Coke who used to live at Bury Court where Piet Oudolf made his first garden. John was running the exceptional Green Farm Plants with Marina Christopher, who has since moved and metamorphosed into the equally exceptional Phoenix Perennial Plants. I met Piet about the same time, so this was probably around 1997. Graham, John and I made a memorable trip over to Piet and Anja's nursery in Holland for a party. It was a great and bonding road trip. We are all musical and listened to Górecki's Symphony No. 3, weeping copiously as we drove across the rainswept flatlands.

This was the first time I experienced being with a unique group of plant enthusiasts all in the same place at the same time, chattering away about cultivars and seedlings and discoveries. Piet and Anja at that time were known for their nursery rather than Piet's now Elvis-like stature as a garden designer. It was a revelation being among these plantsmen and women. Around this time Graham and his partner Lucy Goffin, a textile designer, set up Marchants Hardy Plants. I remember well Graham's robust views on plants. The nursery is on unforgiving boulder clay, and he was interested in growing the heartiest and strongest plants that perform in the best possible way.

The nursery has developed over time and is now one of the most distinguished in the country, with a well-deserved reputation for excellence. It is increasingly rare to find nurserymen who propagate their own plants, selecting and refining in the way Graham and his team do. With the strength, form and colour on display in Graham and Lucy's beautiful garden, literally wrestled out of an initially intractable and now very malleable plot, the plants represent some of the very best grown and sold in the country.

Graham has, with great foresight and generosity, brought a talented team together, a group of quite exceptional plantspeople who can carry his work forward. This is the most important thing we can do in our short lives. Without such uniquely personal specialised knowledge being passed on, the true sensory reality of gifts like Graham's would be lost to all of us forever. None of this work can be digitised. It involves eyes, noses, hands, thought, understanding, sophistication, judgement, intuition, enthusiasm, some manly baritone humming and, most of all, it needs love.

↗ This is a corner of Graham Gough's HQ at Marchants Hardy Plants. I like the filing system for plant labels.

← This kind of plant just screams 'you want me' on a nursery visit. The stunning *Gladiolus papilio*, aka butterfly sword lily, comes in delicate shades of slaty grey, cream and a strange greyish-purple that make it irresistible. You'd never find plants like this in a commercial garden centre, yet these specialist nurseries take the time and care to select jewels that will be treasured in a garden for years.

↱ pp. 164–65: A good perennial nursery is a smorgasbord of delectable — and in Graham's case — indestructible plants, selected and refined in order to be used robustly and confidently in a garden. Genuinely enthusiastic people help you out with a real understanding of each species. It's the horticultural equivalent of a Saville Row suit fitting.

PELARGONIUM
ATTAR OF ROSES

BETONICA OFFICINALIS
EX BLUSH

Propagation

→ The majority of gardeners are enthusiastic propagators. A greenhouse, if you have one, fills quickly with bits of this and that, gifts from friends and surreptitiously swiped cuttings. All this enables the garden to stay fresh and stimulating. It is also a healthy option compared to buying commercial plant products.

There is a ray of light in the perpetual gloom of global destruction. Propagating your own plants is a very pleasant and rewarding pastime. Not only that, but it also tends to make for healthier plants.

A vast volume of nursery plant material is 'micropropagated', which is quite at the other end of the human scale to Graham Gough's beautifully produced plants at Marchants. Micropropagation is how much of the commercial plant industry works. This highly regulated and sanitised laboratory process is now a perfectly normal method of growing plants. I've been to orchid factories in Holland in which millions of identical micro-propagated orchids – the type that you get on the front desk of a posh spa – are grown. The entire process is automated. Acres of glass, hydroponics and machines operated by very few people, move the orchids through their computer-programmed stages of growth until that perfect stem, tilted to the left and covered in flowers and buds is cellophaned and exported. Many of the trees we buy in commercial nurseries begin life in huge micropropagation facilities in Poland. They are then shipped elsewhere to be grown on. This is probably the origin of the majority of plants in any garden centre, a principal achievement being that plants can be produced confidently in vast numbers and with absolute uniformity.

Growing plants from seed is very enjoyable. Seed swaps with friends are a cheap and useful way of bulking up planting. Increasingly, I am interested in growing trees from nuts and acorns. With all the aggressive pathogens attacking trees and a ban on the import of oaks from European nurseries, it makes sense to throttle back to basics. We live near some very ancient woodland and collect acorns from the veteran trees there. They are very easy to grow, and on one of our public projects we are encouraging a big tree-propagating programme with schoolchildren. There are also many walnut trees in our village. For all their misdeeds, squirrels are very good at planting and walnuts shoot up at an alarming rate, alongside 'locally sourced' – that is, from our village trees and hedges – hazels and horse chestnuts.

I have the world's smallest unheated greenhouse, yet still just about manage to propagate all the necessary annuals and grow cuttings from tender shrubs. I have a whole hedge of rosemary and one of its plants is particularly magnificent, so I take masses of cuttings from that. Much commercially grown rosemary is quite disappointing, so I taking advantage of this chunky, glossy specimen.

My soil is poor. It supports subshrubs best and these are not long-lived as a rule, so the continuum is maintained in this way. We also have an annual 'open garden' event in the village and this is excellent for plant bartering, selling on the surplus and swapping notes. This human interaction is part of the ecosystem of gardens, the web of interconnectivity that supports healthy life in all its manifestations.

Plants in Pots

Pots are interesting. Worse, they are fascinating. During the pandemic lockdown, like countless others, I spent unprecedented time at home. Usually, my typical working week involves twenty hours or so of travelling over and above working. I'm never at home in daylight. The pandemic garden lost all interest for me, as summer gardening on a fairly large scale is relatively boring: weeding, mowing, clearing up. My attention turned to pots.

It started innocuously enough. I had already found, and bought at auction, a large collection of Victorian handmade terracotta flowerpots. I've an enthusiasm for the Danish Skagen painter Anna Ancher, who made a wonderful painting of a fisherman's wife sewing. The part of the painting that stands out is the light falling on the straggly red pelargonium in a terracotta pot just behind her. I urgently needed a red pelargonium. Researching pelargoniums of the 1880s didn't get me very far. I found *Pelargonium fulgidum*, a marvellous, rich scarlet with soft greyish leaves. I also got *P. sidioides, P. trifidum, P. abrotanifolium, P. pseudoglutinosum* and I had to have several *P.* 'Ardens' because of the coral red flowers and its impossible behaviour. They arrived, beautifully wrapped, all seven boxes of them. I am not sure how it happened, but I suddenly had more than a hundred fascinating pelargoniums and not quite enough pots. Plus, there were terrible national compost shortages. Pelargoniums look best massed on a table, but I didn't have any display tables, so I made some.

And still the plants came. Standard *Wisteria floribunda longissima alba* 'Shiro-noda' went into two huge old coppers by the front door. Then came the big pots full of agapanthus varieties and vast pots with *Genista aetnensis*. I found a stunning *Euphorbia stygiana* ssp. *santamariae* that grows like a small tree and is relatively rare. Oh Joy! Rare things in pots! Then I had all the tender salvias, such as *Salvia confertiflora* and *S.* 'Phyllis' Fancy' growing on to do their thing in autumn. I had mail-order plants turning up daily from small specialist nurseries. I realised this was all possible because we couldn't leave the house to work or go on holiday. I became a full-time pot skivvy, though not daring to start on pots full of tiny bulbs because that way madness lies. Now the world is back to relative normality I am co-dependent on friends and neighbours, many in the same boat, caring for them all. Obviously, now there is the issue of what to do with the crates of cuttings. My natural disposition leans more towards propagation than gardening, yet I have neither the space nor facilities for it. Pots require time, space and a good greenhouse, a potting table, cold frames and a proper composting set-up – a substantial 'back of house' in fact. All of this has brought sharply to the fore that I am inadequately provisioned for this kind of thing. My garden is all front and there is nowhere to hide anything. I do all my garden work on a small French metal table. My greenhouse is so miniscule I can't get everything tender in it for the winter. Come the great day that I finally address the garden and redesign it, all these necessities will appear.

Planned well, pots will get you through every season of the year splendidly. It makes sense to have handsome evergreen shrubs or small trees in huge planters all year round. These give height to a garden and can add structure in places where you might struggle to plant into the ground. Think of the scale of Versailles planters and go for that level of impact. If you can't afford posh pots in large sizes, buy cheap galvanised dustbins, poke holes in the bottom and off you go. The benefit of big receptacles is that the plants are more stable and need less faffing to stay healthy. Invest in a pot trolley so you can move them about easily. For huge pots, I enjoy the likes of *Arbutus unedo*, olives and citrus, provided there is somewhere to overwinter them. Standard wisteria is very glamorous. Myrtle, *Osmanthus burkwoodii* and *O. fortunei aquifolium*, are good for topiary in the absence of *Buxus*. I underplant the trees with spring bulbs and in some cases with annual bedding. Every garden needs riotous displays of tulips in spring. The parrot- and paeony-flowered varieties are always heart-stopping, especially after long dreary winters. The very rich colours of the parrots are matched by their extraordinary habit of growth as they rise then contort and flop about at this early stage of the year. Beneath my *Genista aetnensis* are *Tulipa sprengeri* and Jekka McVicar's brilliant eponymous thyme.

Through summer, the scented and species pelargoniums make marvellous, long-lasting, trouble-free displays. They are the treasures of the summer pot garden and are just as cheerful inside and out. If you have a greenhouse, keep potted *Rhododendron fragrantissimum* for the same reason.

Autumn is when the salvias come into their own. One summer was so hot, my *Salvia confertiflora* grew to almost 2 metres (6½ feet) and was smothered in flowers – the best I've ever seen it in the UK. Salvia comes in all shapes and sizes and the tender ones are marvellous for bountiful flowers later in the year as they last until the first frosts. The bees appreciate the thought.

Sewing Fisherman's Wife, c. 1890, Anna Ancher (1859–1935)

Things you need

- A greenhouse
- A potting shed or table outside so you don't have to bend down
- A pot trolley for moving the big ones
- A potting tray where you can mix your own compost
- A large receptacle for horticultural grit
- Various scoops for soil and grit for filling and topping pots
- A large sink or access to a tap
- Shelves for storing clean, empty pots upside down
- Gloves
- Labels and appropriate pens
- Plant food, such as a good organic seaweed liquid
- Various sizes of watering cans with roses
- Lots of pot saucers (so you can go away for at least a week)
- A wheelbarrow – taking compost from a barrow prevents you having to bend so far
- Composting facilities
- Plenty of good pots in various sizes

Things you don't need

- Chemical bug sprays or chemicals of any kind

↖ This is one of my numerous plant tables at home, just after liberating everything from the greenhouse in early summer. I have many species of pelargonium, and on the far right is one of my favourites, *P. trifidum*, with its spidery yellow flowers. There are also various aeoniums, some pink miniature marguerites from the farmers' market and a strange little salvia that I've decided I don't much like! Out of sight, but within nostrils reach, are lots of heliotropes.

The Meaning of Flowers

Years ago, in my blushing youth, I was wooed very intently by a handsome doctor. Every Friday he arrived at my shop bearing an incredibly beautiful ikebana arrangement that he had obviously slaved over. Ikebana is the practise of formal Japanese flower arranging. It has, of course, very strict rules. The three main ones are symbolising the sky, earth and man represented through the three pillars of space, depth and asymmetry. I can assure you I knew none of this. The flowers would be presented to me with a deep, enigmatic look and a small bow. The 'way of flowers', or *kado* as it is called in Japan, actually began in China more than 2,300 years ago as a Buddhist practice before being assimilated into Japanese culture. The Japanese coined the term *ikebana*, which means 'living or natural flowers'. Kado is a contemplative practice for studying nature 'as it is'.

I was gradually accruing a large number of glass bowls and special little receptacles as the by-product of these gifts. With panic rising, the elegance of each arrangement only increased my alarm. Worse still, the ever more anguish-making experience was entirely nonverbal. One day I blurted out, 'Do they mean something?' Looking peevish, he replied, 'Of *course* they do.' The spell broke and he never came back.

Flowers have long been used as metaphors for all kinds of emotional conditions. In England, arum lilies are associated with death, whereas in France it is the chrysanthemum. The poor lily has been used to express everything from purity to hatred. Offering a sprig of lily of the valley in early May is meant to bestow good luck. This tradition is still alive and well in France. Red roses represent love. Cheap carnations left in an actress's dressing room meant she had been fired.

The Victorians loved flower meanings and applied them heavy-handedly to anything that bloomed. These days, I think it's pretty much faded away. We still abide by the colour references though: red for love, white for purity or death, pink for romance and yellow for happiness.

Reading about the Chernobyl disaster, I discovered the name translates as wormwood. Wormwood is the common name for *Artemisia absinthium*. The Book of Revelations says that a 'poisonous star of wormwood will fall'. Lots of wormwood grows around the nuclear plant at Chernobyl.

The past master of powerful flower metaphor was undoubtedly Shakespeare. He reduced an entire country's disorder and the obvious psychological deterioration of its ruler, King Lear, to a metaphor of unwanted plants.

'As mad as the vex'd sea; singing aloud;
Crown'd with rank fumiter and furrow-weeds,
With bur-docks, hemlock, nettles, cuckoo-flowers,
Darnel, and all idle weeds that grow
In our sustaining corn.'

← A young Japanese woman in traditional dress from sometime in the nineteenth century is seen making a typical ikebana arrangement. Everything she is doing is highly focused and carefully considered. The accoutrements are specific too, and this presumably adds to the contemplative practice of studying nature.

→ It seems plausible that these sentimental attributes were invented by the printer of the postcard rather than having any greater depth. They were doubtless cashing in on the fashion for sending coy billets-doux to loved ones in the hope they might pick the correct flower and sentiment.

↘ The same implausibility applies to this questionable palette of manly emotions. No wonder she is peering quizzically out at us from the safety of the thumb hole.

↙ An English engraving of wormwood, or *Artemisia absinthium*, the 'poisonous star' of Chernobyl.

The language of flowers
Cornflower Riches
Daisy Attachment
Hundred leaved Rose Sincere love
Violet Modesty
Convolvulus Tender love
Heather Solitude
Geranium Sincerity
Nettle Defiance
Lily of the valley Sensitiveness
Yellow Rose Contentment
Rhododendron Strength
Narcissus Pride
Jasmine Faithfulness
Gentian Gratitude
Edelweiss Cleanliness
Pansy Messenger of love
White rose Purity
Pink Hope

Self-seeders

Self-seeders, often biennials, are magical elements in a garden. I have a collection of self-seeding plants that I enjoy using to pop up and surprise and delight in unexpected places. One of these is *Onopordum acanthium*, the terrifyingly spiny, yet eminently touchable cotton thistle. It appears obligingly where least expected and adds a bit of excitement to things because of its size. Obviously self-seeders need to be managed as some are more enthusiastic than you might wish. Perilous ones being *Verbena hastata*, *Alchemilla mollis* and *Centranthus ruber*. Yet all are welcome with me, I just tweak out any that are getting too familiar. Poppies are welcome, too, in all their forms and are strangely mercurial as they need soil disturbance to stimulate their growth. As we move towards digging less, I imagine they'll just lie still until a disturbance event triggers them into action again. *Stachys byzantina* has been a surprise in the garden, becoming almost invasive on the dry, sandy soil. Alliums of all kinds self-seed and multiply healthily. Verbascum is highly adapted self-seeder and comes in such variety that I tend to leave them all to it. My favourite is *Verbascum blattaria f. albiflorum*, which towers at great heights and is always elegant with seeds pods like little polished marbles.

Here is an alphabetical trundle through some good, reliable self-seeders for the garden that don't look weedy: *Antirrhinum braun-blanquetii*, *Bupleurum*, *Campanula persicifolia*, *Dianthus cruentus*, *Erigeron karvinskianus*, *Eryngium giganteum*, *Foeniculum vulgare*, *Geranium phaeum*, *Knautia macedonica*, *Leucanthemum vulgare*, *Lunaria rediviva*, *Monarda fistulosa*, *Nigella* ssp., *Oenothera sulphurea*, *Origanum* ssp., *Papaver* ssp., *Reseda luteola*, *Salvia amplexicaulis*, *Tragopogon porrifolius*, *Viola odorata*, *Zinnia peruviana*.

See what works in your soil, as that is the true acid test, and enjoy the serendipity of not knowing what will happen next.

Self-seeders are the backbone of many gardens in the summer. Clockwise from top left: *Echium vulgare*, wild viper's bugloss, makes good vertical punctuation and the bees love it; oxeye daisy, also known as 'mathers'; *Nigella*, love-in-a-mist, with *Stachys lanata* and an unknown salvia; a naturalised and self-seeded *Orlaya grandiflora* with an opportunistic poppy; *Stachys* again, combining with the ever-popular *Cerinthe major* 'Purpurescens'; the fleeting showstopper *Papaver somniferum* 'Lauren's Grape' pops up serendipitously beside *Rosa* 'William Lobb' and some catnip.

Caring for Plants

Ultimately, a garden needs a good guardian who will care for it. Nurture is everything. I'm sure the majority of garden owners started out with very little knowledge. It accrues over time, through trial and error and a desire to do better. It is very obvious if a plant is happy or not. It cuts like a knife through the heart if nothing thrives, spurring on the quest for greater expertise.

Our friends Kell and Jacqueline upped sticks during the pandemic and headed off to a new life in France, a country they didn't know. Previously they had an incredibly successful Danish restaurant in London. They bought 14 hectares (35 acres) of land in a rural area famous for growing plums. We held our breath, afraid that they might struggle to adapt to such a massive change from urban living. Not a bit of it – in no time at all, they have become very capable market gardeners and restoration builders. They have established a large greenhouse and vegetable garden, have a productive walnut orchard and are fast heading towards highly organised self-sufficiency. Kell grew up in Denmark surrounded by fruit trees and is a natural-born forager and food lover. 'This thing about doing something for the future,' he says, 'has always fascinated me, after all we are only here for such a short time. I also derive a lot of energy from discovering new things.'

I've asked a few friends about why they garden. Živilė said, 'In short, I don't know, though I come from a place where if you don't grow you don't eat. The relationship enforces mutual care and respect. So, I can see now that I have a choice, I still choose to grow and care for plants. I reckon it's like an umbilical cord supplying information to who I am and what the hell I am doing here. Gardening is my teacher. Helps me stay grounded. This woodcut is my answer.'

We hire a lot of professional gardeners on our projects. These are mostly people who grew up knowing their destiny lay with plants and pursued it as a profession. However, there are a good number who 'got the bug' and decided to apply themselves fully to it. Either way, when asked what it was that got them gardening the responses are similar; a fascination with watching things grow and flourish, a peace of mind from having an active body, breathing good air, watching light change, not worrying about what you look like! There is a clear symbiosis between the act of caring for the plants and caring for others and ourselves.

← These ancient white mulberry pollards, *Morus alba*, are wonderful shade trees in the heat of the continent. The gnarly shapes add instant character and come with their own resident livestock – can you see it? These trees transplant very well and I've never lost one yet. Big commercial nurseries know how to prepare trees like this for moving so the risks are negligible. Just prepare the ground well, make sure reliable people are doing the moving and planting and then water.

↑ Živilė, who worked with me for many years, is currently living in a tent in a far-flung place while renovating her farm and making woodcuts, among other things. She is definitely someone of the earth and living life close to it suits her best. She gardens to eat and her strong aesthetic can be experienced throughout her home. This is one of her woodcuts.

← The peacock butterfly, or *Aglais io*, is one of the United Kingdom's most common butterflies, yet it is still a treat to see any butterfly these days. This one is feasting on sheep's-bit scabious in one of our meadows.

↙ These hives were added to the garden very shortly after we completed it. Given the total transformation of the land from a barren desert – for bees at least – to a fecund and flower-filled paradise, I am confident there will be very good honey yields from healthy and happy hives.

Fauna

All gardens require animals in them, and to be teeming with life at every level. I've been creating more habitats in our garden through planting and other actions. A couple of years ago, I decided to use all the fallen leaves as a dense annual mulch under the shelterbelt. Partly, there is nowhere to compost the leaves and I reasoned they'd rot down in their own time while making a deep insulation layer beneath the trees and shrubs. I've a dim memory of being told it's not a good idea to do this, but since this is what nature does I thought I'd risk the harm, happy to learn the hard way if necessary. Mostly the leaves come from the huge *Salix babylonica* tree so they're quite light and nice to handle. Also, they make a good overwintering place for bugs of whatever kind. I imagined that ground-feeding birds would be delighted by this luxurious store of food, and indeed they are. What I hadn't anticipated is that the warm, leafy mattress is absolutely lovely for the foxes that have chosen to live in one corner. I also hadn't predicted that we would get badgers and hedgehogs. As I've said, the garden isn't large. It abuts fields and I'm completely mystified at how the badger got in, but it has busied itself overturning much of the lawn hunting for worms. I'll tackle that repair job in spring.

Wild animals in gardens require some common-sense management. Not all are welcome if you refer back to the section on pests. I doubt much can be done about the foxes, but I can stop the badger by finding where it's getting in and plugging the gap. The hedgehog is welcome. Muntjacs are not, though, neither are grey squirrels, which we live trap, shoot and feed to the red kites. Wood pigeons are also on my hit list and I'm being taught how to fire an air rifle so I can dispatch them myself. Killing pests is a thorny topic, yet it must be discussed. We had to stop vegetable gardening because the volume of pest predators in the area became too much. Imbalance is rife everywhere.

On projects I work on, I have Bill who comes and helps assess how to deal with infestations of unwanted wildlife. If we are planting large volumes of new woodland – and we do that a lot – it is unconscionable to leave the squirrels, rabbits and deer unmanaged. He loves the natural world, as do I, and is not a mass murderer with no feeling for animals. Everything is highly regulated and properly managed with the best of welfare standards and we eat the meat where relevant.

On a lighter note, the leafmould under the shelterbelt, along with the mixed native hedge planting incorporating immense bulks of *Buxus rotundifolia*, has done what I hoped. It has vastly increased the number of birds in the garden. The thrushes are back and I have masses of small birds now, including sparrows and long-tailed tits. The blackbirds are especially happy flicking through the leaves. Bumble bee numbers are up, and bee numbers in general are very good.

The garden is driven on many levels by wanting to keep bees happy and well fed. It's worth noting that there are definite famine spots in the year for bees. We might think there is always a lot in flower in the countryside, but there isn't. A recent study found that there are significant nectar deficits in the United Kingdom in early spring, around March, and again during the harvest periods of late summer in August and September. These lean periods can be supported by ensuring gardens have plenty going on in those months. It makes plant choices even more enjoyable if you're looking at them not just as things of beauty, but also as a resource.

We still don't get many butterflies here and I'm not sure why that is. The neighbouring fields are managed organically and quite scruffily, so there should be a decent resource both there and in the garden. The Natural History Museum in London reports that almost 50 per cent of native butterflies are on the red list for extinction. Habitat loss and climate change are the biggest culprits, yet they also say that this steep decline could be overturned. One of the biggest issues is that butterflies can't travel very far. If they are exposed to enormous empty fields they literally die trying to get across them. Gardens then become ever more vital for providing stable places for egg laying, caterpillar feeding, pupating and emerging into a nectar-rich environment. Getting to grips with the life cycles in a garden is as vital as any other aspect of what we are doing. Less frequent mowing is also important. Around half of my lawn has been left to convert to long grass and wildflowers. Butterflies lay eggs in long grass, so hopefully this will start to change habits on a tiny scale. I'll probably allow some of the badger-damaged lawn to revert now – we don't need much lawn at all – just for the cockchafers really!

All my bee advice, and honey, emanates from Clare and Ian Nichols at Epping Good Honey. Artists turned beekeepers, they produce stunning seasonal honeys in Epping Forest in an ethical and sustainable way. We have had a lot of hot debates on the new hive fads that are around and we are not enthusiasts. Hive bees need proper care. Clare suggests, 'with these new types of hive, a bait pheromone is placed inside a hollow log to attract scouting bees. A swarm arrives. The colony expands with no place to build and grow, so swarms again. With no disease management in place, any existing diseases spread to neighbouring colonies. It is very irresponsible with regard to the wider ecosystem of wild beneficial pollinators.' Bear in mind that there are 1,500 'wild' pollinators in the United Kingdom alone – not just honey bees but also bumblebees, solitary bees, moths, butterflies and hoverflies live in the wild. Given they could be negatively affected by poor hive hygiene, let's leave honey beekeeping to people like Clare and Ian and other members of The British Beekeepers' Association, all of whom register their hives with the National Bee Unit. These are people who know what they are doing and can monitor collectively the health of this hard-working and threatened species on whom we all depend.

Adding watering holes to a garden, in whatever form takes your interest, is vital. Every type of creature needs access to fresh water. Having a pond is such a source of fascination. Nothing betters dragonflies swooping around during the long hot days of summer. Frogs, toads and newts all bring their helpful pest management to the garden too. I was once told that if you build a pond and do nothing more than fill it with water, it will be completely colonised with all relevant flora and fauna within two years. That would be a worthwhile experiment.

6. DECONSTRUCTING PLANTING

By nature, men desire the beautiful.

—SAINT BASIL (329–379)

PERHAPS THE MOST COMPLICATED ASPECT of making a garden is designing the planting. Every one of us approaches it in unique ways and there is no right or wrong way of doing it. Designing planting involves having a good vision of how you'd ideally like things to look. This is the most brilliant bit about gardening – seeing how other people do it. A good friend has just moved on from the large garden she and her late husband created over many years. The garden was very influenced by their love of Italy and the classics. Their planting style was unique and filled with horticultural references to places, ideas and philosophies. It could be enjoyed purely as a garden but also on many other levels in their company as the stories emerged.

It is best to start with the structural elements of larger trees, hedges, topiary and shrubs, then the infilling of smaller plants can begin. This should take time to put together, lots of mulling, leafing through books and catalogues. Internet scrolling is of course de rigeur these days, though I personally find books much easier to use and more informative. Given this is what I do for a living, and that people seem to like it, it's probably more useful for me to discuss and deconstruct my own planting plans. I can then show how I go about responding to a place, demonstrating my own way of building up the story and showing the end results.

Garden planting that can semi-naturalise a space is my personal preference. It seems to give a relaxed quality that I enjoy. Some say its 'messy' and perhaps it is, although this is – like most things in gardening – a subjective view and bothers me little. Gardens are not the best places for being judgemental, that gift is best left at the door. Someone once told me that they hadn't visited the world-famous private garden of one of our heads of state 'in case I come away disappointed and am then tempted to say so'. I found that astonishing. Gardens are to be enjoyed exactly for their uniqueness. Having always had a very strong affinity with nature, I've looked a lot at how plant matrixes work in the wild. There are wonderful sporadic outbursts and then quieter areas where more jewel-like plants emerge to surprise us. Once, driving across grasslands in Africa, I screeched to a halt. There, in the vast acreage of grass, shone a pyjama lily, *Crinum macowanii*. This great voluptuous pink amaryllis with its rich green fleshy leaves looked incongruous in a vast savanna of dried tawny grass. But that's nature. It's probably still there, looking and smelling gorgeous, to attract a sexy beast.

I find it possible to get a sense of order into a garden through the built structure and the structural planting, so my gardens are highly civilised. I am not trying to emulate nature, I am making a garden and using 'garden' plants – namely those we have tried and trusted – to paint a picture of something loose and relaxed. The 'naturalistic fallacy' was the concept of British philosopher G.E. Moore. He wrote a book on philosophical ethics called *Principia Ethica* (1903). The naturalistic fallacy covers the mistake of thinking something is good just because it is natural. This seems to be what we are in the grips of at the moment, and I do sometimes wonder just to complicate matters further, about who, or what algorithm is driving the definitions of 'good' and 'natural'. However, we are all fully in the grip of this thought. As far as I am concerned, everything on the earth is of the earth so it's all 'natural' – even the stuff we don't like (think back to the dichotomised purpose of bacteria), and we need all of everything. Go and have a read of G.E. Moore and draw your own conclusions.

Four Freshly Made Gardens

The following gardens were all in their infancy at the time of writing. All the photography was accomplished within the first six to eight months after planting. The triumph of the health of these gardens is in the ground preparation. Always spend as much time as you can prepping the ground before planting. It pays off. Weeding in the formative few years is so much easier too as the ground is pliable and receptive. I've chosen new gardens because the plants are still settling down and it's easier to see the combinations in a graphic way.

→ I like space in planting combinations. This airy combination of *Veronicastrum virginianum* 'Album' and *Echinops ritro* is pleasingly structural over a long period. The ethereal colours work well together.

Careful Preparation of the Soil Before Planting a Rose-Bed, c. 1938, William Heath Robinson (1872–1944)

Italy

This was a really fascinating garden to create. The site is an ancient hilltop settlement typical of this part of Italy. It was completely dilapidated and had last been occupied some years previously by a local farmer. Traces of many centuries of occupation were there, yet the place was uninhabitable. What was standing showed almost continuous elements of building from the eleventh century until probably the 1950s. The garden I created surrounds the castle and flows down its terraced slopes, before giving way to olive terraces and recreated wildflowers so typical of the area. There is a tendency to think that Italy only has Mediterranean plant palette because it is hot, but this is not the case. I worked with a local landscape historian to make sure that I chose planting, specifically the trees, that suited the area's unique character. It would be wrong, my erudite client told me, to choose umbrella pine, *Sciadopitys verticillata*. These tend to be planted further south and their distinctive profile on the skyline of this area would be immediately anachronistic. So, too, would the use of silvery Mediterranean plants be out of place. This region is typically coloured with trees and shrubbery of darker greens and reddish-browns. So, the choices we have when planting an area with a profound history and local character is to make a conscious decision to research and emulate that. Obviously, I am not returning the place to its Etruscan past, yet my design does need to settle gently into the wider landscape as it can be seen across the plain on its commanding hilltop. These hilltops are a visual indicator of the local typology of the landscape and protected by law. I chose simple sweeps of shrubbery that we topiarised into loosely corrugated waves. All the trees can be topiarised or pollarded, the exception being the Italian cypress, *Cupressus sempervirens*, which lends its typical spires to the skyline as it emerges from the scrubby oak woodland. This is, of course, a decorative garden though the manner of planting is relaxed. In support of the age of the place, I included lots of herbs, fruit trees and edible plants that will naturalise into their setting.

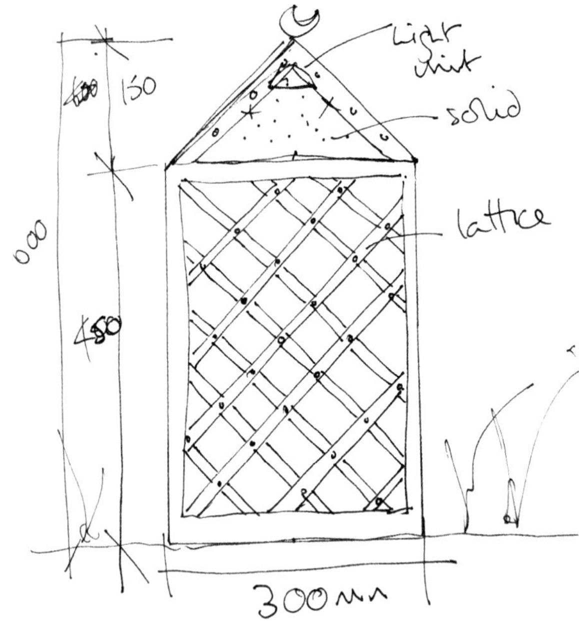

↑ I designed this simple lantern to sit among the planting and to give a gentle wash of light at night, just to support traversing the garden. The crescent on the top is from the old coat of arms of the original owners so I kept it. The lantern's rusty patination helps it disappear among the plants.

↙ The tree here, just seen on the right, is a *Cercis siliquastrum*, or Judas tree. In England, we suggest that Judas hanged himself from an elder bush but he is more likely to have chosen a *Cercis* as they grow across the Mediterranean and into the Middle East. It is a lovely tree. Below it, I planted various types of *Cistus* to form a flowery, shrubby understorey. Here we have *Cistus creticus* and *C.* × *purpureus* 'Alan Fradd'. Behind the lantern is a myrtle that will eventually get very large. I anticipate a rolling programme of replacing the *Cistus* plants as they grow old. We will start taking cuttings.

↲ pp. 184–85: There was nothing here at all when I started, just a vague suggestion of a level change with no walls. I created a raised *orto botanico* – a little herb garden with the myrtle, *Myrtus communis*, in pots. The distant *Quercus ilex* was already there, but terribly overgrown, so I had it reshaped. This is a garden of texture so I introduced, from left to right, *Morus alba* pollards with their wonderful craggy trunks, a rather tall, stringy bay tree and, in the foreground, *Arbutus unedo* for its winter flowering and wonderful scent. Evergreens are always welcome in a hot place.

→ Things begin to get flowery at ground level. The paving is planted with many different varieties of prostrate thyme. At the edges, where the paving meets the beds – all of which were mulched in gravel after planting to keep them cool – I introduced slightly taller thymes and helianthemums, which then support the deep blue *Aquilegia alpina* and *Dianthus carthusianorum*. All of these plants are prolific self-seeders.

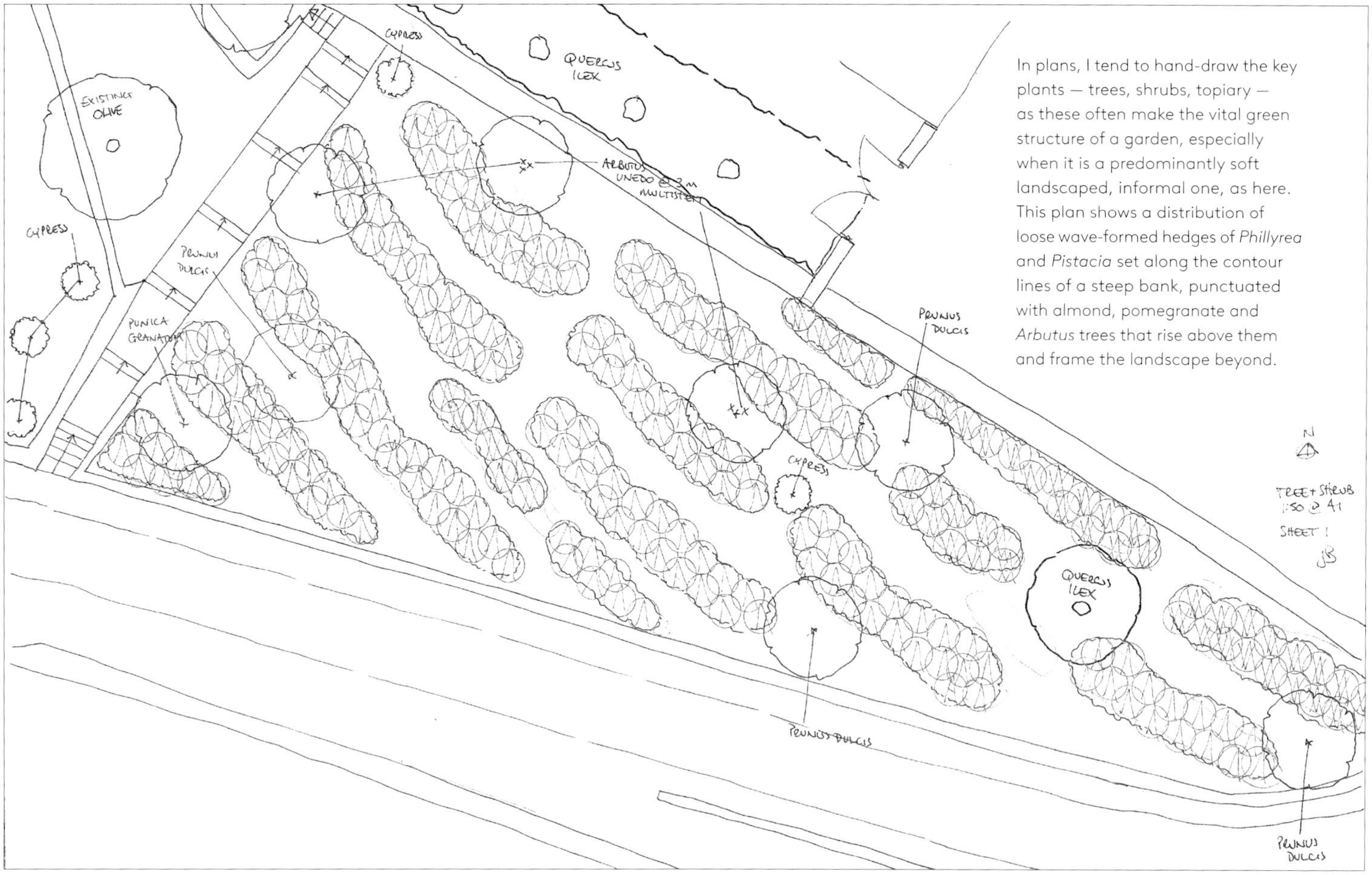

In plans, I tend to hand-draw the key plants — trees, shrubs, topiary — as these often make the vital green structure of a garden, especially when it is a predominantly soft landscaped, informal one, as here. This plan shows a distribution of loose wave-formed hedges of *Phillyrea* and *Pistacia* set along the contour lines of a steep bank, punctuated with almond, pomegranate and *Arbutus* trees that rise above them and frame the landscape beyond.

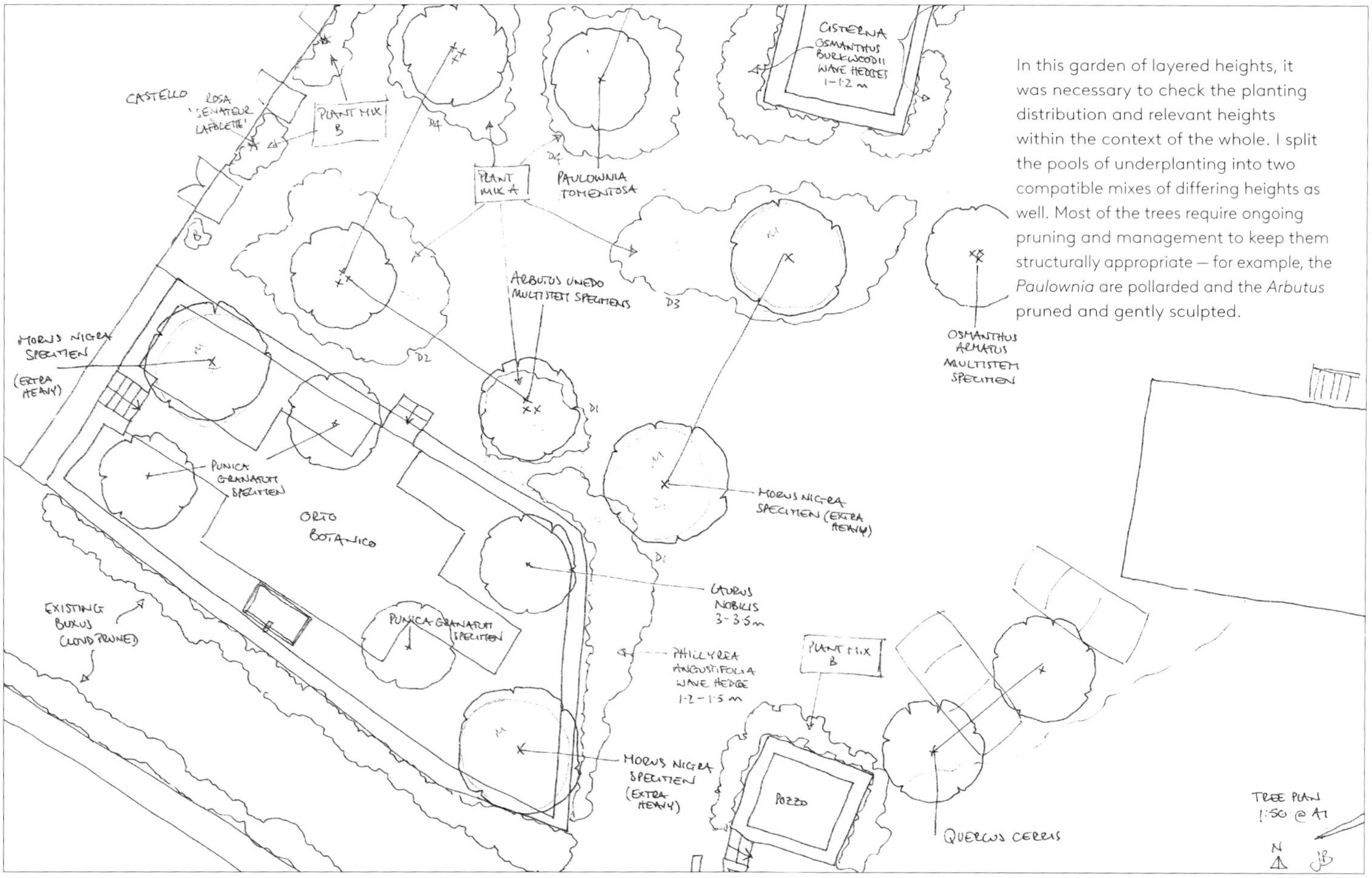

In this garden of layered heights, it was necessary to check the planting distribution and relevant heights within the context of the whole. I split the pools of underplanting into two compatible mixes of differing heights as well. Most of the trees require ongoing pruning and management to keep them structurally appropriate — for example, the *Paulownia* are pollarded and the *Arbutus* pruned and gently sculpted.

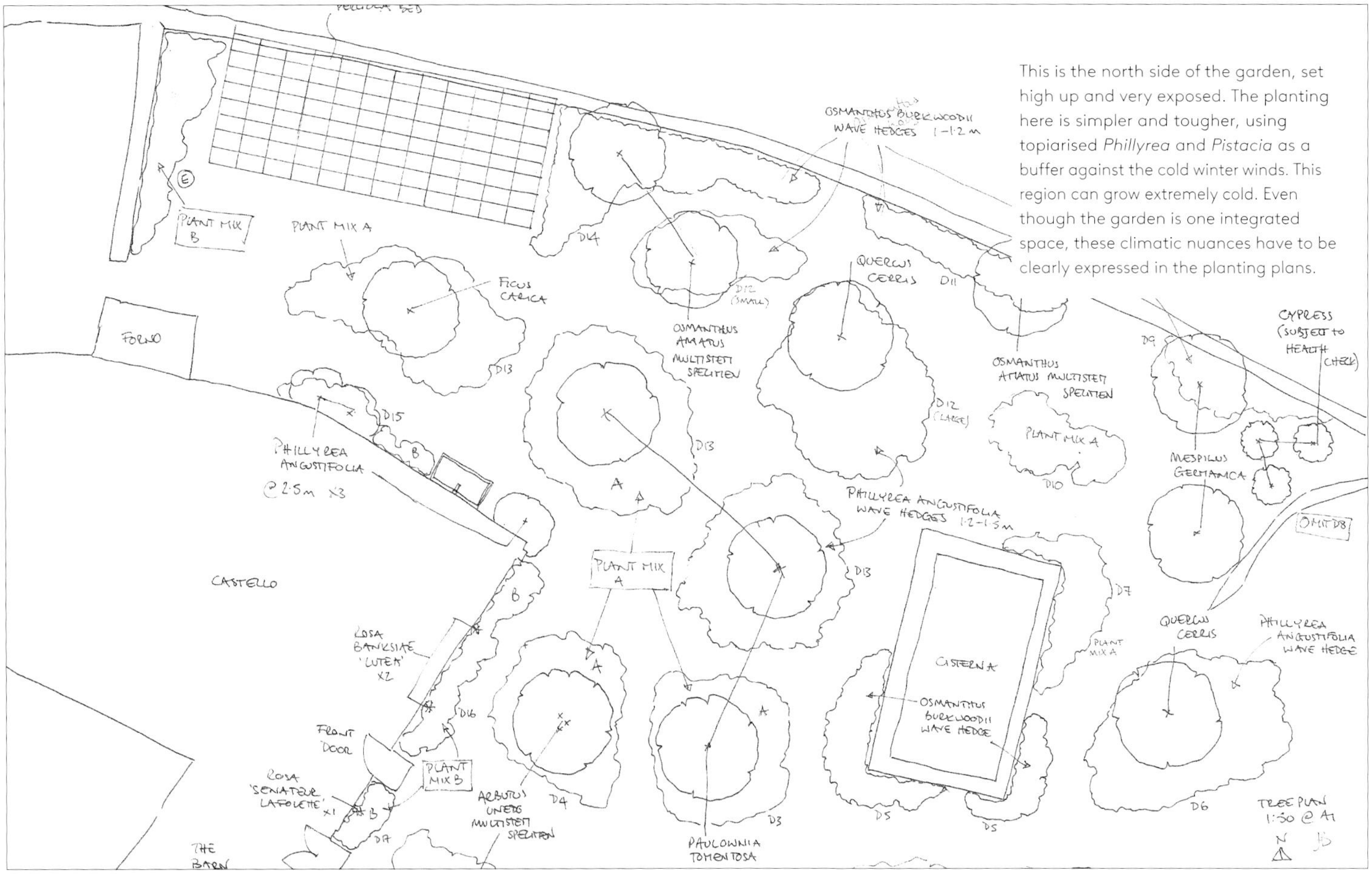

This is the north side of the garden, set high up and very exposed. The planting here is simpler and tougher, using topiarised *Phillyrea* and *Pistacia* as a buffer against the cold winter winds. This region can grow extremely cold. Even though the garden is one integrated space, these climatic nuances have to be clearly expressed in the planting plans.

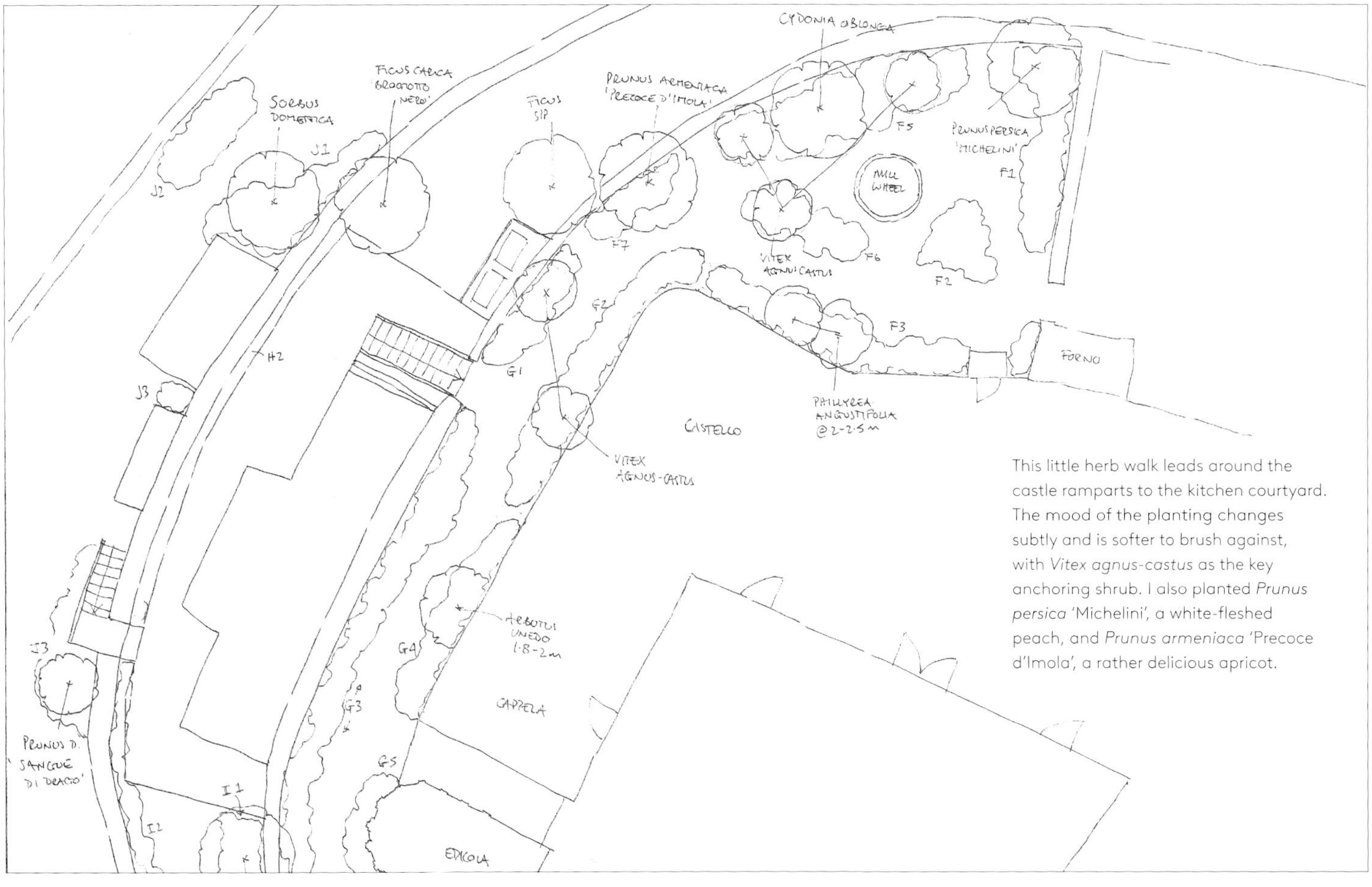

This little herb walk leads around the castle ramparts to the kitchen courtyard. The mood of the planting changes subtly and is softer to brush against, with *Vitex agnus-castus* as the key anchoring shrub. I also planted *Prunus persica* 'Michelini', a white-fleshed peach, and *Prunus armeniaca* 'Precoce d'Imola', a rather delicious apricot.

→ The ground is smothered in thyme throughout, with as many varieties as I could lay my hands on. The individual types matter less than the overall effect. The plants crush underfoot, releasing their wonderfully varied scents.

These are the plants I used:
Thymus herba-barona
Thymus coccineus
Thymus mastichina
Thymus praecox
Thymus serpyllum
Thymus serpyllum 'Minor'
Thymus serpyllum 'Pink Chintz'
Thymus serpyllum 'Snowdrift'
Thymus vulgaris 'Silver Queen'

↘ In the *orto botanico*, I used very straightforward plants such as sage, *Salvia officinalis* 'Purpurescens', and tarragon with chives, fennel and all the other necessary pot herbs for the kitchen. We have seasonal large pots of basil too.

← I set large terracotta pots throughout the planting, and we swap bitter winter oranges like this one with lemons in summer so there is a constant layer of citrus in the garden, with flowers in spring through to the fruit in late winter.

↙ Throughout the gardens, I used a selection of trees that would feel complicit with the local landscape. I planted big old apricots and almonds here. The flowering season is long and the fruit of both delicious. Scale is very important and often fruiting trees maintain a comfortable domestic size. In the foreground is a fig. I've planted this as a standard so we can control its growth. Figs are a nuisance when they become shrub-like and get into the stone walls; they are violently strong and very difficult to control.

↑ This valiant *Mespilus germanica*, or wild medlar, was the only surviving shrub on the site when I arrived. In a way, it set the tone for the whole garden. Medlars are beautiful, sophisticated plants, yet at the same time have a wildness that is very attractive.

↘ Here, in the background, is one of the huge, pollarded white mulberries I planted, *Morus alba*. At its feet is a hedge of *Pistacia* that I am clipping into soft, mounded shapes. In the foreground is one of many pomegranates, *Punica granatum*, that I planted in the *orto botanico*. They are small trees that we keep in bounds with regular hard pruning. The flowers of pomegranate are a beautiful rich red.

↖ These *Allium schubertii* work wonderfully in this garden as there is enough space for them to show off. They feel naturalised popping up out of the gravel here and there. This plant originates from Syria, Israel and Libya so is at home in this dry, arid place. It is interesting that plants from tough environments often give a dazzling performance.

↑ We had great difficulty getting accurately named varieties of *Iris germanica*, so in the end I accepted substitutes. This was supposed to be *Iris germanica* 'Chartreuse Ruffles', but is it? Does it matter? Not especially. I just wanted masses of irises in various shades blasting up through everything like a spontaneous visit from Barbara Cartland.

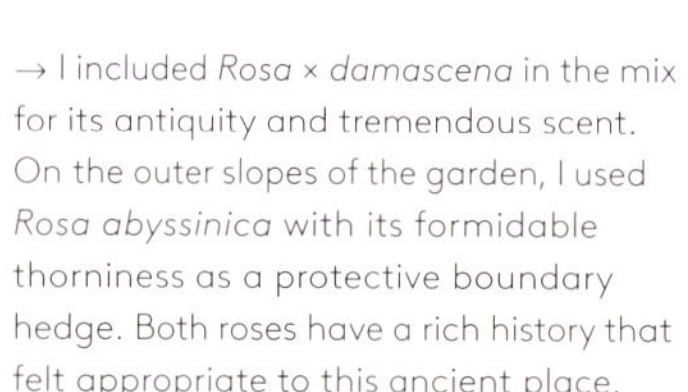

→ I included *Rosa × damascena* in the mix for its antiquity and tremendous scent. On the outer slopes of the garden, I used *Rosa abyssinica* with its formidable thorniness as a protective boundary hedge. Both roses have a rich history that felt appropriate to this ancient place.

← Planted against a hot, south-facing wall, this little *Arbutus* × *andrachnoides* tree will grow very fast, making a stunning contribution provided it doesn't get too hammered by frost. It is one of my favourite trees, its red bark smoothly sinuous and eminently tactile. It is evergreen and presents trusses of sweet-smelling white flowers in winter.

→ I filled the bed edges, and other areas where I wanted a bit more substance at low level, with helianthemum – this one is 'Wisley Cream' – *Thymus vulgaris* 'Silver Posie' and lots of *Dianthus deltoides*.

←The common almond, *Prunus dulcis*, is another great favourite. It has an elegance in every season. Narrow leaves filter sunlight attractively, yet long before they appear, the tree blossoms on bare twigs in winter. I've seen whole hillsides in the Atlas mountains of Morocco seemingly snow-covered in almond blossom. The fruits are covered in grey-green down.

↘ We all have bad habits and *Rosa* × *odorata* 'Mutabilis' is one of mine. This plant just never stops flowering. The habit is lovely – I am very fond of light twiggy things with plenty of space and air in and around them.

→ I included quite a few *Phlomis italica* plants throughout the garden. It grows very well in a hot dry climate. In the United Kingdom it gets leggy too fast and our winters are too damp for it. It survives, but not always attractively, so it is a treat to use in its happy place.

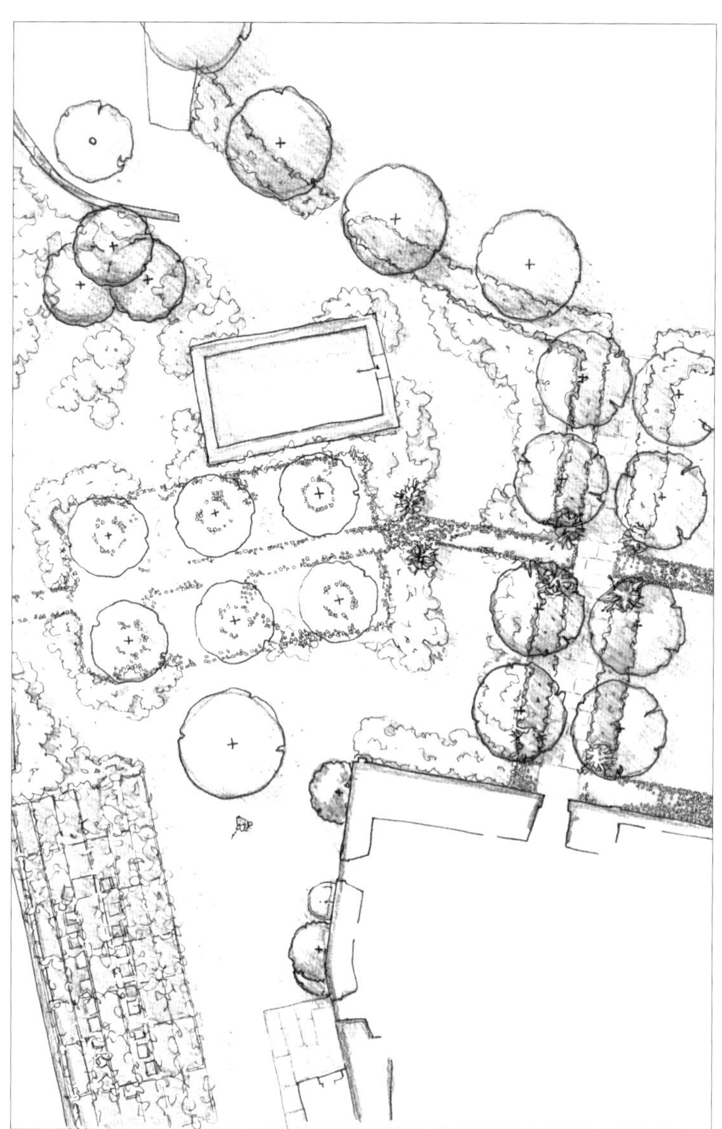

↙ This was an early layout drawing for the garden, in which I was considering using only planting for both structure and decoration. In the end, I abandoned this rather formal plan for something a lot looser — still using plants as structure, but in a much less formal way. Sometimes, it takes a while to relax into a place and understand what it really needs. Below is the plan for the *orto botanico* and this didn't change. It is a functional herb garden near the kitchen and serves as a place for pottering among the plants.

→ The *orto botanico* is elevated by about 1 metre (3 feet) above the garden, which gives a very useful height dynamic to the scheme as a whole. The ancient mulberries are presented as though on stage and have a presence throughout the gardens. They contrast very well with the cypresses. The dense green shrubbery between them is topiarised *Pistacia*, which lends its strong yet natural form to the garden all year round. This garden functions very well in winter.

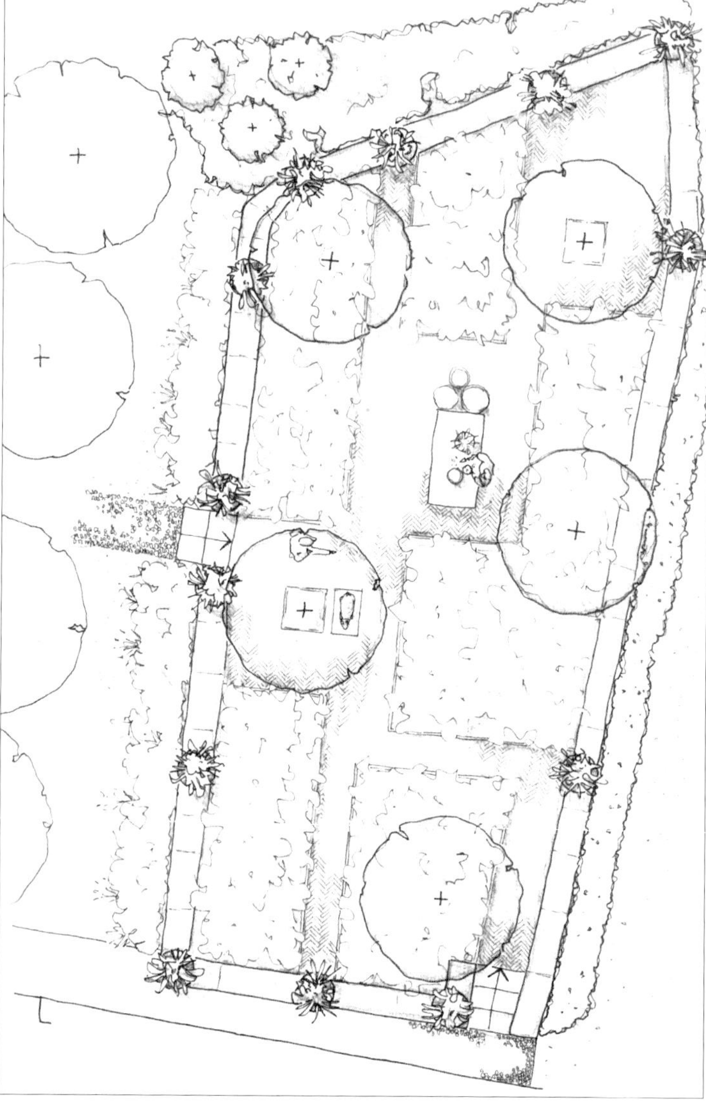

England

When the flower blooms, the bees come uninvited.

—RAMAKRISHNA (1836–86)

There literally wasn't a single plant in this garden when I met my clients. No flower beds, nothing. They had just bought the house and the previous owner had imported a highly conceptual international designer for the place but had subsequently never lived there. The garden had deconceptualised quite quickly! My aim was to bring as much life as possible back into the garden and wider landscape while retaining the existing hard landscape. There was no good reason for ripping out all the laborious work that had been done. It was a wonderful prospect for me as usually we build for years before the planting starts. Apart from reconfiguring the spaces and making flower beds where none had existed, this was all pure planting. The aspirations were high. As well as lots of beautiful flower gardens there would be arboretums, foraging gardens, orchards, vegetable gardens, a greenhouse or two, composting areas, meadows, lakes and wetlands and huge native, fruit-rich hedgerows. All of it was designed to tie the land, which is very steep and quite exposed, to the house in a commanding spot at the top, and then back into the local landscape. The soil was absolutely appalling. It quickly became clear that most of the builder's rubble had been levelled and topped with grass. This gave us an opportunity to solve the mess and create wonderful new beds full of compost-enriched soil. The planting is generous. I chose a top layer of flowering shrubbery, including *Syringa vulgaris* 'Mme Lemoine', *Malus* 'Evereste', *Cirsis siliquastrum* and *Arbutus unedo* against the house and many others giving a long flowering season through the year. Abundant rose banks give nesting opportunities for birds and plentiful supplies of hips for mice in winter. The borders are all colour themed and wash into one another on your walk through the gardens. The return of wildlife in all its forms was instantaneous. 'If you book them, they will come', says Jim Morrison memorably in *Wayne's World*.

↙ I have a soft spot for *Agastache foeniculum*. This is an exposed and very windy site and yet this plant stands up to it. You can just see *Perovskia* getting going – it will take over later in the summer. In the middle is my beloved *Kniphofia caulescens* to add the much-needed warmth of soft terracotta orange in among the blues.

↵ pp. 196–97: We planted the garden in October and this image was taken the following June so this planting, in its entirety, and over the next few pages, is eight months old. There was quite literally nothing here before I started. All the flower beds are new, allowing us to make up proper soil, which has enormous benefits. The planting is unstable inasmuch as the shrubs and roses will take a while to catch up with the herbaceous plants. In the short term, therefore, it all looks very frothy.

→ The house looked incredibly severe when I arrived, stripped of any green. I tucked *Arbutus unedo* into the niche by the bay for a bit of darkness. The opposite side of the bay has a *Wisteria venusta* 'Alba'. The foreground is three separate beds but as you descend this steep site they all start to work together. For this first season, I planted a slightly overenthusiastic quantity of *Cosmos* as a buffer, but needn't have worried as it is so full, with *Lychnis coronaria*, *Salvia verticillata* 'Purple Rain', *Viola cornuta* 'Boughton Blue', *Allium amethystinum* 'Red Mohican', a slightly suffocated *Syringa* and loads of roses battling their way through. The house looks as if it is floating on a big pink hovercraft.

↗ Drawings such as these are very helpful, not just for the client, but also when it comes to balancing the planting intensity across the site. For example, we added a greenhouse to hide the garage and to bring that function closer to the house. I also added trees around the drive and omitted the arches, which felt too overblown. I also added some height in the shape of *Cercis siliquastrum* and lilac around the top lawn.

↑ This is how the initial stages of a planting design look, before everything gets refined, drawn and presented to a client. I work quickly, decisively and scruffily, visiting the site often and in all weathers. Here I'm using a CAD plan as a base. Ideas for planting are really multi-dimensional. Seasons, years, months orientation and weather conditions have to be considered, as do colours, to ensure that areas wash into each other comfortably without jarring. The house is on top of a hill, so the gardens fall away and are pretty much visible all at once – it takes skill to make the segues work.

→ This image expresses how the planting needs to constantly take account of the wider landscape into which it is being slotted. In every direction the view changes – here we are looking across three areas of the garden towards the mature *Tilia cordata* in the background. In summer they are a darkish green that benefits from these soft washes of colour, and the atmospheric morning mists, lightening the foreground. I enjoy the punctuation that the *Allium sphaerocephalon* give.

↱ p.203: I do use this clematis rather a lot. It is a wonderful plant. *Clematis viticvella* 'Purpurea Plena Elegans' indeed lives up to its name with elegant masses of nicely spaced muddled flowers in a beautiful dusty greyish magenta.

→ I've kept all the colours quite soft in this garden. The beds are terraces on a steep hill, so it's important that the colours flow reasonably gently into each other without also becoming a bland nothingness. *Achillea* 'Lilac Beauty' has a good blending colour and fades nicely. It also nods to the wild *Achillea millefolium* in the meadows. I like repeating textures.

↘ *Perovskia* 'Blue Spire' is a tough plant. Placed well, its aggravating habit of keeling over can be managed. This is a windy and exposed garden and has been planted with this in mind. *Perovskia* is a useful early host for other plants, such as this little *Allium sphaerocephalon*.

↗ *Echinacea purpurea* is a marvellous plant. Here, I've underplanted it with *Nepeta grandiflora* 'Dawn to Dusk', which I am also partial to — a soft plant with a useful colouring that works well with lots of things.

→ The unusual pinkish-brown calyces are what give *Nepeta grandiflora* 'Dawn to Dusk' its depth from a distance. It blends effortlessly with the slender spires of *Veronicastrum virginicum* 'Album', without blocking them out. The two provide a useful compatibility of heights in a big border.

↖ A magnet for bees, *Knautia macedonica* needs no introduction. I use it unreservedly as it is an uncomplaining, attractive and airy plant. In summer, I cut it back and let it go again for a later blast. Cutting back tends to deal with mildew too, although this is not a big problem.

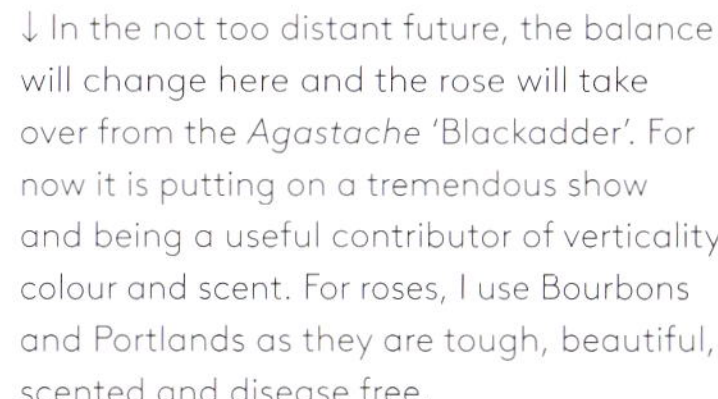

↓ In the not too distant future, the balance will change here and the rose will take over from the *Agastache* 'Blackadder'. For now it is putting on a tremendous show and being a useful contributor of verticality, colour and scent. For roses, I use Bourbons and Portlands as they are tough, beautiful, scented and disease free.

← I treat *Gaura lindheimeri* almost as an annual, although it does chug on in some gardens. I think it exhausts itself with exhibitionistic flowering. It's a good pairing with this *Salvia verticillata* 'Purple Rain'.

→ I used *Cosmos* as an annual filler while everything else got itself settled. Here we have *Achillea* 'Cerise Queen', *Salvia guaranitica* 'Amistad', the reed-like leaves of *Dierama pulcherrimum* 'Blackbird', *Penstemon* 'Garnet' and my favourite, *Sedum* 'Matrona'. In due course, the roses will get stronger for these are ultimately old rose borders with the herbaceous as a supporting cast.

↖ This site plan shows the scale of the place. We had a lot of land to bring to life, including a spring-fed lake. The top field lent itself very naturally to becoming an orchard and vegetable garden. The planting is held closely to the house, as this is where its greatest effect is felt, and then we filled the empty enormity of lawn with trees and meadows, the former providing much needed succession planting on the previously empty hill.

Scotland

This magnificent place is high in the Cairngorm Mountains in Scotland. I wish I could show you what it looked like before we started. There were piles of old fridges, a half-smashed concrete curling rink and mountains of builders rubble 3 metres (10 feet) tall. The hedges were overgrown, the trees were sad and there were weeds everywhere. Yet this is a whimsical spot with wonderful, natural character. The old Fife Arms Hotel is a glorious Scottish Baronial granite building sitting proudly on the rocky banks of the tumbling Clunie Water. It is in the centre of Braemar in Royal Deeside, only moments away from Balmoral Castle. Iwan and Manuela Wirth are great fun to work with. They are interested in ideas and after our initial animated conversations they let me loose.

The site is quite complicated, and like any hotel, the demands on a garden space are legion. The idea for the drumlins came not just from my love of the natural forms in Highland landscapes – I've worked in Scotland a lot now – but they solved a practical problem. I needed to create elevation in the garden to present the planting well. It's far too small to keep as a flat plane. There was a need to screen views from one another to give differing experiences of outside when viewed from inside. I also wanted to create little routes and discoveries through to the lower area where we had a flat meadow lawn. The character of the hotel was conceived by Russell Sage as Victoriana on steroids and mirrored in the graphic design by Mark Paton, himself a Scot. We shared ideas. That's important if an entire place is to be cohesive. I chose a planting palette that was redolent of both Highland folklore and also the Victorian plant hunters. Native rowan, Scots pine and downy birch are the trees, interspersed with bog myrtle shrubs to keep the midges away and wild broom. I used loads of *Rhododendron luteum* for its glorious scented yellow flowers and fiery autumn colours. Scotland is all about autumn colour so this garden is packed with it. It's a magical place, so go and see for yourself.

'When my husband Iwan and I are in the early stages of planning a project, the surrounding landscape and its unique relationship with the local architecture is always our first consideration since these elements go hand-in-hand to create the unique atmosphere of a place. Our goal is to create an environment which seamlessly blends with the local character, whether that is a garden in Menorca, Somerset or, in the case of the Fife Arms, the Scottish Highlands. At The Fife Arms, it was clear that the magic – and the challenge – of the place stems from the incredible surrounding landscape and that integrating it into the project would be a vital ingredient in its success.

From our first conversations, Jinny showed her true depth of understanding of the special character of the Highlands, its native plants, and the challenges that each season brings. It was important that the design would be sustainable and that elements of the wild beauty of the Cairngorms vistas would blend with the garden through the use of native plants and scrubs. Overlooking the River Clunie, the sights and sounds in the garden combine with the planting to create a Gesamtkunstwerk *for all the senses. The graceful design is an extension of the landscape you see beyond the hotel. It is a garden that is utterly captivating in each season, providing interest all year round. In summer, the stunning wildflower meadow at the bottom of the garden is in full bloom. We love it equally in the winter when its elegant structure stands against the dramatic backdrop of the snowy mountain views beyond.'*

—MANUELA WIRTH

↙ I installed these steps to separate the lower meadow from the 'banks and braes' of the main gardens. Besides a lavish use of coppery *Rhododendron luteum*, I used a huge quantity of the wonderfully acidic, yellowy grass *Sesleria autumnalis*. In the low light of the Highlands it is illuminating, giving lift and luminous accents to the garden.

↲ pp. 207–08: To confirm the spirit of the place, this photograph was shot in heavy drizzle. Scotland performs well in rain, and I love to see everything weighed down with glistening droplets. This juvenile planting scheme is settling in well in its Highland home. I wanted all the trees to have resonance to the place so chose rowans, Scots pine and downy birch. The whole garden is filled with a muddle of native plants such as bog myrtle alongside Victorian favourites such as hydrangea, *Rhododendron luteum* and potentilla, which I used in prodigious quantities. A sturdy bank of *Euphorbia robbiae*, *Deschampsia cespitosa* and *Geranium macrorrhizum* holds everything together.

→ The genteel Coalbrookdale cast-iron furniture is leavened by its place in the meadow. Tucked in little oases between the shrubbery, these places are there for people to enjoy intimate drinks and chats. The scents and textures are unique to Scotland, as are the early shades of autumn appearing here.

→ *Pinus sylvestris*, or the Scot's pine, was once the core of the great Caledonian forest and remains the essence of Scotland. I chose it for its place in the myths and legends of the country – spells have been woven around and under this tree. It is Scotland's only native timber tree.

↗ The rowan or mountain ash, *Sorbus aucuparia*, is another Scottish tree with strong associations with the legends of the country. A benign tree that protects people from evil, its bitter berries have several health benefits though none that really survive to this day. I used it here for its quintessential Scottishness and stunning colouring.

↘ I have a sentimental attachment to potentillas. This one is *Potentilla fruticosa* 'Elizabeth' and I planted lots and lots of them, along with *P. f.* 'Daydawn' and *P. f.* 'Sunset'. The colours are beautiful in the soft light of the Highlands, and they have a sweet character with their ferny leaves and little flowers that come continuously for ages. They are tough, dependable and adaptable. Small birds love nesting in them too.

← A local optimist told me that hydrangeas would never survive in this garden. They have and they do. *Hydra* obviously means 'water' — they have plenty of that and are capable of withstanding the cold. I hedged my bets by planting *Hydrangea paniculata* and *H. aspera* subsp. *sargentiana* — both in rude health and enjoying Highland life.

↗ This image shows three of my favourite plants living harmoniously. The first is *Rosa pimpinellifolia*, the burnet rose, with its charming feathery foliage and beguiling, jet-black hips. A suckering shrub, it is busy binding the steeper banks together. In front of the rose is a red-hot poker, *Kniphofia* 'Tawny King'. The colour of the smouldering, orange, torch-like flowers is unforgettable. Behind the *Kniphofia* is a frothy mound of *Potentilla fruticosa* 'Elizabeth' flashing sunlight into the drizzly garden.

↓ Scotland is not Scotland without a thistle and I use *Cirsium rivulare* 'Atropurpureum', a magnificent mass of glowing, deep-crimson flowers and a plant that loves the summer moisture and cool air.

↗ I made this sketch to see whether it was possible to screen out the north face of a very large, dark grey granite building. This view is from the lowered meadow. There was nothing here before I began work, except a vast pile of rubble and a broken concrete curling rink — curling is an ancient Gaelic sport. It took a little imagination to see it as a fairy woodland full of berries, birds and beauty.

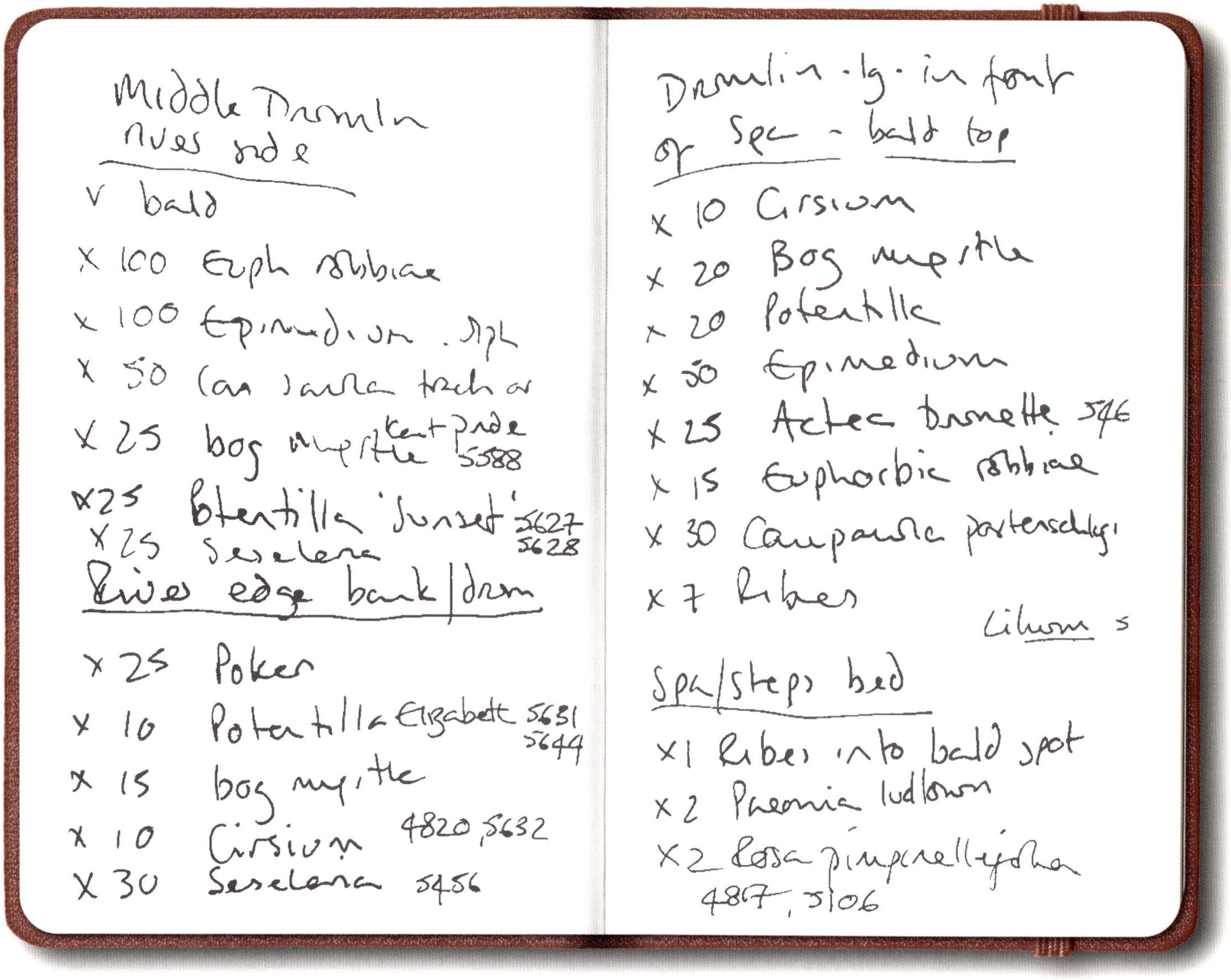

↖ I make endless lists. These are some of my original notes on quantities and species per drumlin. I readily see planting combinations in my mind and rarely draw out extensive planting plans, especially on a project like this, where I know I'll be doing all the setting out on site myself. The lists allow me to create sweeps of planting that morph into one another. I can punctuate easily with shrubbery. My answer to box plants on Scotland is bog myrtle, *Myrica gale*, which has a pleasing shape, texture and wonderful aroma.

↗ There is a gentle planting combination throughout the gardens. I wanted lots of textures and colours to marry easily together. The near-constant moisture in the air influenced the choices I made. Here, the broom on the left holds drops of water on its slender stems as do the furry soft leaves of the *Geranium macrorrhizum* 'Album'. Warm shades of russet and red in the rowans and *Rhododendron luteum* warm up the pallet, linking the garden seamlessly to the Cairngorm hilltops beyond.

City

Urban gardens are fun to create. My client on this one was adventurous and that's a great gift to a designer. Furthermore, the architect on the project is an old friend of mine, and we hadn't worked together for years so that was an extra treat. So, from the start this was a very happy project. David was designing not just the house, but also a stunning new garden room at the rear of the space. This is not a big garden and is viewed pretty much from all sides. The property also has very tall windows on both sides, necessitating tall planting, yet not so big that it swamps the place, stealing all the light. Light is a vital consideration in small gardens. 'Definitely no grass' was part of my brief, as the kids needed to be able to tricycle and roller skate all through the garden. Hard surfaces are definitely necessary in a garden and allow for lots of different styles of human activity to be tucked into separate areas. I chose a jungle theme for the planting as it needed a strong evergreen structure to carry the seasons. In the city, it stays warm enough all year for the core of this kind of planting. It can be shot through year-round with all kinds of excitement by using seasonal plants. My old favourite *Salvia confertiflora* is perfect for this type of space, as is *Melianthus major*. Both have a strangely musty smell so need siting carefully away from seating. This garden is a wild agglomeration of different continents colliding: the Antipodes, South Africa and South America. Yet isn't that the joy of gardening in a temperate climate? A mad mashup doesn't have to be confined to music!

↙ The idea was to create several completely separate areas, simply by using plants. Centrally here, is the trunk of a tree fern, *Dicksonia antarctica*. To the left are the leaves of a sumac tree, *Rhus typhina*, and to the right the unusual, triangular leaves of my favourite wattle, *Acacia pravissima*. In the lower foreground are the huge palmate leaves of *Tetrapanax papyrifer*. In the city these plants tend to hold leaf for most of the year.

↲ pp. 218–19: The wonderful thing about city gardens is how warm they are. In this one, I really wanted to play with a different plant palette to make a year-round space with lots of textural differences. This photograph was taken a few months after planting. Some of the plants will take a while to stabilise and settle, yet overall it is quite well balanced.

→ Tucked away in the depths of this garden is a large oak pergola with a seat swing. We have bananas, *Pittosporum tobira* 'Nana' and huge white *Agapanthus africanus*. The frothy blue on the left is *Verbena rigida* 'Bampton', a prolific self-seeder. Peering out behind the pergola to the left is *Melianthus major*.

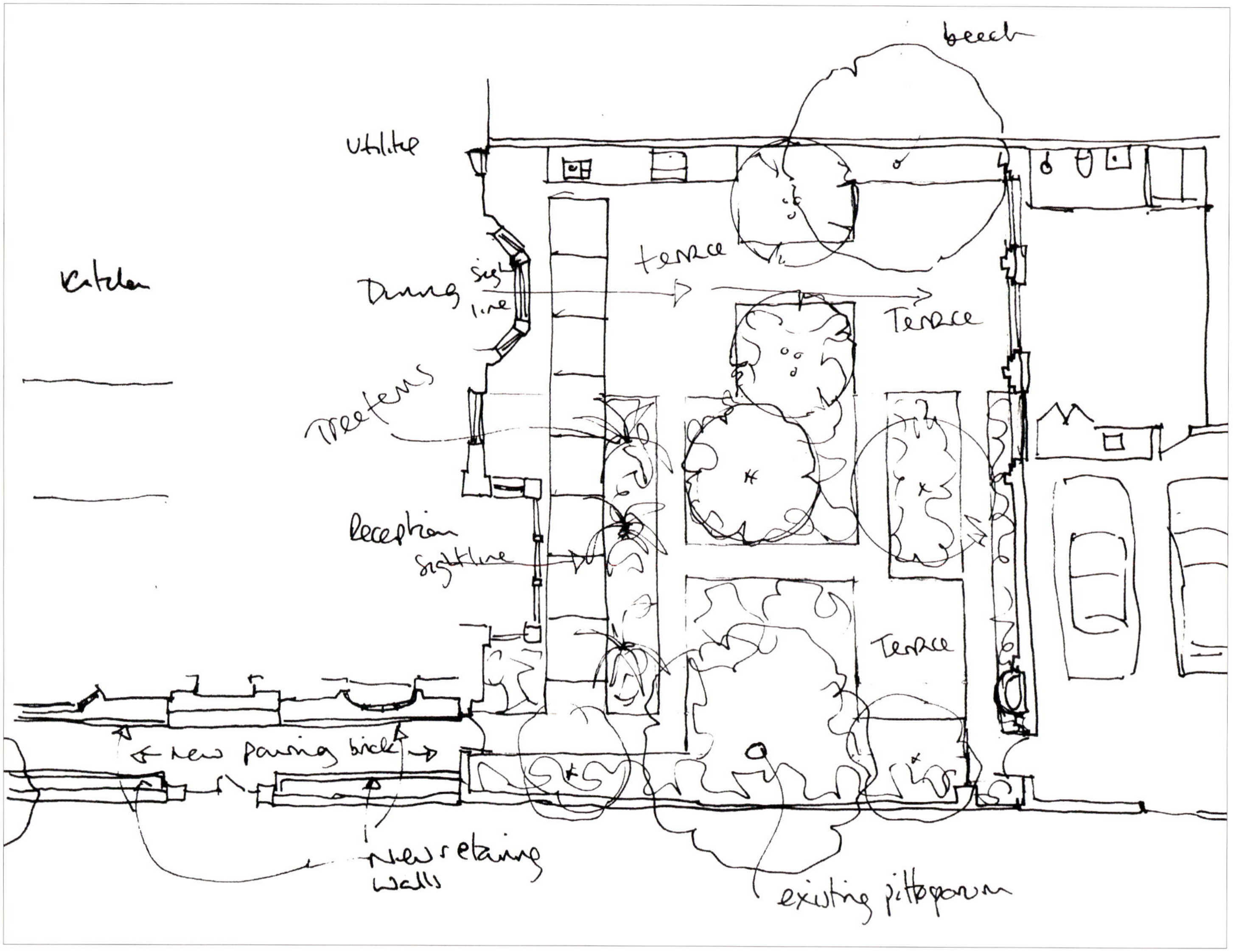

↖ This first sketch I made worked very well. I tend to feel things quite quickly and like to get them down on paper fast. Roughed-out key views, hidden terraces and a sequence of linear paths seemed to click into place. A large, existing *Pittosporum* tree set the tone for what was to come. It needed the companionship of compatible plants, and plenty of them, managing a series of different canopy heights and leaf textures. Overall it needed to stay light and appealing through the year.

← The trees are vitally important and, in particular, their scale. The sumac can be managed easily to stay in bounds; it is not a tree that overshades. However, it does make a space feel more intimate and that is important. We humans appreciate the protective cover of a garden; it helps us relax.

→ The Japanese-inspired bridge is made of pegged oak in a traditional manner. The pine is a lovely, tactile thing. It smells delicious and perfumes the rooms each side. To the right, I have planted *Schizophragma hydrangeoides* 'Moonlight', which ultimately will smother the walls up to the third floor. It has a strange pewter cast to the leaves, and I find it very attractive in the right place.

← At the heart of the house is a large lightwell that can be viewed from three sides. Here, I planted a clipped and tiered pine, measuring about 4 metres (12 feet) tall. It sits on a rocky outcrop studded with small, clipped azaleas, ferns and epimediums. I added the little oak bridge later, so now it's possible to pass through the garden between two rooms. It has added a bit of excitement and a place for the kids to hang out.

→ This was an experiment using *Verbena rigida* 'Bampton' and *Aster × frikartii* 'Mönch'. I like both very much, but not together. You live and learn. I have separated them now. Both habits are quite good in this garden for low down froth.

← *Melianthus major* is best grown as a foliage plant. I tend to cut the flowers off and reduce it in size in spring so it rejuvenates well. Since it can get leggy and woody at the base, I plant several and rotate their hard pruning so there is always a good show of both height and leaf cover. It can grow to 2 metres (6 feet) in a year – allow it some space to get going.

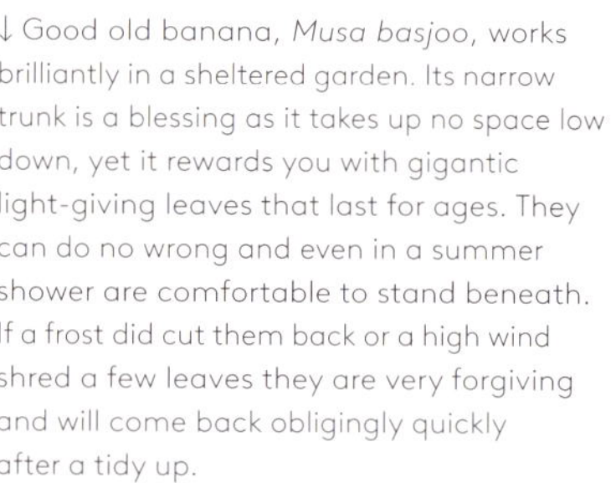

↓ Good old banana, *Musa basjoo*, works brilliantly in a sheltered garden. Its narrow trunk is a blessing as it takes up no space low down, yet it rewards you with gigantic light-giving leaves that last for ages. They can do no wrong and even in a summer shower are comfortable to stand beneath. If a frost did cut them back or a high wind shred a few leaves they are very forgiving and will come back obligingly quickly after a tidy up.

↖ This is *Pseudopanax ferox*, or lancewood, quite a fearsome plant from the antipodes. I was first introduced to it by New Zealand garden designer James Fraser, who lived near me in South London and planted his vast garden to look like a chunk of his homeland. It was my first proper look at plants from that part of the world and they are addictive. Keep soil away from the base of the trunk and generally read up before you start, as they are sensitive in spite of their fiercely sharp lances.

→ Tree ferns, *Dicksonia antarctica*, cast quite a dark shade, so it's important to remove old fronds and generally take care of the canopy so things can survive beneath them. Here I have used two tough customers, also from New Zealand. *Phormium tenax*, aka New Zealand flax, is a handsome plant. It has long been used for ropemaking as the leaves contain immensely strong fibres. Below it is another strong yet beautiful grass, *Stipa arundinacea* or *Anamanthele lessoniana*, aka New Zealand wind grass, or pheasant's tail grass. It has gorgeous russety tips and is as tough as nails. I prefer combing it out to cutting it back though that can be done every few years. It also self-seeds attractively.

← A narrow bed at the back of the garden is shady and damp — perfect for a strip of luxuriant *Zantedeschia aethiopica* or *Brosimum aethiopica*, calla or arum lilies. These grow to about 1 metre (3 feet) tall, with healthy, glossy leaves topped with abundant white flowers from spring to summer. They are amphibious and I tend to keep them wet. Poking up through the leaves is *Persicaria amplexicaulis* 'Orangefield', a new, compact variety with a soft orange flower spike.

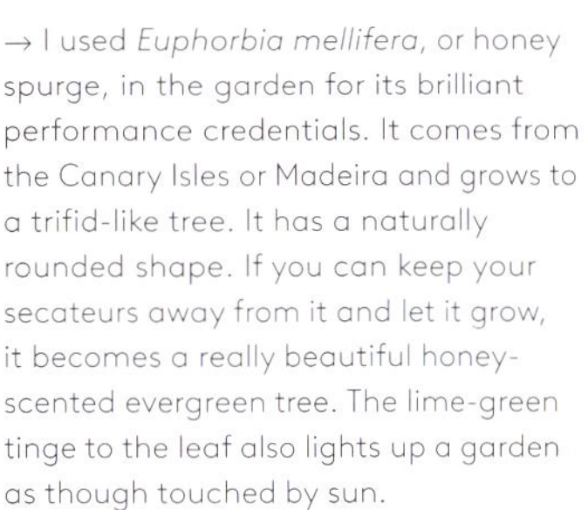

→ I used *Euphorbia mellifera*, or honey spurge, in the garden for its brilliant performance credentials. It comes from the Canary Isles or Madeira and grows to a trifid-like tree. It has a naturally rounded shape. If you can keep your secateurs away from it and let it grow, it becomes a really beautiful honey-scented evergreen tree. The lime-green tinge to the leaf also lights up a garden as though touched by sun.

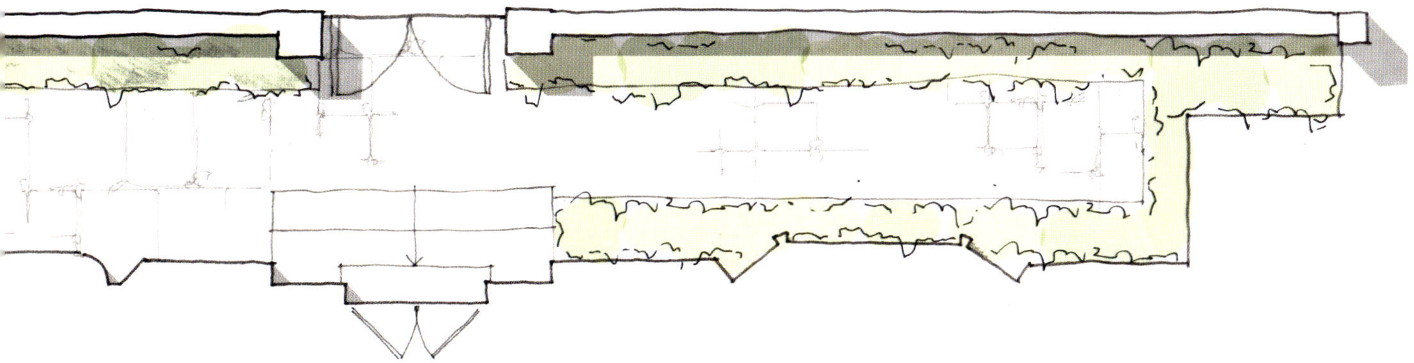

The main idea for this garden was to make sure that greenery is visible from every window. So often in gardens, plants are pinioned to the edges, leaving a great empty space in the middle – usually full of stuff you'd rather not be looking at. I'm a great believer in making people go on journeys, so deliberately planted a long bed of tree ferns and phormiums right outside the French doors to the drawing room. This gives a view of deeply layered jungle-type planting through which the route to the pergola becomes more interesting. The same applies for the two main terraces – a dining terrace by the house with an outdoor kitchen, and a summerhouse terrace. The choice of trees in a small garden is important as they need to stay in bounds. I have used two *Rhus typhina*, a beautiful *Koelreuteria paniculata* and *Acacia pravissima*. All have multiple stems and attractive rounded canopies and can easily be kept in scale. To the right of the drawing is the little garden in the lightwell. This house has many views and each of them is filled with planting. We included lots of large houseplants to blur the boundaries even further.

↘ This little sketch is useful for showing how the garden blends together when viewed from inside. The main canopies of the trees and tree ferns sit just above human head height at about 2.5 metres (8 feet), so the garden has an intimate atmosphere. Luckily this is a leafy part of the city, so we borrow screening from bigger trees outside the garden.

↗ I love how this path has worked out. I wanted the children to be able to play games and chase each other through the garden in close contact with the planting. We don't worry about things flopping over the stone as they are soft and easy to push through. I included lots of scented plants, such as the *Pittosporum tobira* 'Nana', which smells incredible and scents the whole garden.

Time

Part 3

Introduction

Everything we have been busily creating is now finished. The garden is done, the buildings complete, the plants in the ground. We take a few steps back, allowing time to take over and reveal the secrets of what has been made.

Time is our daily measurement, marching continually forward, ticktock, ticktock, ticktock. It shapes our inexorable sequence of existence from which there is no deviation and no escape other than the inevitability of death. Time is irreversible. We move successively through it – developing, as we go, an increasing past, a present and a decreasing future. After the three dimensions that make up our physical space – height, length and width – comes time, the fourth dimension. We need time in order to describe 'events' that move and evolve through and between the other three dimensions. Time is growth, evolution, progress. Time applies patina and beauty.

Time destroys the speculation of men, but it confirms nature.

—MARCUS TULLIUS CICERO (106–46 BC)

This view has remained unchanged for centuries. Humans have lived, farmed, died, fought wars, fallen in love, built things and destroyed things. Empires have waxed and waned, and with them their riches and poverty. Nothing has left a discernible trace on this timeless and beautiful landscape. The mists of morning linger here, the sun and moon move on their arcs through the heavens, time exhales gently over all of this.

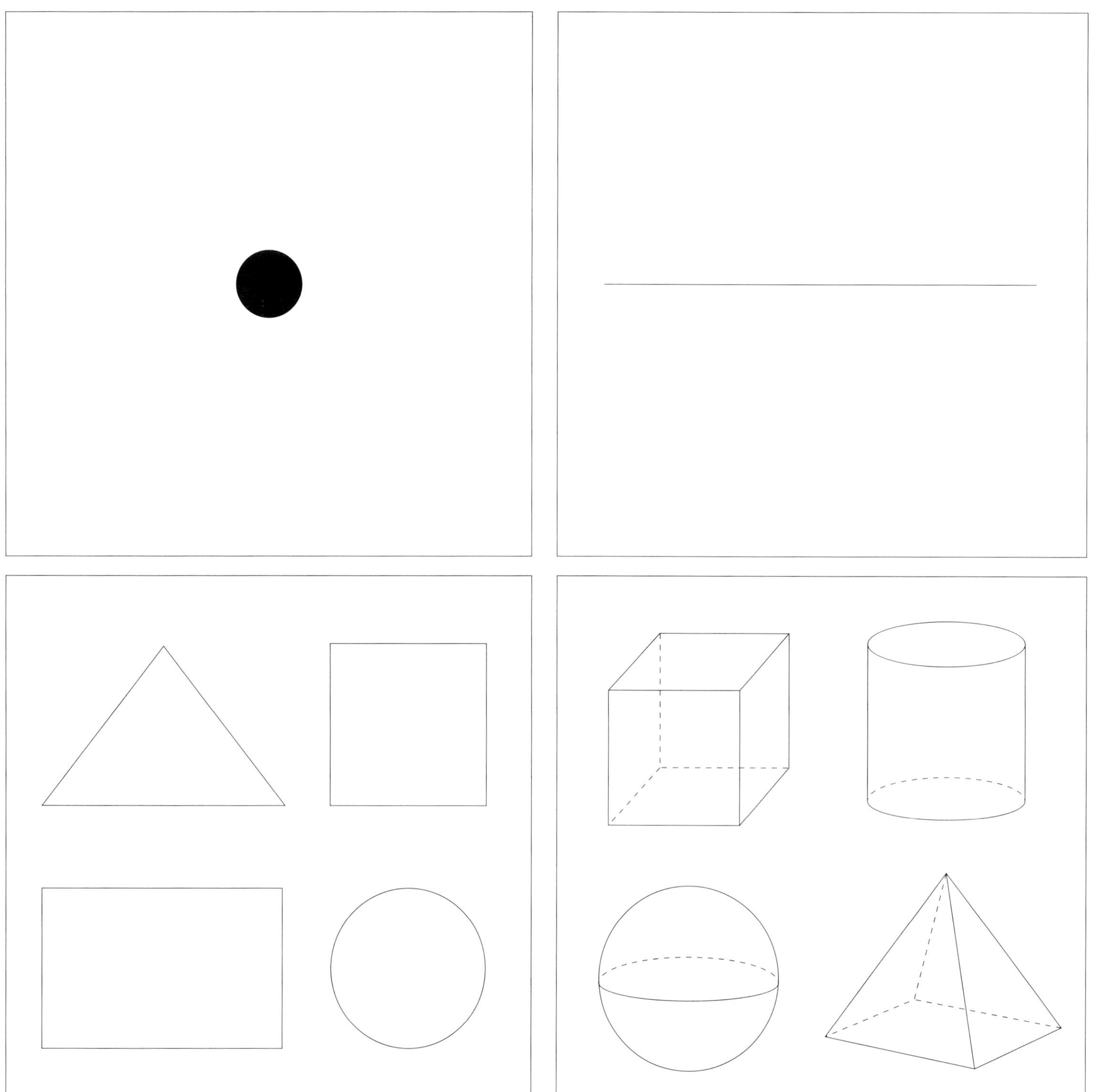

Moving Through Space

Gardens are four-dimensional spaces. The process of creating a garden certainly moves through the dimensions. From the original thoughts are developed two-dimensional drawings. These progress through to the three-dimensional manifestations of the garden when it is built. And then time, the fourth and most mysterious dimension, takes over. With the planting comes the continually moving event of growth and change that creates, or destroys, the act.

A garden is a unique artform. It relies on the passing of time to be able to give of its best. When I complete a garden, I always tell people it will need at least five years to settle down. Yes, there is a 'finished' garden with planting – some of it quite mature – at the end of the building process, but it won't really start to show its true character until time has worked on it. Time is transformative. Materials need to take on patination. Plants need to settle into their locations, develop their structure and personality and relax into harmonious collaboration with each other. Gardens need the passage of time to allow them to mature. When I hand a garden over, I usually refer to it as a 'baby' garden. It is really important to instil into the owners the idea that their garden is a vulnerable living thing that needs elegant nursing if it is to grow into exceptional adulthood.

We have all been children. We are born defenceless. Without the constant instinctive care of our parents to fulfil our most basic needs, we would fail to thrive, wither away and die. In human nature, neglect of the defenceless is an absolute taboo. It is unthinkable to allow a baby to die. The analogy applies perfectly to new a garden.

In the 1940s, American psychologist Abraham Maslow cooked up his eponymous hierarchy of needs in his well-known paper about human motivation. He didn't originally express it as a pyramid, though its commonly drawn as one. I have always found it a very useful time map for human advancement and aspiration. If we grow securely through the developmental phases, with appropriate care, education, socialisation and so on, we can ultimately achieve our full potential as humans. I also think we can achieve a great deal even if we are 'bonsai'd' by events – growth isn't always straight and true. Humans, like plants, have a burning will to live and can warp themselves around obstacles and still achieve fulfilment. This is why we love underdog stories, tales about people who have overcome difficulties to succeed. There is added beauty in a story about someone who has found a way to thrive against the odds.

Trees are akin to humans to some extent. It is important to try and inculcate the same connectivity and love when we plant a tree so that the person caring for it understands the tree as though it were a defenceless child. Trees live a great deal longer than we do; they are vulnerable and have basic needs that need attending to in order that they survive. An excellent planting pit, regular water, food and stability are essential and must be consistently given until a tree becomes self-supporting. Its long-term safety and security is catered for by choosing the location carefully at the outset so that it can live out its days undisturbed. Honestly, this is getting much harder as very little on earth is now undisturbed for very long. Humans are fickle creatures who tend to consider their own drives and desires to be of greater importance than anything else. However, let's remain optimistic and idealistic and hope a planted tree will be able to enjoy its fullest lifespan in health and peace.

It feels appropriate to place gardens at the top of the pyramid of human needs, at Maslow's pinnacle spot of self-actualisation and fulfilment. Being at one with a garden that you have striven to create and care for is self-actualisation at its best. It takes a long time in life to get there, and this maturation of ourselves, our comfort with the passage of time, our pleasure in creative activity is easily the peak of our human potential. A garden can't be rushed or forced, or time will, as Cicero so well expressed it, 'destroy the speculation of men and confirm nature'.

Seasons

Beauty is the only thing that time cannot harm. Philosophies fall away like sand, creeds follow one another, but what is beautiful is a joy for all seasons, a possession for all eternity.

—OSCAR WILDE (1854–1900)

The diurnal motion of the planet on which we live governs all aspects of a plant's growth as it spins slowly through space. The seasons flow through time, carrying all aspects of nature with them, influencing the growth of things through flowering and decline to re-emergence. Every gardener's annual map is laid out in tune with this unstoppable progression. Before we wore watches to tick away our minutes for us, our bodies, synchronised with the rising and falling of the sun, the waxing and waning of the moon, knew instinctively what time of day it was, what the season was, what to expect. Almanacs printed afresh each year contained the phases of the moon, the times of sunrise and sunset, the solstices and equinoxes and other important information for farmers and gardeners alike. I have friends who still use them, swear by them in fact.

We Westerners only really became deracinated from this simple understanding of diurnal biology during the Industrial Revolution. It was Dr Rudolph Steiner, scientist and philosopher, who in the 1920s reintroduced the concept of farming and gardening in tandem with 'nature', or more accurately, with time. He called it biodynamics. Many detractors still claim Steiner was a pseudoscientist and a mystic. However, he was the progenitor of what we now consider 'organic' growing and using lunar phases as a guide for planting and treating the soil. With the benefit of hindsight, he was prophetic. We were, as we became less and less tied to the land losing our instinctual seasonal connection to the land. We were losing our feeling for nurturing it and increasingly saw it as an inert commodity. These days, as more of us are city dwellers and fully urbanised, our connection with the seasons and the moon cycles is all but lost too. We might rush outside for a quick 'ooh-er' at a supermoon, but that's about it. And it has to be a 'supermoon', or we won't summon sufficient interest for even a brief look.

I lived for a time in the south of France in a small *vendangeur*'s hut. I had no modern conveniences, no plumbing. Pruning vines all winter, I woke with the sunrise and worked through the day. I stopped for food when I got hungry and went to bed as the sun set. It was astonishing how little I needed. Given where I was living, once I'd finished my days pruning, I spent a fair chunk of time foraging for food and firewood. With the assistance of my pruning colleague (who lived a normal life in a regular house with his family and thought I was quite mad), I became expert at finding food in surprising places, even in winter. The thing that was most astounding was the night sky. If you live without electricity, your eyes adapt to an extraordinary degree and the night sky – heaving with stars – becomes a familiar place. I knew the basic constellations thanks to my *Observer's Book of Astronomy* – every child of my generation grew up with these indispensable *Observer's* pocketbooks. Staring deep into the night sky was captivating; time and space becomes very absorbing at night when you can literally feel, and definitely see, the motion of all the celestial bodies moving together.

As a result of this reductionist experience, which lasted for several cold wet winter months, I became overwhelmingly connected to plants. The vines I was pruning were well over a century old. They had lived in this unforgiving stony ground for all that time. Every year each one had to be carefully pruned by hand. In winter the soil was sodden, the vineyards being on land reclaimed from the sea not more than 300 metres (980 feet) away. As the estuarine river rose with autumnal rainwater, turning it a muddy brown, we flooded the vines to wash away the summer's accumulated salt, freshening the soil. Glooping strenuously through the resulting mud while pruning gave me time to consider each snip of the secateurs, and to reflect on the cuts of the hundred preceding winters. I felt responsible. My uncle wouldn't let me prune his own vines a few kilometres away – he said his harvest mattered too much to let me loose on them. That comment rattled my nerves. I had no reason to believe I was naturally gifted at pruning having never done it before. I felt the weight of my decision-making and the impact it would potentially have on the next grape harvest many months in the future. After a while my confidence grew and I enjoyed the task of caring for these venerable old characters. Having harvested the same vineyards a few months earlier, I had clear knowledge of how the year would flow out from here. Spring weeding, light summer pruning and tying in and late-summer harvesting followed by the alchemy of wine-making. I found the sequence of care very grounding. All the same qualities that are needed for domestic gardening were here in the vines. It isn't farfetched to say the year spent with the vines changed the course of my life.

Annual movement of the Sun
Summer solstice
NORTH POLE
Sun
Celestial sphere
E
First point of Aries
N
S
Horizon
Autumnal equinox
W
Equator
SOUTH POLE
Winter solstice
Ecliptic

↱ pp. 238–39: It feels all the more poignant these days to find a tree that has had time and space to grow as this *Tilia* ssp. has. It is still relatively juvenile and I can only hope that it manages to live on undisturbed in its glade.

↘ This is a shadow map that we produce in the studio. We make them to ensure that we have fully understood the impact the sun will have. Before technology, I would work this out on paper. It's an important part of the job. This image shows a feature I am making in a garden and its sole purpose is to catch the warmth of a glowing sunset.

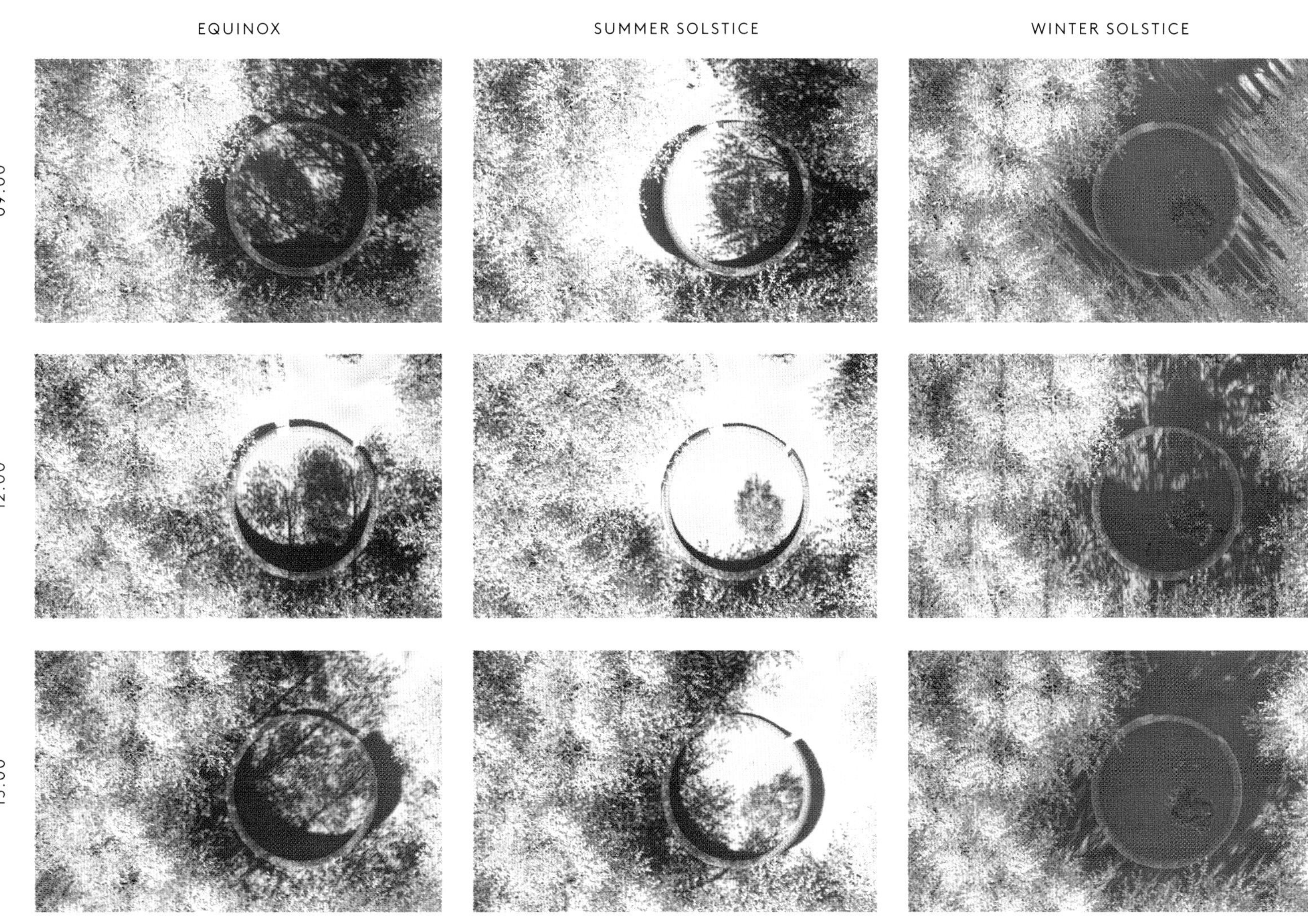

Light

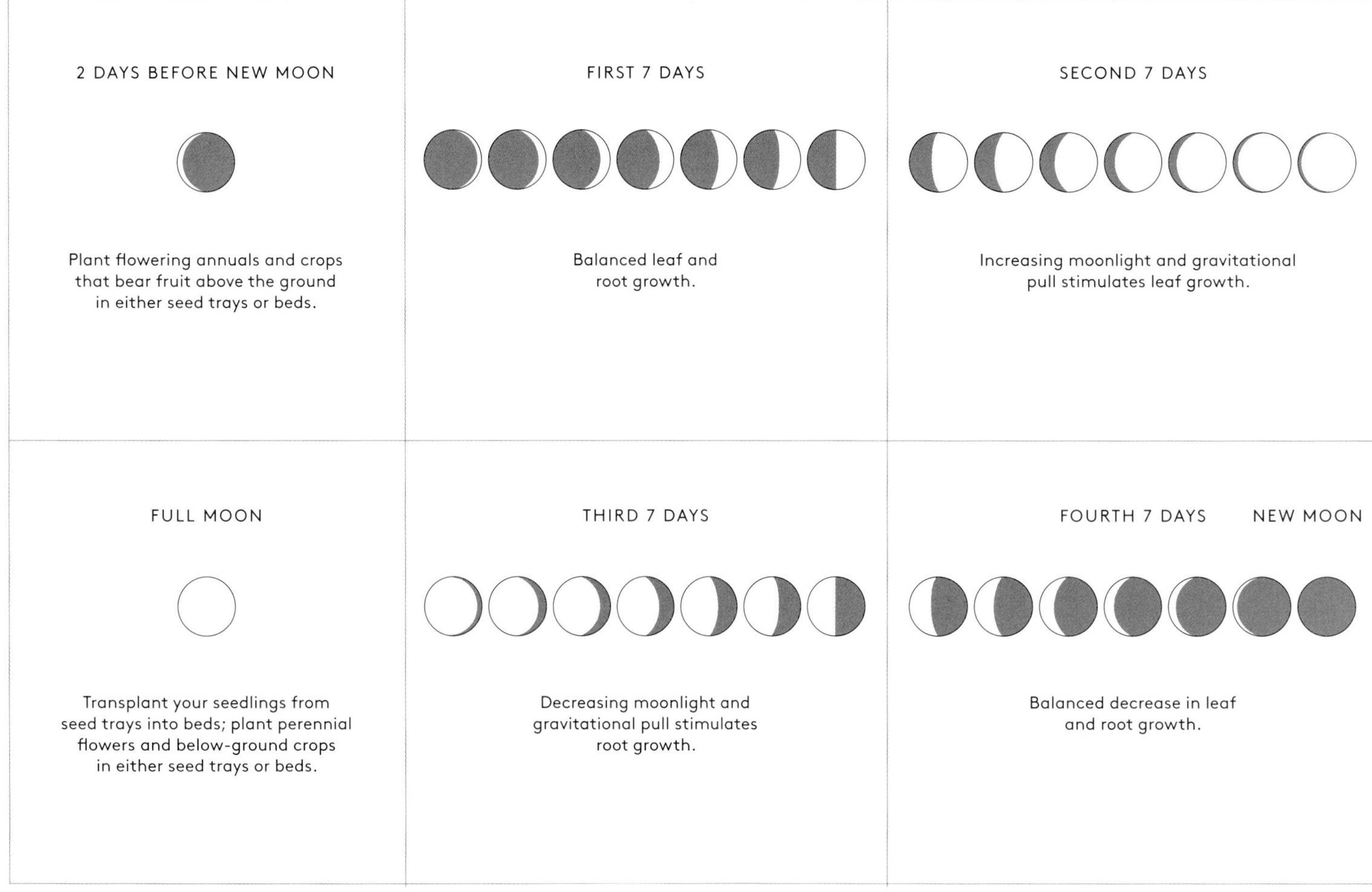

LUNAR LIGHT AND GRAVITY

Lunar Light

Many people grow vegetables and flowers using the lunar phases as a guide. It seems entirely logical. Clearly the tides are affected by lunar gravity – after all we are on an orb spinning on an axis with a predisposition to fall. The force of gravity keeps all of the planets in our solar system in orbit around the sun rather than twirling off into the great dark blue yonder. This is just physics. It's not mystical, it's real.

So, growing by the moon phases makes a great deal of sense as nocturnal light is greater as the moon waxes. It stands to reason that it would encourage the growth of seeds. Encourage children to follow this simple logic. Try following the sequence illustrated here and see how you get on.

Planisphere based on the Copernican system, with the sun, not the earth at the centre of the solar system, 1660, Andreas Cellarius (c. 1596–1665)

Solar Light

Electromagnetic radiation creates light, and the human eye can't really see that much of it. This luminous energy to which our eyes reacts travels at a speed of 299,792 kilometres (186,282 miles) per second as a constant stream of particles What we see is called 'visible light'. Without light we are blind. How we see light varies during the course of a day and through the seasons. Our colour perception alters as light levels drop. For example, in the early evening as light fades, our perception of ultraviolet increases and blue flowers, having more ultraviolet, are more noticeable at dusk.

Fellow creatures see things very differently as they are attuned to frequencies of radiation we miss. Some birds, bees and most butterflies and insects mainly see ultraviolet light. Given the iridescence of butterfly wings I wonder what they do see? It must be stunning. Bullfrogs, fish and snakes see the world through infrared radiation, allowing them to navigate in the dark or through opaque muddy waters.

Light has a direct influence on the growth of plants through photosynthesis. Plants with sufficient natural light generate their own food and oxygen and develop in a strong, healthy way. Plants are the principal producers of energy in every ecosystem, bringing in new power to support life. All this is managed by the influence of the sun as sunlight conducts photosynthesis.

If you would like to see the transformative effects of sunlight and photosynthesis, watch Wim Wenders remarkable film *The Salt of the Earth* about Sebastião Salgado, the acclaimed war photographer. At the end of the film, Salgado and his wife return to Brazil to the family farm that his father decimated by deforestation in order to pay for his children's education. What happens next is not a miracle because it is real. All it takes is sun and photosynthesis.

Artificial Light

↖ An advert from Joseph Swan and Thomas Edison's first company making electric light bulbs. It was indeed the 'parent of a new and great industry' and a revolution in electricity and light. In this poignant image, a handsome young man sits at a workbench, making blown-glass candle bulbs — all lovingly hand-finished — for illuminating homes of wealth and taste.

This all changed in the mid-1800s when my distant cousin Sir Joseph Swan started experimenting with creating artificial light. He was an independent inventor and one of the first to develop an incandescent lightbulb. By 1881 his lightbulbs were illuminating homes and even the Savoy Theatre. As an aside, he also lit up his own home in Gateshead and that of the great inventor William Armstrong, 1st Baron Armstrong, a magnificent house called Cragside, in Northumberland. If you haven't been, you really must go. It was a pinnacle achievement for Victorian green technology. With his ingenious abilities with hydraulics, Armstrong powered not only the house, but all the waterworks too. He was forceful in his opinion that coal should be replaced by hydropower as a 'green' and ultimately better, cleaner alternative. However, the main reason for visiting his house is to the see the staggering gardens. They are the work of an immensely capable, practical mind, but also a great aesthete, as they tie together the eponymous crags and the stunning moorland with state-of-the-art technology and brilliant gardening.

Swan couldn't have lived to see his invention replace the suns' rays, or even have considered it as a possibility. His incandescent bulb generated a technology that has developed to such an extent that it removed the need for the sun, or day and night, or the rolling forward of the seasons in the propagation and production of plants. Visiting the vast automated hydroponic production glasshouses in Holland and around the world is an eye-opener. Many of our houseplants and garden plants – and indeed many of our foods – are produced without recourse to soil, sun, weather or seasonal harvests. If you wonder why the cheery cellophane-wrapped plant gifted to you by Aunt Doris seems to wither and die the minute she leaves the house, ask yourself how it was produced. It was generated from micropropagation on a conveyer system modulated to the minute. In a glasshouse perhaps covering several acres bathed in artificial light twenty-four hours a day, seven days a week, the plant never sleeps. It is drip-fed nutrients and its production digitally programmed to the nth degree. Plucked from the conveyer at peak bud, it is wrapped and shipped. These impressive mutants sometimes struggle to live outside their freakish man-made universes. The still lifes of plants, fruit and insects that the Dutch Masters are so famed for have been supplanted by a denaturised factory production of outlandish proportions. This is how most 'developed' countries are sustained now.

Roses, Tulips and Other Flowers in a Glass Vase on a Stone Ledge, 1709, Rachel Ruysch (1664–1750)

↑ I have always found these Dutch flower still lifes captivating. I get sucked into them, identifying flowers, enjoying the water droplets frozen in time, seeking out ants and ladybirds. I marvel at the deftness of the artist's touch, the mastery of colour and the sheer beauty of these works. For me, they always summed up Dutch art and my fantasy of the Dutch way of life. Calm, ordered, intelligent and beautiful.

↗ This is the Dutch flower art I am more familiar with these days – the hectares of gigantic glass houses presided over by robots and illuminated by Swan's now deviant electric lights, which stifle the nighttime so these poor, mad flowers can be created nonstop to feed rapacious markets. This is not just the fate of flowers, of course, but of many of our foodstuffs as well, grown with no soil, no air, no sun.

The British Character, Enthusiasm for Gardening, 1938, Graham Laidler Pont (1908—40)

CODA: THE LONG VIEW

My library is heaving with books new and old on gardens, on horticulture, on garden history, on geology, on herbalism, on crafts, arts, the countryside around the world and many other related subjects. The comprehensive question as to what makes a garden is fascinating, far-reaching and all-consuming. The thread that runs through it all is our very human desire to pass on what we know, to tell stories of learning and experience. The books hold snapshots of the time in which they were written, the notions of those days, the condition of society at the time. The societal view is often as present as the factual information they describe. Attitudes are definitely changing, though. We are all affected by how our recent and current generational actions will impact the lives of those who will follow.

If you think about it, our predecessors rarely lived half as long as we do, yet they handed on a great deal more in terms of shared knowledge. Oral traditions were typical, 'learning at your grandfather's knee' was expected. Venerating the older generation was a vital function of a co-dependent society. Experience mattered so much it could save you when things got tough. These ancestors of our near and far past understood the future needed investing in. They had a true grasp of the fragility of life and took the generational relay race seriously.

Now we live long and solipsistically in a world in which self-broadcasting swiftly confirms personal thoughts as fact. Only individual, often short-term concerns are matters of any importance. This epoch of narcissism is dangerous for future generations. Social media, the modern pulpit of self-important verbiage, gives voice to all this nonsense and makes it scintillatingly true – at least for a moment before it passes into digital oblivion. Gardening in this arena has committed itself with missionary zeal to the idea that we are in the grips of Armageddon and humankind is substantially mentally unwell. While there are grains of truth in there to be dealt with seriously, surely the reality is more nuanced.

Luckily for us garden enthusiasts, garden-making cannot be digitised. It can't easily be flipped into instant gratification endorphin shots. Gardening will always be a multidimensional event undertaken slowly in the fresh air. It benefits from being sociable. It takes a long time. It enjoys that. It demands that we plan the coming year and often many years beyond – even beyond the span of our own lives – giving our egos some much needed perspective on our place in the scheme of things. It keeps us healthy, sustaining our relationships, bodies, minds and emotions. Gardens insist we care for them as much, or more, than ourselves.

Garden-making puts us all in the comfort zone of being part of the positive continuum of earth. Our small contributions are part of the baton race to keep our natural world going. We are our ancestors' children and the sum of what they passed on to us. The honourable thing is to pass it on to those who follow in good heart and in better condition than we inherited it. Leave them with something wonderful, something beautiful, something worth respecting.

FURTHER READING

Find below a list of highly recommended reads. Some of these titles may have fallen out of print, but are well worth tracking down a copy if you can.

David Bourdon, *Designing the Earth: The Human Impulse to Shape Nature*, Harry N. Abrams, Inc., 1998
Jane Brown, *The Art and Architecture of English Gardens*, Weidenfeld & Nicolson, 1989
Ronald Brunskill and Alec Clifton-Taylor, *English Brickwork*, Van Nostrand Reinhold, 1983
Thomas D. Church, *Gardens are for People*, University of California Press, 1995
Alec Clifton-Taylor and A.S. Ireson, *English Stone Building*, Gollancz, 1983
Rick Darke, *The Encyclopedia of Grasses for Livable Landscapes*, Timber Press, 2007
Rick Darke, *The American Woodland Garden: Capturing the Spirit of the Deciduous Forest*, Timber Press, 2002
Jonathan Drori, *Around the World in 80 Trees*, Laurence King Publishing, 2018
Linda Farrar, *Ancient Roman Gardens*, The History Press, 2011
Christopher Grey-Wilson, *Poppies*, Batsford Ltd, 2000
Mrs M. Grieve, *A Modern Herbal*, Dorset Press, 1992
Anna N. Griffith, *Collins Guide to Alpines and Rock Garden Plants*, HarperCollins, 1972
Geoffrey Grigson, *The Englishman's Flora*, HarperCollins, 1975
Suzie Grogan, *Shell Shocked Britain: The First World War's Legacy for Britain's Mental Health*, Pen & Sword History, 2014
Kenneth I. Helphand, *Defiant Gardens: Making Gardens in Wartime*, Trinity University Press, 2008
Donald Insall, *The Care of Old Buildings Today*, Architectural Press, 1972
Barbara Jones, *Follies & Grottoes*, Constable & Co Ltd, 1979
Fritz Kuhn, *Wrought Iron*, George G.Harrap & Co Ltd, 1965
Mark Laird, *A Natural History of English Gardening*, Yale University Press, 2015
Clare Leighton, *The Farmer's Year*, Little Toller Books, 2018
Clare Leighton, *Four Hedges: A Gardener's Chronicle*, Little Toller Books, 2010
Christopher Lloyd, *Meadows*, Pimpernel Press Limited, 2016
Todd Longstaffe-Gowan, *English Garden Eccentrics: Three Hundred Years of Extraordinary Groves, Burrowings, Mountains and Menageries*, Paul Mellon Centre for Studies in British Art, 2022
Richard Mabey, *Food for Free*, HarperCollins, 2012
Michael Marriott, *RHS Roses: An Inspirational Guide to Choosing and Growing the Best Roses*, DK, 2022
Thomas Hayton Mawson, *The Art and Craft of Garden Making*, B.T. Batsford LTD, 1926
Ellen Miles, *Nature is a Human Right: Why We're Fighting for Green in a Grey World*, DK, 2022
Mary Mycio, *Wormwood Forest: A Natural History of Chernobyl*, Joseph Henry Press, 2005
Piet Oudolf and Henk Gerritsen, *Dream Plants for the Natural Garden*, Frances Lincoln, 2013
Régine Pernoud and Georges Herscher, *Jardins de Monastères*, Actes Sud, 1996
Roger Phillips and Martyn Rix, *Wild Food*, Macmillan, 2014
Roger Phillips and Martyn Rix, *Perennials Volume 2: Late Perennials*, Pan Books, 1993
Roger Phillips and Martyn Rix, *Perennials Volume 1: Early Perennials*, Pan Books, 1991
Roger Phillips and Martyn Rix, *Bulbs*, Pan Books, 1989
Roger Phillips and Martyn Rix, *Shrubs*, Pan Books, 1989
Roger Phillips and Martyn Rix, *Roses*, Macmillan, 1988
Oleg Polunin and Anthony Huxley, *Flowers of the Mediterranean*, Chatto & Windus, 1990
Jonas Reif, Christian Kress and Jürgen Becker, *Cultivating Chaos: How to Enrich Landscapes with Self-seeding Plants*, Timber Press, 2015
Sylvan T. Runckel and Dean M. Roosa, *Wildflowers of the Tallgrass Prairie: The Upper Midwest*, University Of Iowa Press, 2009
John Sutton, *The Gardener's Guide to Growing Salvias*, Timber Press, 1999
Michael Symes, *The Picturesque and the Later Georgian Garden*, Redcliffe Press Ltd., 2012
Graham Stuart Thomas, *Ornamental Shrubs, Climbers and Bamboos*, Frances Lincoln, 2004
Lawrence Weaver, *Houses and Gardens by E.L. Lutyens*, Country Life, 1914
Keith Wiley, *On the Wild Side: Experiments in New Naturalism*, Timber Press, 2004
Ron Wilson, *The Hedgerow Book*, David & Charles, 1979

IMAGE CREDITS

Key: t = top; b = bottom; l = left; c = centre; r= right; and variations thereof.

© Britt Willoughby: cover (main and author photo); endpapers; half-title page; title page; 1, 4; 20–21; 30–31; 33; 39; 40; 44; 49; 50–51; 52; 60–61; 64–65; 80; 82–83; 92–93; 94; 95; 97; 100; 103; 108l; 113; 114–15; 124; 125; 128bl; 128br; 130; 131; 135b; 143; 147; 150–51; 157; 160; 162; 163; 164–65; 167; 170–71; 174–75; 176; 178; 183; 184–85; 187; 190–91; 192–93; 195; 196–97; 199; 202b; 203; 204–05; 207; 208–09; 211; 212–13; 217; 218–19; 221; 222b; 223t; 224–25; 229; 232–33; 238–39.

© Jinny Blom: 17; 26; 56–57; 63; 70; 74–75 sketches; 84; 85; 87; 102; 106; 110tl; 110bl; 110br; 117; 120–21; 122 sketches; 128t sketches; 138; 154–55; 161; 166; 186; 188–89; 194; 200–01; 202t; 206; 214–15; 220; 222t; 223b; 226–27; 228; 237b.

All other images:
7 CSU Archives/Everett Collection Historical/Alamy; 8 © Christo and Jeanne-Claude Foundation. Photo: Wolfgang Volz. © ADAGP, Paris and DACS, London 2023; 11 © ADAGP/DACS/Comité Cocteau, Paris 2023. Photo: Michael Parkin Gallery/Bridgeman Images; 12 Tuul and Bruno Morandi/Alamy; 15 Heritage Image Partnership Ltd/Alamy; 18t © The John Barrett Collection/Mary Evans Picture Library; 18b Sunny Celeste/Alamy; 22 UIG/Bridgeman Images; 25 J. Paul Getty Museum (public domain); 29 superclic/Alamy; 36 © Natural History Museum, London/Bridgeman Images; 43 images/Alamy; 45 © Tom Mannion; 54t G. Dagli Orti/© NPL – DeA Picture Library/Bridgeman Images; 54b Photo © Agnew's, London/Bridgeman Images; 55 Granger/Bridgeman Images; 66 © Institut océanographique, Fondation Albert Ier, Prince de Monaco/Michel; Dagnino; 69t DcoetzeeBot (public domain); 69b Art Heritage/Alamy; 73 Didier Descouens (CC BY-SA 4.0); 76 © Royal Academy of Arts, London; photographer: John Hammond; 89t The Artist's Estate; 89cl Photo © CCI/Bridgeman Images; 89br Bridgeman Images; 90 cristina.sanvito (CC BY 2.0); 99 Bridgeman Images; 104 David Valinsky Photography/Alamy; 108r Casa colonica; 110tr Dinodia Photos/Alamy; 119 unknown/Alamy; 122 background MM_photos/Shutterstock; 126–27 © Laura Ford. Photo: Peter Lennby.; 128t background Suradech Prapairat/Shutterstock; 132 © Iberfoto/Bridgeman Images; 135t © British Library Board. All Rights Reserved/Bridgeman Images; 137 Photo © Underwood Archives/Bridgeman Images; 144 History and Art Collection/Alamy; 148t © NPL – DeA Picture Library/Bridgeman Images; 148b Prismatic Pictures/Bridgeman Images; 152 Christophe Coat/Alamy; 159 © Becky Crowley; 169 Villy Fink Isaksen (public domain); 172t Picture Alliance/DPA/Bridgeman Images; 172b © Look and Learn/Bridgeman Images; 173t © Amoret Tanner/Alamy; 173b © Look and Learn/Bridgeman Images; 177 © Živilė Maciukaite; 182 © Look and Learn/Bridgeman Images; 216 background Daboost/shutterstock; 241 © British Library Board. All Rights Reserved/Bridgeman Images; 242 Pictorial Press Ltd/Alamy; 243l 1Veertje (public domain); 243r iStock/Getty Images Plus; 244 © Look and Learn/Bridgeman Images.

While every effort has been made to credit photographers, Quarto would like to apologise should there have been any omissions or errors, and would be pleased to make the appropriate correction for future editions of the book.

ACKNOWLEDGEMENTS

Firstly, my thanks go to my clients without whom I would never have had this extraordinarily satisfying life. Special thanks are offered to those generous enough to let me shoot the gardens and use the photos here. You know who you are. No one else does!

My husband, Marc Fox, for his unfaltering support, love, brilliant ideas, tea (etc.), unblocking blocks and sitting in the dark for a month during a blistering heatwave while I got started.

Thank you to Maureen Doherty, William JR Curtis, Julie Harrod, Rosalind Caldecott, Angela Palmer, Ptolemy Dean OBE, Michael Blom, for gifts of guidance and good ideas all of which have been followed.

To my commissioning editor at Quarto, Philip Cooper. Skilled with the ability to offer succinct comment that helped every time and especial thanks for unravelling the knots as they arose. Also, to Laura Bulbeck and Anna Southgate for deft editing and editorial support.

To Fiona Lyndsey, my agent at Limelight Celebrity Management. Onward and upward.

To Britt Willoughby for all the unique photography of my work in here. Always stunning.

To Jacqui Small, for making me write the first one and your generosity and friendship always.

To Here Design for another wonderful experience creating the book. It's been a pleasure – again. Mark Paton, Eleanor Robertson, Thomas Boswell, Romy Leonard-Parsons.

To my studio associates who have been brilliant throughout as always. Amy Harley Jepson, Daniel Ridgway, Xijie Tao, Lina Braouch, Elke Maynard, Adrienne Johnson, Tom Ruff, Frances Costelloe, Chris Page, Sam Wing, Esther Akehurst, and the outriggers Laura Diggens, Zivile Maciukaite, Richard Keys, Anneka Thom, Maude Pinet and the original Jared Lockhart.

To dear friends and collaborators who have contributed in many diverse ways:

Anna Dudziak, Gunner Petersen, Clare Foster, Pam Coote, Graham Gough and Lucy Goffin, Piet and Anja Oudolf, John Coke, Selvi May Akyildiz, Omar Mullick, Adam Nicklin, Alex DeRijke, Dominic Myland, Alex Evans, Tim Walker, Robert Crocker, Mike Veness, Neil Attride, John Crouch, Phil Hall, James Brooks, Mark Pittman, Potop Ionut, Phil Wraight, Chris Green, Tom Mannion, Tim Boyd, Alex Michaelis, Carrie Donald, Tom Dodge, Steven Collins, Luis LaPlace, Tom Croft, Steve Westmore, Olivia Outred, Ptolemy Dean OBE, Ronnie Sonneborn, Brian and Astrid Hall, Julia Blackburn, Clare German, Michael Marriott, Alex Pasley-Tyler, Napoleon Villatoro, Brian Eno, Bro. Paul Jakeman, Bro. Simon Hurst, Bro. Flora Roberts, Emma Robertson, Becky Crowley, Bee Emmott, Calandra Caldicot, Richard Podd, Gilbert Stirling-Lee, Steve Melville, Eddie McPhilips, Laura Ford, Janet Mavec, Jacob Hepworth-Bell, Rob Orford, Pippa Shirley, Fiona, Rupert, Rose, Evie and Felix Hardcastle, Henry Estorffe, Joan Lonborg, Dr Paul Jenkins, John Danzer, Alejandro Saralegui, John Tanner, Jan Hendzel, Jayne Kersten, Kendra Wilson, Lee Mallett, Pete Fane, Philip Flockhart, Robert Sabella, Cathy Haynes, Rosie Oliver, Russell Sage, Scott Sansum, Pernille Bisgaard Jensen, Ole Smith, Todd Longstaffe-Gowan, Udo Heinrich, Tom Taw, Zoe Traill. Prof. Susan Downes, Melanie Pappenheim, Dr Amanda Salisbury, Veere Grenney, Natasha Greig. Amin Taha, Rafal Szczepaniak, David Money, Trystan Hawkins, M. et Mme Roux, Bro Rachael Matthews, June and Jon Summerill, Bolko von Schweinichen, Lorenzo Venturini, Doriano Cappaci, Giovanni Lebono, Morag Hood, William Smalley.